Labour and racism

Labour and racism

Annie Phizacklea *and* **Robert Miles**

Routledge & Kegan Paul · London, Boston and Henley

First published in 1980
by Routledge & Kegan Paul Ltd
39 Store Street,
London WC1E 7DD,
9 Park Street,
Boston, Mass. 02108, USA and
Broadway House,
Newtown Road,
Henley-on-Thames,
Oxon RG9 1EN

Set in 10/11 Phototronic Baskerville by
Saildean Ltd Molesey, Surrey
and printed in Great Britain by
Biddles Ltd, Guildford, Surrey

British Library Cataloguing in Publication Data
Phizacklea, Annie
   Labour and racism.
   1. Alien labour – Great Britain
   2. Blacks – Great Britain – Politics and
   government
I. Title   II. Miles, Robert
331.5'44   HD8398.N5   80-41085

ISBN 0 7100 0678 0
ISBN 0 7100 0679 9 Pbk

CONTENTS

TABLES

ACKNOWLEDGMENTS

Our greatest thanks must go to all the people in Brent who gave up their time to talk and extended their hospitality to us. In particular we want to thank the staff and clients at Harlesden Advice Centre, everyone at Brent Law Centre, and the management and shop stewards at 'Food Co.' We owe a particular debt to Martin Bailey who sacrificed a great deal of his valuable time to help us interview and to Dolly Sewell who provided us with support throughout the research. We also want to thank Rawle Boland, Ian Carr, Martin Davies and Daphne Smalling for their practical help.

We would also like to thank all our colleagues at the Research Unit on Ethnic Relations at the University of Bristol, especially Michael Banton, Glen Gocoul, Sarah Pegg and Susan Whitmore, for five years of help, heated discussion, humour and entertainment.

We are very grateful to the following for their advice and support: Geoffrey Alderman, Ezra Bennathan, Percy Cohen, Ivor Crewe, Betty Gittus, Danny Lawrence and Theo Nichols.

We are particularly indebted to those who have read and commented on various parts of this manuscript – Elizabeth Bird, John Eldridge, Hazel Flett, Dave Frisby, Stephen Green, Barbara Littlewood, Bert Moorhouse, Richard Sargent and Jackie West.

We want to thank Philippa Brewster, without whose encouragement this manuscript would not have been published, and Doris Macey and Josie Satterthwaite without whose skills there would not have been a manuscript at all.

Most of all we want to thank Steve, Veronica and Ben for their patience.

Author's note

This volume does not represent the views of the Social Science Research Council, nor does it necessarily reflect those of all members of the Research Unit on Ethnic Relations at the University of Aston.

CHAPTER 1

Capitalism, class and migrant labour in Britain

The object of this book is to consider the position of black migrant labour in the British political process. Given that the majority of black workers are structurally part of the working class, such consideration must proceed from an understanding of class politics in a capitalist social formation. It follows that, in order to understand the position of black migrant labour in the political process, it is necessary also to understand the position of the working class in the British political process. Hence, the analysis in this book is comparative and proceeds against the background of a theory of the economic and political structure of British capitalism.

Given this object, there are three general themes that run through the book. First, we argue that an understanding of the presence, position and circumstances of black workers in Britain must begin by taking account of the fact that Britain is a capitalist social formation with a history of colonialism and imperialism. But, having argued that, we believe, second, that an explanation for the presence, position and circumstances of black people in Britain is not completely or ultimately reducible to class relations in the sense that black workers are only workers. That is to say, we maintain that there are structures and processes in the British social formation which must be comprehended as real phenomena 'in themselves' and not as being only the reflection of some broader and more important structure or process. Third, we believe that in so far as black workers in Britain are geographically concentrated in the so-called 'inner cities' of the major conurbations, then their presence, position and circumstances must also be understood and explained in terms which take account of both the reasons why such areas exist and the processes (both economic and political) which are operating within and upon them. The theoretical arguments which support these themes will be outlined in this and the subsequent two chapters, prior to presenting our data in the remainder of the book. But, given our specific subject-matter, the reader may be wondering why we do not begin with the concepts of 'race' and 'race relations'.

Despite the use of these concepts in contemporary public and political discussion as if there is consensus about what they refer to (as for example when a national daily newspaper can run a headline such as 'Another race war warning by Enoch'), their meaning is in fact uncertain and ambiguous. If, as we shall recount, 'race' has no reality other than as a social construction, then what has to be explained is not 'race in itself' but a social process. Moreover, in so far as this social process is not an inevitable or universal feature of social formations, then its occurrence must be traced and explained historically and specifically for each formation. Given this context, to begin an analysis with the concept of 'race' is to begin with a concept which refers to a conjunctural phenomenon. We believe that it is methodologically more satisfactory to begin with concepts which identify the structural features of a social formation rather than those which presuppose such features. Hence, we do not locate our analysis within the framework of a 'sociology of race relations' as such.

To understand what this means, it is useful to consider the intentions and framework of one of the principal 'race relations' texts, *Race, Community and Conflict* (Rex and Moore, 1967). This work had the general aim of wishing to 'throw light on problems of race relations' (ibid., p. 11) in Birmingham but within the context of certain strands of sociological theory, particularly that concerned with the analysis of urban situations (ibid., p. 17). We wish to offer an alternative form of analysis from that outlined in this work which differs in four major respects. First, Rex and Moore begin with a theoretical proposition which might be described as Weberian: we begin by considering the goals of typical actors representing the various host and immigrant groups, the various politico-economic classes and more specifically what we have called 'housing classes' (ibid., p. 6).

We believe that 'the goals of typical actors' can only be understood in the context of a prior analysis of structural characteristics of the social formation in which those 'typical actors' live. We shall therefore argue below, following Marx, that analysis should begin with an analysis of class structure and class relations, not as determined by the marketplace but by the relationship to the means of production.

Second, Rex and Moore, although objecting to a mode of analysis derived from an 'immigrant/host' framework, nevertheless retain 'immigrant' as a major analytic category (e.g. ibid., pp. 10-11, 14 276). We believe this is misleading inasmuch as the concept of 'immigrant' implies intentional and permanent settlement within the 'host population'. Yet the intention of the immigrants with which Rex and Moore (and ourselves) were concerned was temporary settlement for the purpose of material and social advancement in the 'home country' upon return. This notion is grasped by the concept of 'migrant labour'. Such an omission is particularly interesting in the light of the authors' concern with 'the goals of ... actors' because, as others have observed (e.g. Dahya, 1973, 1974), the behaviour of 'immigrants' in Britain has to be assessed in relation to their intention of return. That there has been a change in circumstances (in so far as the migrants now realise that their migration is no longer short-term) can be grasped by the concept of 'black settlers' (cf. Sivanandan, 1976) and does not require resort to 'immigrant/host' framework. But despite this partial change of orientation over time, the facts that the motivation for migration was to sell labour power in the British social formation (if only on a temporary basis) and that capital desperately required semi- and unskilled labour constitute the central dynamic in explaining the presence of black workers in Britain and, as we shall argue, in explaining their class position.

Third, Rex and Moore were particularly concerned with certain strands of argument derived from urban sociology. This is not in itself 'wrong' but does constitute a somewhat narrow perspective because it de-emphasises the relevance of the means by which the migrants obtain their livelihood and the impact that this has on their political consciousness. We do not deny that discrimination in the process of housing allocation is a crucial factor in determining the economic and social fortunes of the migrants. But it is also relevant to this process that the migrants are wage labourers. This is important not only because it has implications for the level of resources available to meet housing needs but also because the impact of discrimination on the migrants' political consciousness has to be assessed in relation to the impact of wage labour on political consciousness. Hence, we are particularly concerned with migrants as wage labourers as well as residents.

This takes us to our fourth and final point. Rex and Moore's text is conceived as one about 'race relations' (e.g. ibid., pp. 1, 11, 17), with the consequence that they focus on the factors that encourage conflict between the 'races' (in particular, racial discrimination). We see little value in such an approach, not only because of doubts about the theoretical validity of utilising the concept of 'race' (even if it has been divested of its biological connotations), but also because it leads to a form of analysis which seeks to explain the beliefs and behaviour of the migrants almost solely in terms of racism and discrimination. In other words, the migrants are too often viewed primarily as objects of processes of racial exclusion. We believe (and we present evidence below to support this belief) that we first need to grasp the fact that the migrants are wage labourers and that this too has implications for their beliefs and behaviour before we can assess the impact of racism and discrimination.

We are therefore offering an alternative framework of analysis, one that begins with the concepts of capitalism and class and then proceeds by introducing the concept of migrant labour. This warrants reference to the extant debate about these concepts and this chapter consequently has a rather abstract character. Those not interested in such theoretical debates may prefer to accept 'on trust' that a case can be made for conceiving of black migrant labour as a fraction of the working class and move straight to chapter 2 where our analysis begins the process of focusing down on West Indian migrant labour and then (from chapter 3) on Willesden in North West London as the location of our research.

Concerning capitalism and class relations

The Marxist tradition defines classes in relation to the process of production, and argues that the capitalist mode of production gives rise to two major classes, the bourgeoisie and the working class. This formulation has been attacked by both Marxists and non-Marxists for taking insufficient account of political and ideological relations. We do not wish to directly enter this debate but we do want to draw upon it for the purpose of establishing that (1) class is an objective structural phenomenon which exists independently of a consciousness of class position and (2) that Britain is a capitalist social formation.

This first proposition is clearly articulated by, amongst others, Poulantzas, who additionally argues that while the individual's economic place within the relations of production plays a principal role in determining social class, 'the places of political and ideological domination and subordination are themselves part of the structural determination of class' (1975, p. 16). There are, however good reasons for not uncritically accepting Poulantzas' analysis of class boundaries (see Wright, 1976; Hunt, 1977) and we here follow Wright when he suggests that class relations can be understood in terms of three processes underlying the social relations of production: control of labour power, control of the physical means of production and control of investment and resources (ibid, p. 31)

The capitalist class controls all three processes while the working class is without control over investment or the physical means of production, sells labour power (mental and manual) for a wage and does not control the labour power of others (ibid., pp. 20–3, 32–5). According to this definition, the working class includes not only manual workers selling their labour power for a wage but also, for example, those non-manual workers (e.g. clerks) employed in unproductive sectors (e.g. wholesale and retail trade, finance, insurance) of the economy. These positions stand in the same relationship to capital as positions in the productive sectors and so constitute neither a 'middle class' nor part of a new petit-bourgeoisie. We would add that the working class also includes those not directly involved in the wage labour relation, but who are dependent upon that sale (Gardiner, 1977).

Wright additionally argues that structural changes in the course of capitalist development have led to the emergence of contradictory locations between the bourgeoisie and the working class. These locations (e.g. top management, supervisors) can be identified by virtue of their having the characteristics of more than one position in the relations of production and so cannot constitute a distinct and unambiguous class. For this reason, political and ideological relations have a determining role in their alignment to one or other of the two main classes in a capitalist formation. So, for the purposes of the analysis to be pursued in subsequent chapters, we are arguing that classes are structurally determined in relation to the productive forces and that the capitalist mode of production produces and reproduces two 'unambiguous' classes, the bourgeoisie and the working class, and certain contradictory locations between these two classes.

Can such classes be identified in Britain? And is Britain a capitalist social formation? Westergaard and Resler concluded from their study of the class structure of Britain that:

> The continuing predominance of capital makes for deep fissures in the social structure. The economic order draws major lines of cleavage between people whose life circumstances and share in influence contrast, however they themselves may see their position and respond to it (1976, p. 346).

Their empirical analysis shows that the ownership and control of capital is concentrated amongst a very small proportion of the population, leaving the vast majority dependent upon the sale of their labour power as the means of obtaining their livelihood (ibid., pp. 107–17). They also show, despite ambiguity in their terminology (e.g. pp. 98, 350), that a large proportion of routine non-manual labour shares with manual labour the same relationship to capital and so does not constitute a separate class (ibid., p. 96). Finally, they demonstrate one aspect of the reproduction of classes by showing how the children of the working class and the bourgeoisie generally occupy the same class position respectively as their parents. In sum, this and other evidence assembled by Westergaard and Resler demonstrates that Britain remains a capitalist formation, the two main classes being the bourgeoisie and the working class.

Class fractions

Having adopted criteria for analysing the structure of class relations, we now introduce the concept of class fraction as a means of identifying the base of stratification within classes. We will use the concept of fraction to refer to an objective position within a class boundary which is, in turn, determined by both economic and politico-ideological relations.[1] That is to say, class boundaries mark the objectively different structural positions in economic, political and ideological relations, but these relations also have independent effects within these boundaries. For example, some forms of wage labour occupy a relatively (within the class) advantageous economic position (e.g. skilled manual labour) which has corresponding politico-ideological effects (e.g. a craft ideology). Thus the structure of class determination simultaneously defines the position of one class vis-à-vis another and cleavages within a class, with the consequence that a fraction, along with the class of which it is an integral element (that is to say, it is not 'firstly' or 'mainly' a fraction before it is part of a class), is determined by economic and politico-ideological factors. Moreover, aspects of these structures of class determination are always undergoing transformation (because a mode of production is not a static structure but a structure of processes) and these transformations can serve to reinforce the basis of, or even bring into existence, these cleavages within classes. It follows that an analysis of fractions depends upon a prior analysis of the structure of class determination or, in other words, that fractions are always only class fractions (although this does not mean that they do not or cannot have autonomous effects *qua* fraction).

All classes are objectively fractionalised. They are not first homogeneous and then divided by virtue of the independent intervention of some other class. Certainly, a class can be said to have objective interests in relation to that other class with which it shares an antagonistic relationship but in any given social formation class relations are simultaneously relations between class fractions and this applies both within and between classes. The precise nature and effect of these relations between fractions of classes, and hence between classes and classes, is an historical and conjunctural question which cannot be determined by prior theorising.

Capitalism and gender: women as a class fraction

Our concern in this section is to argue, albeit briefly, that women constitute a class fraction. Our main argument is that it is only through an understanding of the legal and economically dependent conditions under which women perform the role of an actual or potential domestic labourer that the subordinate position of women under capitalism can be understood, particularly their subordinate position as wage labourers.

Most women perform a dual role in production, one as a wage labourer (most working-class women are employed for some or for all of their lives), the other as a domestic labourer. In the first instance a woman will sell her labour power for a wage, while in the second she provides the only comprehensive means for the maintenance and reproduction of labour power.[2] In the latter role she 'services' (cooks, cleans, provides physical and psychological support for) those wage workers within her family unit, and she gives birth to, cares for and socialises children for the next generation of wage workers, all of which is unpaid. Her contract in the latter case is usually one of marriage symbolising the dependent relationship of wives to husbands.

From the nineteenth century onwards it is possible to identify a basic contradiction between capital's need for female wage labour and its parallel need for the working class to reproduce itself. At various conjunctures the state has attempted to manage this contradiction through legislation. For example, the Factory Acts of 1834 restricted the hours worked by women: while they were seen to provide protection for women (who became defined as minors) they also provided a legal underpinning to the notion that a woman's rightful place was in the home caring for her husband and children (Wilson, 1977, pp. 18–22).

During the two world wars women were encouraged to become wage labourers and particularly during the Second World War many provisions for the care of children were introduced to this end. The state was at this point willing to bear some of the costs of the reproduction of the labour force (CSE, 1975, p. 27).

But in 1942 the Beveridge Report made it very clear that women were once more expected to fulfil their primary responsibility for the reproduction of the labour force. 'Official' thinking at this conjuncture was in fact reflecting a body of opinion in child care which stressed the importance of mother–child relationships. Ideological pressure was backed up with limited material rewards (maternity benefit and child allowances). The establishment of the Welfare State did directly benefit the working class in terms of health, education and social security, but it did not alter women's dependent and therefore subordinate status in the realm of political-legal relations (see Wilson, 1977). The ultimate contradiction in the post-war period is that while women were being defined in their primary role as domestic labourers, increasingly large numbers of married women were becoming wage labourers as well, their entry into the labour market meeting the expanding demands of capital *and* the state for service workers in particular.

Since 1945 there have been fundamental changes in the labour market – traditional industries have declined while the service sector and white-collar work has expanded. According to official figures for the mid 1970s it is in the expanding sectors that half the female wage labourers are now employed compared to only a quarter in the manufacturing industries (Mackie and Pattullo, 1977, p. 40).

But whatever the sector, women are concentrated in low-pay industries so that the sexual division of labour within the family is replicated and reinforced in the economy through the creation of whole sectors of women's jobs commanding low rates of pay. The term 'industrialised housework' aptly describes many of the jobs performed by women in the public and private service sectors which were traditionally duties reserved for the domestic labourer in her home. Other jobs which are becoming increasingly female, such as clerical work, have suffered a reduction in both status and wages in comparison with, for example, skilled manual work (Counter Information Services, 1976, p. 10).

The relationship between domestic and wage labour creates a vicious circle for an increasing proportion of women, particularly married women whose numbers in the workforce doubled between 1951 and 1971. Because women are viewed primarily as actual or potential domestic labourers (wives and mothers), their work is considered secondary and temporary and their opportunities for training and promotion are correspondingly reduced. Furthermore, in the absence of day care provision for all under-fives, the vast majority of women are forced to find wage work which enables them to also meet childcare responsibilities. It is therefore hardly surprising that two-thirds of women wage labourers are part-time workers, a particularly vulnerable section of the workforce.

So far we have made no distinctions between women on the grounds of nationality or colour. A recent survey has shown that there is a lower incidence of discrimination among black female applicants for jobs as compared to black men:

> Women seem to face less discrimination than men in the more junior jobs in which they have traditionally worked. This conclusion fits closely with the actual pattern of employment, for the gap in terms of job levels and earnings between the minorities and whites is much greater among men than among women. The explanation is probably that women are already discriminated against as women, and this tends to restrict them to more junior and less well paid jobs; they are therefore not regarded as a threat, and there is less need for employers to discriminate against them on the ground of colour as well, in order to keep them in a subordinate position (Smith, 1977, pp. 120–1).

Later in this volume we will examine in some detail the work patterns of West Indian women, but within the context of the present discussion it is relevant to note that even according to official figures on female employment for women aged between 16 and 54 years, we find that 75 per cent of West Indian women are working, compared with 55 per cent of all women (Smith, ibid., p. 65). Additionally, the difference in the proportion of West Indian, as compared to all, women engaged in wage labour is highest during child-bearing years. In short, West Indian women in Britain are more likely than women taken as a whole to perform a dual role in production.

In sum, we are arguing that women's role as an actual or potential domestic labourer is used ideologically (in the form of sexism) to determine her structurally subordinate position as a wage labourer. Sexism, like racism, is a concept which refers to a process of social categorisation. Hence, we use sexism to refer to those beliefs which set women apart by attributing significance to some biological or other 'inherent' characteristic(s) which they are said to possess, and which attribute other physical and/or social characteristics in a deterministic manner to women. Women therefore occupy a distinct position in economic, political and ideological relations so as to constitute a class fraction.

Our attention must now turn to a consideration of another class fraction, that of migrant labour, one which includes men and women.

Migrant labour and capitalism: the case of Western Europe

We shall here designate as migrant labour that labour which is geographically mobile for the purpose of individual self-advancement but which simultaneously satisfies the demands of capital where there is an inadequate supply of 'local' labour. In contrast to indentured labour or slavery, it is 'free' labour in the sense that there is no physical or political compulsion, although there is a sense in which one can talk of economic compulsion in so far as the 'sending' formation is characterised by structural unemployment and underemployment. The concept of 'migrant' indicates that there are temporal limits, either self-imposed or imposed by contract (or both), to the movement although evidence indicates that in certain circumstances there is a strong tendency for economic migrants to become permanent settlers (e.g. Bohning, 1972; Sivanandan, 1976; Ballard and Ballard, 1977).

Historically, migrant labour has assumed two forms, intranational (or internal) and international (or external), the former involving movement within a national boundary, the latter involving movement across national boundaries. Moreover, international migrant labour can take on one of two forms, colonial or proximate. In both historical instances there is a relationship between the two nations of economic domination/dependence but the nature of the related politico-ideological domination/dependence is different. The colonisation process has had as one of its features the direct politico-ideological domination of the colonised social formation such that there was direct or indirect political rule and the development of an ideology alleging the inferiority of the dominated. As Rex has emphasised (1973) this has had important implications for the perception by indigenous labour in the dominant formation of migrant labour from the dependent colony or ex-colony and we shall return to this point later in the chapter. Migration from the Caribbean to Britain is an example of this form of international migration.

In the case of proximate international migrant labour, there is or has been no direct politico-ideological domination of the economically dependent formation, although economic domination will also entail aspects of politico-ideological domination, particularly when the dependent formation is predominantly rural with only small industrial centres (e.g. advertising sponsored by firms located in the dominant formation). Rather, for various historical reasons, the two formations have entered into an unequal economic relationship and their (relative) proximate geographical relationship, in the context of greater facilities for and speed of travel, makes it possible for the inequality of this relationship to be further expressed by the movement of labour from the dependent to the dominant formation. Migration from Greece and Turkey to Germany is an example of this form of international migrant labour (e.g. see Paine, 1974).

When migration takes an international form, we can talk of the internationalisation of the exploitation of labour as a structural feature of the contemporary capitalist mode of production. Commenting on Western European capitalism Castells (1975) has argued that this structural feature needs to be seen from the perspective of both the dependent and the dominant formations. As far as the former is concerned, migrant labour has become a permanent feature because of the decomposition of backward productive sectors, structural unemployment and the higher nominal and real wages in the dominant capitalist formation. Concerning the latter, Castells argues that immigration is determined by more than a shortage of labour because there is a long-term trend of a growth of migrant labour, despite the appearance of structural unemployment. Moreover, migrant labour now constitutes an important and permanent part of the labour force in the productive sector and is not utilised only in periods of rapid growth.

In much of Western Europe (particularly Germany and Switzerland) there is direct recruitment of migrant labour into low-grade jobs. Economic subordination is paralleled by disadvantage in other spheres, such as housing, education and political rights.

These factors have led Castles and Kosack to argue that migrant workers should be viewed in terms of this common social and economic situation, which is independent of their particular group characteristic (skin colour, language, religion). They argue that migrant workers, although sharing a common class position with indigenous workers who stand in the same relationship to the means of production, are nevertheless objectively a distinct stratum of the working class because of their disadvantaged economic, social and political position. Moreover, this objective division within the class is paralleled by a subjective division: the indigenous working class, due to its authoritarianism (itself the product of repressive socialisation, argue Castles and Kosack) and a fear of competition, are highly prejudiced towards migrant workers and this serves to divide the Labour movement, to the advantage of the dominant class (1973, pp. 430–77).

Let us accept this argument to the extent that it asserts that migrant labour has a specific objective place in both economic and politico-ideological relations such that they constitute a class fraction. But the specific economic and social circumstances to which we refer do not in any way alter the class determination of migrant labour, that is, their general relationship to capital. Hence, we argue that migrant labour constitutes a distinct fraction of the working class. We suggest that Castles and Kosack's analysis is misleading when they identify

> two strata within the working class: the indigenous workers, with generally better conditions and the feelings of no longer being right at the bottom of society, form the higher stratum. The immigrants, who are the most underprivileged and exploited group of society, form the lower stratum (1973, p. 477).

It is equally misleading to suggest that there is a marginal and a mainstream working class (Leggett, 1968, pp. 14–15) without also indicating that the racial or ethnic cleavage to which these terms refer is only one of many lines of cleavage within the working class. Both these formulations abstract and reify only one line of cleavage (i.e. one class fraction) because they fail to grasp theoretically at the outset the full complexity of class relations as being simultaneously relations between class fractions: the working class was not, prior to the migration of labour, first united and then divided by its arrival.

The most important structural tendency of contemporary capitalist formations which is central to understanding migrant labour as a class fraction is the post-war economic growth and accumulation of capital. This, because of the associated technical progress and increased production of services, has led to, amongst other things, changes in the occupational structure (Castles and Kosack, 1973; Bohning, 1972; Nikolinakos, 1975). The expansion of service industries, along with the emergence of new industries requiring either skilled or less arduous labour (or both) has, in the context of full employment until the late 1960s, attracted labour away from what were, comparatively speaking, undesirable and low-wage jobs in other sectors of the economy. There has, therefore, been a shortage of labour in certain sectors of the capitalist economy, a shortage that in the context of full employment in the national economy has been overcome by the internationalisation of the labour market, although, as Bohning has pointed out, this was not the only option open to capital. He suggests that higher wages could have been paid to attract labour into the less desirable jobs (ibid., p. 56), but in so doing he ignores the possibility that certain sectors of capital have been dependent upon migrant labour as a 'source of the excess profit necessary to compensate for their below average rate of profit' (Castells, 1975, p. 58; also Cohen and Jenner, 1968, p. 55). A further option open to capital was to draw upon women as a reserve army of labour. We know of no data which clearly illustrates why this option was not adopted, although we would speculate that it would have necessitated the provision of child-care and other social facilities which may have been more costly than the establishment of the contract labour system as in the case of Germany, France and Switzerland, and the use of migrant labour from the New Commonwealth in the case of Britain. Certainly, in the latter case, the migrant labour solution involved little or no expenditure on social capital because, as is now clear, many of the problems' consequent upon migration were due not to the character of the migrants themselves, but to the failure to provide additional housing, social and welfare facilities.

In Western capitalist formations the migrant labour solution produces its own effects, the first being that migrant labour tends to occupy a specific economic position within the broader category of wage labour: it is not only concentrated within the manual working class, but in semi- and unskilled sections of the working class. To this specific position in the labour market corresponds a parallel position in the housing market. Thus, on the basis of the available evidence, we argue that migrant labour in Western capitalist formations occupies a distinct economic position within the working class.

Migrant labour also occupies a distinct position in political and ideological relations. Although the specific features vary from one formation to another, migrant labour occupies a subordinate *de jure* or *de facto* legal political situation; for example, migrant labour has been prevented from participation in the political process; in some Western European countries has been denied permanent residence rights, has been prevented or discouraged from being accompanied by families, and has been denied access to certain institutions and services (Castles and Kosack, 1973; Castells, 1975). The subordinate position in ideological relations is evident, at one extreme, in that they have become the object of agitation by right-wing and neo-Nazi political parties, ascribing migrant labour with negatively valuated physical and cultural characteristics, often as a means of justifying discriminatory action against such labour.

It is relevant to stress that there is a certain consistency in the position of migrant labour in these three different sets of relations, to the extent that one might suggest that migrant labour is over-determined as a fraction of the working class. It is because migrant labour, at least initially, has been conceived as contract labour to be employed for a limited period and then returned to the country of origin (that is, conceived as a 'guest' worker) that it has been denied rights of citizenship. In addition, both capital and labour have, in certain circumstances, concluded that it is in their mutual interests to maintain migrant labour in certain sectors of the labour market, both consequently ascribing inferior characteristics to migrant labour as justification for their action. Put in other terms, a self-fulfilling prophecy is in operation: migrant labour, having been 'produced' by the demand for labour in socially undesirable and low-wage sectors of the economy, is confined to those sectors, often by specific policies and practices which are partially justified by the ascription of inferior characteristics, the consequence then being viewed as a vindication of the ideology.

On the basis of this argument, we assert that migrant labour constitutes a fraction of the working class in contemporary Western capitalist formations. The position of migrant labour in the British formation is, however, distinct in a number of respects.

Black migrant labour in Britain

It is here that we must establish the specificity of the international context of British capitalism which had important consequences for the nature of the solution which arose in response to the problem of labour shortage in certain sectors of the economy, beginning in the mid 1950s. A central feature of this context was the legal legacy of the British Empire, one important aspect of which was that Commonwealth citizens shared with citizens of the United Kingdom and Colonies the right to live and work in Britain. Hence when the shortage of labour developed, it was much easier for Commonwealth citizens to come to Britain to sell their labour power than for, say, southern Europeans who were legally aliens and were obliged to obtain a work permit. Moreover, the shortage of labour in Britain coincided with developments in certain Commonwealth countries which encouraged at least a proportion of their citizens to consider migration to Britain for economic reasons (Peach, 1968). Thus there began in the early 1950s an economic migration from the Caribbean, to be followed slightly later by a similar migration from the Indian sub-continent. The facts and details of this migration have been well discussed elsewhere and do not require repetition here (e.g. Deakin, 1970). What we wish to establish is the extent of the similarity (and hence, dissimilarity) between the migration of labour to Britain compared to migration to the other Western capitalist formations.

The source of migrant labour is similar in so far as the countries of origin occupy a subordinate position in the world capitalist economy: they all have a large, even predominant, agricultural sector which, where it does exist alongside an industrial sector, not only serves to demonstrate its own uneven, internal development, but also the underdevelopment of the economy as a whole in comparison with the formations to which labour migrates. Finally, at least at the outset of the migration process, the majority of migrant workers have been 'target workers', though as we have already noted, there are strong tendencies at work which encourage the migrant to be a settler.

Black migrant labour and legal relations

But there are also important dissimilarities relating to politico-ideological relations which other writers have either ignored or played down, all of which relate to the distinction drawn earlier between colonial and proximate migrant labour. In the case of Britain, for reasons already explained, from the early 1950s until 1968 most migrant labour originated from the New Common-wealth, that is, from those countries which had most recently exchanged colonial for Commonwealth status. For various impor-tant historical reasons, the formations in question all had predomin-ntly black populations, with the consequence that the majority of migrant labour to Britain has been black. Moreover, with the exception of the recruitment office set up by London Transport in Barbados (Brooks, 1975a), the initial phase of migration to Britain from the New Commonwealth was not officially organised or selective. Certainly, companies advertised for labour in newspapers in New Commonwealth countries but labour was not selectively recruited on a contract basis as, for example, in most other EEC countries (Yannopoulos, 1975). This feature of migrant labour is, in turn, related to the fact that, until 1962, New Commonwealth migrants had the right to live and work in Britain without restriction and, moreover, upon arrival had the same political-legal rights as the indigenous population. Although the rights of residence and access to employment for New Commonwealth citizens have been gradually removed, with the result that, since the 1971 Immigration Act, Britain now has a contract labour system similar to that pertaining in the rest of the EEC (Sivanandan, 1976), those who actually migrated prior to the legislative changes continue to have the same *de jure* political-legal rights, except with respect to the rights of certain dependants to live with them in Britain (e.g. Moore and Wallace, 1975; Dummett, 1976).

These differences are of considerable significance in relation to the claim of Castells that the greater exploitability of migrant labour derives from its inferior legal-political status and that the specificity of migrant labour as a class fraction is defined by the fact that they are both workers and foreigners (1975, pp. 53–4, 57). Nikolinakos also draws attention to the fact that migrant labour in the EEC lacks the political rights of indigenous labour (1975, p. 7). If both inferior legal-political status and status as a foreigner are interpreted in a precise, *de jure* sense, then Castell's analysis does not apply in all aspects to the British case. For example, despite the provisions of the 1971 Immigration Act, it is not yet possible to deport *en masse* the vast majority of black workers who arrived in Britain in the 1950s and 1960s as a means of eliminating an unemployment problem. Moreover, migrant labour from the New Commonwealth did not have, again until 1971, the legal status of 'foreigner' (or in British legal terms, alien). It has therefore been much easier for New Commonwealth migrants to settle permanently in Britain, either by simply not returning or by consciously deciding not to return to the country of origin, and in so far as they have been able to bring with them or form families after migration, a new generation of black British has been created. Thus, by virtue of the legal status of Commonwealth citizens prior to the legislative changes of the 1960s, migrant labour from the New Commonwealth, given its specificity as a fraction of the working class, is reproducing itself as part of the working class, not as migrant labour, but as black indigenous labour. And, finally, unlike migrants in the remainder of Western capitalism, migrant labour from the New Commonwealth has always had the right of full political participation in the formal sphere of electoral politics. In sum, then, the position of black migrant labour from the New Commonwealth in political relations is different in important aspects from that of migrant labour in other western capitalist formations.

However, if we consider not only the *de jure* but also the *de facto* position of migrant labour in political relations, its subordinate position in these relations in Britain is clear. Firstly, there has been (e.g. Daniel, 1968) and still is (e.g. Smith, 1977) substantial discrimination against black workers in employment, housing and the provision of services. Up until 1966 racial discrimination was not illegal, from which we argue that black migrant labour was legally disadvantaged in that it was legally unable to counter its subordinate position. Moreover, it is questionable whether the provisions of the 1966 and 1968 Race Relations Acts really did alter that subordinate position because of the nature of the process established to gain redress and the field of application of the legislation; in this respect, the 1976 Act has more to be said in its favour, although its actual impact and effect has yet to be demonstrated. One should also recall in this connection that not all discrimination was the result of individual purposive action but of the effects of rules and procedures formulated and practised before the arrival of migrant labour; for example, it has been argued that a residential requirement for access to council housing is an example of institutional, indirect discrimination against black migrants (Rex and Tomlinson, 1979). Finally, there is evidence available to suggest that black migrant labour and the migrants' children occupy a second-class status in the law enforcement process (Humphrey, 1972; Pulle, 1973; Select Committee, 1977). This is particularly evident in the way in which Section 4 of the Vagrancy Act, 1824, is being used to prosecute black youth on 'sus' charges (Demuth, 1978).

Our argument is, therefore, that although black migrant labour in Britain does not formally occupy a subordinate legal-political situation, it does so in a *de facto* sense. In concentrating only on the *de jure* legal-political situation of migrant labour, Castells and Nikolinakos ignore this important dimension and so exclude New Commonwealth migrant labour from their terms of reference. We believe that this is inappropriate and misleading because a focus only on the content of the law tells us nothing about how law is interpreted and used in practice, nor about what areas of behaviour are not at any specific point in time subject to legal restraint.

This adds substance to the earlier claim that a distinction be drawn between proximate and colonial migrant labour, a distinction which, we have suggested, is particularly important in identifying the specificity of the British situation, although it also has relevance to France, Holland, Belgium and Portugal in that these formations have also had to respond to colonial migrant labour.

Black migrant labour and economic relations

So far in our consideration of the position of migrant labour from the New Commonwealth in the British class structure, the emphasis has been upon its place in legal-political relations. We now want to consider its place in economic relations, and here we wish to contest the view of Westergaard and Resler that immigration from the New Commonwealth has not introduced 'a significant new dimension to the pattern of stratification in Britain' (1976, p. 356). Although we agree that black migrants as a whole do not constitute an 'under-class' and that 'stratification by colour' has not replaced 'stratification by class', we believe that they have overestimated the extent to which black migrants are 'equally' distributed throughout the economic structure. In their concern to show that 'coloured people are not uniformly concentrated at the bottom of the economic order' (p. 356) by questioning the 'conventional assumption' that the majority of black migrants are in unskilled jobs, they gloss over the extent to which they are concentrated within the manual working class and, compared with all workers, concentrated within the semi- and unskilled sections of the working class.

Their argument hinges upon their claims that the majority of male, black workers, with the exception of Pakistanis, are in skilled or non-manual jobs, a claim based upon the work of Castles and Kosack and, indeed, subsequently supported by the work of Smith (1976, p. 64). However, closer attention to the occupational distribution of black workers, using Smith's data, shows that this is so only because of the large proportion of black migrants, particularly West Indians, in skilled manual jobs; in other words, only a very small proportion of black migrants are in non-manual employment. Thus, of the male black migrant workers (excluding African Asians) in the PEP study, 42 per cent were in semi- or unskilled jobs, with a further 45 per cent in skilled manual jobs, compared to 18 per cent and 42 per cent for white, male workers respectively (Smith, 1976, p. 64). For women, 63.5 per cent of black migrants were in manual occupations, compared with 45 per cent of white working women; this disparity reflects, in the main, the fact that 45 per cent of black working women are in semi-skilled manual jobs, compared with 24 per cent of white working women (Smith, 1976, pp. 69, 215). A study of employment in Walsall shows a similar if not more extreme, picture, the author concluding:

> Black workers, both male and female, are overwhelmingly in the semi-skilled and unskilled grades. Excluding the health service area, very few black workers are to be found higher than at the skilled manual level. . . . Black concentration in semi-skilled manual occupations in particular is very marked. Few are found in supervisory posts ... (Brooks, 1975b, p. 10).

Our first point, therefore, is that not only are black migrants predominantly manual workers, but also that more than two-fifths of them are in semi- and unskilled jobs (see also Unit for Manpower Services, 1977, p. 43).

Second, black migrant workers are not only disproportionately concentrated in manufacturing industries but in certain types of manufacturing industry. For example, Smith's study showed that of his sample 47 per cent of black male migrants and 36 per cent of black women were employed in manufacturing industries, compared with 33 per cent of white men and 25 per cent of white women (1976, p. 73). Within manufacturing, one finds disproportionate numbers of black migrants in shipbuilding, vehicle production, textiles, construction and food manufacture (ibid., pp. 74, 219; see also Unit for Manpower Studies, 1977). When Smith analysed his data regionally, he found a substantial disproportionate concentration of black migrants in the textile industry (Yorkshire and Lancashire) and a lesser concentration in metal manufacture (Midlands) (1976, p. 75). Moreover, where black migrants are employed in the service sector of the economy, they are disproportionately represented in transport and communications, hotels and catering and the National Health Service, sectors in which semi- and unskilled labour predominates (Smith, 1976, p. 73; Unit for Manpower Studies, 1977, pp. 55–69).

Third, these manufacturing industries and services in which black migrants are concentrated share several, if not all, of the following characteristics: shortage of labour, shift working, unsocial hours, low pay, and an unpleasant working environment (see Unit for Manpower Studies, 1977, pp. 44–69; Smith, 1976, pp. 64–81). These characteristics correlate with each other in an important way: there is shortage of labour because the work involves unsocial hours, low pay and an unpleasant environment. Moreover, at least in the case of the textile industry, low wage rates are a function of its low profitability in the face of international competition, and Cohen and Jenner have argued that it is probably because migrant labour has been willing to work for low wages that the industry's rate of contraction has been slowed down (1968). Given a shortage of labour, employers in these sectors of the economy have been only too willing to employ black migrant labour (Smith, 1976, p. 37). In other words, black labour tends to be replacement labour, employed in socially undesirable jobs vacated in the context of full employment by white indigenous labour.

Finally, there is now some evidence to suggest that the concentration of black labour in the manual working class is being reproduced, partly because of racial discrimination. Not only is there still considerable discrimination at the point of employment, particularly for both unskilled manual and non-manual jobs (Smith, 1977, pp. 108–11, 119–21), but also in connection with promotion (ibid., pp. 185–90), leading Smith to conclude that 'there is little evidence that racial inequalities in the employment field will be quickly corrected by upward mobility of Asians and West Indians' (ibid., p. 190). Even where black people born in

Britain have entered and completed higher education, they experience considerable discrimination when trying to find employment and the evidence suggests that black graduates tend to only obtain employment commensurate with their qualifications when they are not in competition with equally well-qualified whites (Ballard and Holden, 1975). What actually happens to black graduates is not yet known, but it is not unreasonable to speculate that the black, manual working class may not only include a substantial proportion of black immigrants who obtained degrees prior to migration (Smith, 1977, pp. 75-6), but also black British who obtained degrees in Britain.

On the basis of this evidence, we argue that although the majority of black workers are not concentrated in unskilled jobs in Britain, neither are they randomly distributed throughout the working class. In other words, although the majority of black migrants are structurally part of the working class, there is a systematic pattern of economic 'stratification' within that class. We argue that this is so, and indeed, is to be expected to be so because migrant labour was attracted to Britain precisely to fill a labour shortage in certain sectors of the economy. The most recent accentuation (first manifest by the late 1960s) of the long-term historical decline of British capitalism has probably allowed only a very small proportion of black people to move out of those sectors of the economy characterised by low pay, shiftwork, poor conditions, etc. Westergaard and Resler fail to acknowledge that black labour is migrant labour and that its presence and position in the British economy must therefore be evaluated in the context of the structural demand of the capitalist mode of production for migrant labour. We argue that it is by locating migrant labour in terms of the structural tendencies of the capitalist mode of production that one can explain its economic position in Britain, a position which is sufficiently structured to warrant description as a class fraction.

Black migrant labour and ideological relations: racial categorisation
But migrant labour constitutes a class fraction not only because of its position in political and economic relations but also because of its position in ideological relations. There are two levels to this position, levels which are intimately connected in reality, but which should be considered separately for analytic clarity. The first concerns the fact that the arrival of black migrant labour in Britain has been said to have produced a 'race relations' situation: that is to say, the migrants are perceived to belong to 'races' which, by

implication, are distinct from the 'race' of the perceivers. We have suggested elsewhere (Miles and Phizacklea, 1979, pp. 4–5) that this definition came to prevail for the following reasons. Viewed historically, the 'race' concept has tended to be used when people are being classified in terms of their physical characteristics: thus, if a population consists of two groups which are clearly physically distinguishable, and significance is attached to some aspect of this distinguishability, it is usually concluded that the two groups belong to different 'races'. The idea that the world's population can be divided into permanent and distinct racial types (Banton, 1977, p. 27) has been shown to be without justification (Banton and Harwood, 1975) but this has not prevented politicians and public from defining the situation in Britain following the arrival of black migrant workers as one where 'races' were relating. This definition has been encouraged by the development of mass communications on an international scale, enabling attention to be focused upon apparently similar relations elsewhere in the world (Hartmann and Husbands, 1974, pp. 133-6) and so confirming the validity of the definition in Britain.

This explanation is undoubtedly incomplete but there is nevertheless evidence to support the argument that the designation of a 'race relations' situation in Britain since the 1950s is a social construction, hence Banton's useful notion of racialisation (1977, pp. 18–19). Thus, when a population is racialised (or racially categorised), as was the case in Britain by the 1960s, we are dealing with a strictly ideological process for there is no adequate scientific evidence to support a division of population into exclusive racial types. In other words, black migrant workers in Britain have a specific place in ideological relations because social significance is attached to their physical appearance, a significance which leads to their being categorised as a 'race'.

It is analytically important to stress that the significance that is attached to physical differentiation could be positive or negative although in fact the historical evidence shows that the significance has been negative, at least for those groups which have been the object of racial categorisation. This leads us to the second aspect of the position of migrant labour in ideological relations, racism, a concept about which there has been much argument and confusion.

In the late 1960s Banton defined racism as 'the doctrine that a man's behaviour is determined by stable inherited characters deriving from separate racial stocks having distinctive attributes and usually considered to stand to one another in relations of superiority and inferiority' (1970, p. 18) and suggested that the denial of equal treatment to 'outgroups' which does not appeal to biology should be labelled as ethno-centric (p. 31).

Although Banton has now departed from this definition (1977), it has been subject to substantial criticism, notably by Rex. He argued that the position outlined by Banton was unnecessarily restrictive because deterministic theories which refer to sociological or historical factors in justification of the inferior treatment of a particular group have the same function as if they had referred to biological factors. Consequently, Rex defined as racist those beliefs which posit a deterministic relationship between membership of a specifically identified group and possession of certain qualities which draw upon biological, sociological, cultural or religious evidence to justify the exclusion of the minority (1970, pp. 12 144–60).

We have previously argued (Phizacklea and Miles, 1979) that racism should be defined as those beliefs and arguments which give rise to the identification of a negatively evaluated racial category and what immediately follows is a modification of that analysis. We use racism to refer to those negative beliefs held by one group which identify and set apart another by attributing significance to some biological or other 'inherent' characteristic(s) which it is said to possess, and which deterministically associate that characteristic(s) with some other (negatively evaluated) feature(s) or action(s). The possession of these supposed characteristics is then used as justification for denying that group equal access to material and other resources and/or political rights.

We use 'inherent' to indicate that, although the characteristic(s) in question may not be biologically based, it is nevertheless regarded as innate or 'natural'; that is, it is not actually hereditary but it is perceived as if it were so (as in the instance of the belief that 'all Jews are usurers'). Hence, the characteristic(s) to which significance is attached can be biological or social/cultural: what matters, as Rex has argued, is that the group's possession of the characteristic(s) is said to be determined (1970, p. 159). To make the same point differently, the group is said or implied to possess a (negatively evaluated) characteristic(s) which, even if it is social/cultural, is as much ineradicable as a characteristic which is governed by genetic inheritance.

According to the definition advanced here, racist beliefs can be held about groups which are not distinguishable by colour, an important theoretical consideration given the history of hostile sentiment in Britain about Irish migrant workers and Jewish refugees (see, for example, Benewick, 1972; Nugent and King, 1979)

But this is not to ignore the significance of skin colour to racist beliefs: by its very nature, skin colour is an immediately obvious feature to which significance can be attached and this goes some way towards explaining the prevalence and apparent potency of the racism articulated from within all classes in Britain since the 1950s.

It is important to stress that our definition of racism does not require the beliefs and arguments in question to be systematically or logically ordered. One might usefully mention Gramsci's notion of common sense which refers to the incoherent conception of the world which is dominant within any given social formation (1971, pp. 323 ff., 419 ff.) rather than ideology or belief system, both of which imply a logical and hierarchically organised set of beliefs. Racist beliefs are often vague and contradictory so that in the British context one can often find the reference of an argument shifting from allegations about the 'coloured' to the 'Asians' and then to the 'immigrants' without it being made clear whether these terms are being used to refer to the same group. Indeed, it is just this vague and shifting quality of the beliefs that prevent them from being effectively challenged by argument (Rex, 1970). We have stressed this inchoate aspect of racism in our analysis of working class racism when we drew a distinction between systematic and piecemeal racism (Phizacklea and Miles, 1979, p. 117; cf. Husbands, 1979).

It is the ascription of the 'race' label and the articulation of racism in the British social formation which ensures that migrant workers have a particular position in ideological relations. This is not the place to show in detail why and how this is so but there is evidence to demonstrate that governments, individual politicians, neo-fascist political organisations, the mass media, employers, institutions of the labour movement and sections of the working-class in Britain have all acted and articulated racist beliefs which have identified black migrant workers as an excluded racial category (Hartmann and Husbands, 1974; Evans, 1976; Sivanandan, 1976; Schoen, 1977; Miles and Phizacklea, 1977a, b, 1978, 1979).

Conclusion

In this chapter we have outlined a case for conceiving of black migrant labour in Britain as a fraction of the working class. The theoretical context of our study is therefore an analysis of Britain as a capitalist social formation which, like other Western European capitalist formations, developed a need for migrant labour as a solution to labour shortage in certain sectors of the economy. Once we have established this context we then consider it necessary to consider the fact that, since their arrival, the migrant labourers have been racially categorised. The implications of this process for the political strategies available to black migrant labour are considered in the next chapter.

Notes

1 It should be recognised at the outset that the notion of divisions within classes is not a new one. Lenin, for example, spoke of the working-class aristocracy (1963) while an American sociologist has referred to the internal stratification of the working class (Form, 1973), but there have been few attempts to systematically theorise about these divisions. The work of Poulantzas is perhaps a major exception, although his early theorisation (1973) is far from clear and does not easily accord with his later analysis of classes in contemporary capitalism (1978). For example, in his earlier work he argues that social categories and fractions are both distinct from strata in that the latter, unlike the former, do not constitute 'social forces' (1973, p. 84), while in his later analysis he suggests that all three have the potential of becoming 'social forces' (1978, p. 23). Moreover, the precise (and obscure) definitions offered in the early text of categories, fractions and strata (1973, pp. 84–5) are not reproduced in the later theoretical formulation (1978, p. 23) or clearly followed in the analysis of classes in the French social formation (1978, pp. 303–26). This is a serious criticism given his expressed desire to eliminate the obscurity of Marxist analysis on this issue (1973, p. 84).

In this context, the concept of social category is of little relevance if it is used to refer to 'social ensembles ... which ... may become social force whose distinguishing feature is based on their specific and over-determining relation to structures other than economic ones' (1973, p. 84), that is, defined by their place only in political and ideological relations (1978, p. 23). Hence, if we are to argue, as we will, that the position of black workers has to be defined by their place in economic and political and ideological relations, then they cannot be defined as a social category, along with bureaucratic officials and intellectuals. But what of the concepts of fraction and strata? Unfortunately, the distinction between these two concepts is problematic because they both refer to places in economic, political and ideological relations: Poulantzas specifically denies that the distinction between fraction and strata is a distinction between the effects of the economic and of the politico-ideological respectively and argues that the identification of fractions can depend on the political level while the identification of strata can be located in the economic (1973, p. 85). But after dispensing with the argument that a fraction, unlike a stratum, has the potential for constituting a social force, we have no means of identifying one from another. This is made evident when Poulantzas writes that both fractions and strata are distinguished 'on the basis of differentiation in the economic sphere, and of the role, a quite particular one in these cases, of political and ideological relations' (1978, p. 23). Thereafter, in his most recent work, Poulantzas distinguishes strata of the working class (1978, pp. 198, 276, 279) and fractions of the bourgeoisie (1978, pp. 91–2) and of the new petit-bourgeoisie (1978, pp. 303–26) without justifying the conceptual distinction.

But this later work does offer us some criteria for identifying fractions, at least within the new petit-bourgeoisie. His argument, in essence, is that the structure of class determination not only determines the boundary of the petit-bourgeoisie but also cleavages within this class and, morevoer, that elements within that structure of determination are undergoing transformation, with corresponding effects on the internal cleavages. It is as a consequence of identifying five different transformations within the sector of non-productive wage labour (within the determinants of the class boundary of the petit-bourgeoisie) that Poulantzas identifies three major fractions of the new petit-bourgeoisie which have 'an objectively proletarian polarisation'.

While not wishing to necessarily accept the validity of this specific analysis of the so-called new petit-bourgeoisie, nor the supposed distinction between fraction and stratum (because we cannot find a clear reason in the analysis for such a distinction), we do believe that Poulantzas' theory does provide us with a means of identifying the bases of 'stratification' within classes. Hereafter, therefore, we use the concept of fraction to refer to an objective position within a class boundary.

Much debate has surrounded the question of whether or not domestic labour contributes to the value of labour power and therefore indirectly to surplus value through its role of maintaining and reproducing labour power (Seccombe, 1974; Gardiner, 1975; Coulson, Magas and Wainwright, 1975; Smith, 1979; West, 1979). None of those party to this dispute deny that capital benefits from domestic labour which performs services for which there are no or inadequate substitutes. Domestic labour can be viewed as a way of subsidising working-class wages (see Conference of Socialist Economists, 1975) because the latter are not equivalent to the total labour performed in the reproduction of labour power (see West, ibid., p. 7).

CHAPTER 2

Migrant labour and the political process in Britain

So far we have argued a case for considering black migrant labour as a racialised fraction of the working class and this has involved brief consideration of the position of black workers in Britain in political relations. In this chapter we intend to consider this position in much greater detail, with the overall aim of designating the political strategies which are open to black migrant workers as a consequence of their fractionalised class position. In so doing, we shall narrow our focus from the general category of black migrant labour to one group which constituted that category in the British case, that is, black migrant labour from the Caribbean.

We must stress at this point that this narrowing of a focus also specifically excludes consideration of the place in political relations of the children of black migrants, a large proportion of whom are now British born. We believe (Miles and Phizacklea, 1977a, p. 49; 1979, pp. 15–16; Miles, 1979) that the political ideology and practice of black youth in Britain has to be considered in somewhat different theoretical context, because black youth are either not themselves migrants or are not migrants in a self-willed sense but find themselves in Britain because their parents brought them here.

The national political context

We do not wish to recount in detail the formal political response to the arrival of black migrant labour from the Caribbean, the Indian sub-continent and from East Africa for the story is, if not well known, certainly much written about (e.g. Deakin, 1970; Hiro, 1971; Katznelson, 1973; Moore, 1975; Miles and Phizacklea, 1979; Rex and Tomlinson, 1979). In addition to defining the consequence of the arrival of black migrant labour as the creation of a 'race relations' situation, this response involved the imposition of immigration controls which were specifically aimed at black migrant

26

(and were therefore racist) and the formulation and initiation of a policy of 'integration' which had as its aim the establishment of 'good race relations'. This latter policy has had a number of specific strands: anti-discrimination legislation, the formation of state institutions to encourage positive 'community relations' (the Community Relations Commission, the role of which has now been subsumed by the Commission for Racial Equality), and various programmes of material assistance to areas where the majority of migrants have settled (the most recent of which focuses on the 'inner city', which will be discussed in chapter 3). Both the Labour and Conservative parties, despite disagreement at various times about specific details of these policies, have agreed that (black) immigration control is essential to ensure 'good race relations', a proposition that is both logically and practically unsound (see Moore and Wallace, 1975). There is therefore a considerable degree of unanimity within the formal political process about the terms on which black workers should enter and live in Britain and in so far as both parties have advanced and perpetuated racist policies, there are limitations on the extent to which black workers can expect to improve their disadvantaged position by involvement in and support for either of these two parties.

A more specific limitation follows from one specific strand of government policy, the formation of the Community Relations Commission which, at the local level, both reorganised existing and stimulated the formation of new committees concerned to encourage 'good race relations'. It has been argued that these committees have acted as a quasi-colonial buffer institution, supposedly serving as a forum for the articulation of specifically black grievances and thereby indirectly linking the black population to the political structure. The result is that the community relations apparatus serves as an instrument of social control, ensuring and attempting to enshrine the political marginality of black migrants and their children (Katznelson, 1973, pp. 175–208; for a critique see Lawrence, 1974). There is other evidence available to support this conclusion. For example, in his assessment of Birmingham Community Relations Committee, Newton argues that 'the Committee has contributed to the whole issue's being de-politicised. It has been removed from the main political arena and shunted off into a little siding where it can be easily forgotten' (1976, p. 216). That this is so is due also to the related fact that British political parties focus on and organise around class issues and rarely sponsor issues of specific concern to black people, especially if that issue is expected to receive an unfavourable reaction from the respective white electorate.

Newton argues that the result is that in Birmingham, black people, as a racialised fraction of the working class, do not have a voice in Birmingham politics, at least not in the formal sphere. There is no obvious reason why this conclusion should not hold for the other major areas of settlement of black migrant labour.

It might be objected that the establishment of the Commission for Racial Equality under the terms of the Race Relations Act, 1976, has changed this. However, given its terms of reference and continuing sponsored form of representation of black interests, it is difficult to see how it can perform a role other than that of 'domestic neo-colonialism' (Sivanandan, 1976). As long as the machinery exists, the main political parties can attempt to bypass many of the issues of concern to black workers while the latter remain sceptical about the expediency of using the machinery. Indeed, in a recent study in our research borough in London, 76 per cent of the black people interviewed had not even heard of the local Community Relations Council (Morrison, 1976, p. 102).

In sum, events within the formal political process in Britain have had two major effects on the place of black migrant labour in the political process and therefore upon the political strategies available to that labour. First, it has assisted in the racial categorisation of black migrant labour through the implementation of racist policies (particularly in the area of immigration control) and through its legitimation of the 'race relations' framework in which the consequences of the migration have come to be perceived and discussed. Second, it has attempted to channel the demands and grievances of black migrant labour through alternative institutions. Both imply that the formal political process is unlikely to be an effective arena (at least in itself) for the articulation and advancement of the interests of black migrant labour.

Black migrants and political action in Britain

We have elsewhere argued (although we no longer adhere to the form in which some of our points were expressed) that the political action of black migrant labour should be viewed in the context of three possible political strategies being available to them (Miles and Phizacklea, 1977a): class unity, ethnic organisation and black unity. This first strategy recognises that black migrant labour is, structurally, part of the working class, from which it can be concluded that the specific interests of black workers will be articulated and advanced through working-class political institutions. In the field of formal politics, this would mean that black workers would join and participate in the traditional organisations of the working class, while in the informal sphere it would involve membership of and participation in revolutionary parties, rank and file trade union movements and locally-based protest and direct-action groups. The other two strategies place greater emphasis upon the fact that black workers are migrants and constitute a racialised fraction of the working class, from which it is concluded that they will initiate and express their specific interests through quite separate processes or organisations in both the formal and informal sphere of politics. This requires more detailed discussion.

Hitherto our category of black migrant labour has been used in such a way as to perhaps imply that those persons to whom the category applies are characterised by social and cultural homogeneity. This is not the case, and it is at this point that our analysis must first take cognisance of the social and cultural diversity of the groups in Britain which we designate as migrant labour. The most publicly recognised distinction is between migrants from the Caribbean and from the Indian sub-continent, but within these large groups further distinctions have to be made. Migrants from the Caribbean are usually described as West Indians, although in the late 1950s and 1960s this was not a term used much by the migrants themselves but was a label attached by the indigenous population (Midgett, 1975, pp.76–7). The migrants were more aware of themselves in terms of their island of origin and, more specifically, the area of that island where they had been born and/or had lived (e.g. Philpott, 1973; Midgett, 1975; Sutton and Makiesky, 1975; Pearson, 1977; Foner, 1979). Although these migrants were coming from a colonial context in which racial categorisation was a central feature, their expectations rarely included any notion that they would experience racism and discrimination in the 'Mother Country' (e.g. Sutton and Makiesky, 1975; Foner, 1979). Rather, they saw themselves as British (indeed, the colonial government had encouraged them to hold such a belief), as well as holding to a national island identity, and it has been their experience of racism and discrimination which has played an important part in their developing a 'West Indian' identity.

In certain respects the same argument applies in the case of migrants from the Indian sub-continent and from East Africa. These migrants are commonly referred to as 'Asian' yet this notion glosses over a wide range of cultural diversity which, again, is taken account of only by referring to both the national and regional origins of the migrants (e.g. Khan, 1976). In their daily lives it is the regional and, indeed, village origin which is of greatest importance, at least in relation to their interaction with 'fellow' migrants. The notion of Indians or Pakistanis as an ethnic group is therefore a misnomer, such collectivities best being expressed as a national grouping, reserving the concept of ethnic group for reference to Mirpuris, Sikhs etc. (Khan, 1976, 1977; Ballard and Ballard, 1977). It is only in their contact with British society, and particularly when this contact is expressed through racism and discrimination, that these migrants too are made aware of their being perceived as a single racial and 'ethnic' category. This is of particular significance in understanding political processes within the respective national and ethnic communities (e.g. Le Lohé, 1979), processes which do not always articulate with or have relevance to the British political process but which are bound up with the migrants' continuing ties with their country, region and village of origin (e.g. De Witt, 1969).

But our concern here is with the British political process and with the fact that the racial categorisation of migrant labour has important implications for the relationship of these migrants to this process. The important point is that if we can conceive of West Indians as constituting an ethnic group in the sense described above and if we note that migrants from the Indian sub-continent can only sensibly be viewed as an ethnic group in terms of their region (and even village) of origin, then we can return to our discussion of ethnic organisation and black unity because we have now recognised that, in so far as political action implies the recognition of common interests, the common interests of black migrant labour in Britain result from a complex equation of racial categorisation overlaying considerable social and cultural diversity. Our categories of ethnic organisation and black unity consequently involve simplification for the purpose of analytical clarity, but it is enough to stress here that the boundary of the respective ethnic group in question has to be designated in each empirical instance. We shall do this ourselves later in this chapter by focusing our interest solely on West Indians.

Thus we refer to ethnic organisation as a political strategy when migrant workers pursue political interests on an ethnic basis: that is to say, a group believes that a specified political goal can best be attained by organising with other individuals who are defined as belonging to the same ethnic group. At the level of formal politics, this can take the form of voting for representatives of ethnic political organisations at local or national elections; voting for an ethnic candidate adopted by one of the three main bourgeois political parties who specifically seeks to utilise ethnic ties as a basis for recruiting support and votes; members of ethnic groups standing for election on a platform relevant only to the specific ethnic group; organising an ethnic block vote, or withholding such a vote; or, finally, establishing an ethnic organisation to represent ethnic interest within the formal political process. Ethnic organisation in the informal sphere of politics can take the form of an extra-electoral protest group, an ethnically-based revolutionary party, or, at the place of work, ethnically-based trade union organisation.

Finally, we refer to black unity when black workers conceive of themselves as having sufficient interests in common to justify organisation over and above the ethnic boundaries that otherwise divide them. This would entail joint recognition of their position as a racialised fraction of the working class. The recognition and expression of these interests could take the same political forms as outlined in relation to ethnic organisation.

Which of these strategies best describes the political action of black workers in Britain? In order to answer this question, we ought to begin by taking note of the available evidence which, in fact, is not extensive. Lawrence (1974) argues that class unity is unlikely in the present circumstances because of the extent of racist sentiment within the working class. In addition he argues that, while West Indian workers are the closest of all migrant groups to the indigenous population in terms of culture and self-identity, his findings suggest that they are the least likely to adopt a class perspective in approaching politics (ibid., p. 57). Concerning ethnic organisation, he suggests that this is a possibility for Indians and Pakistanis because of their comparatively greater communality. He doubts that black unity is possible in the present circumstances because of the mutual suspicion and hostility between the respective ethnic and national groups in Britain. His overall conclusion is that black workers will withdraw from participation in British political institutions because of their experience of racism and discrimination and their original intention not to settle permanently in Britain. Katznelson (1973) agrees that class unity has been ruled out by racial exclusion, particularly after it became institutionalised by successive Conservative and Labour governments. The alternative that he conceives, that of direct bargaining by black people, has been achieved 'only in the highly inadequate form of uni-directional buffering institutions' (ibid., p. 184).

Rex (1979) poses the problem rather differently, although he arrives at a somewhat similar conclusion. He argues that because British politics are essentially expressed in terms of class divisions, there is little scope for black workers to buy themselves into the political system through ethnic organisation in the way that migrant groups did in the United States. The only 'way in' for the working-class black migrant is to gain acceptance by the indigenous working class and its relevant institutions and to enjoy the protection which these institutions provide. Given the poor record of British trade union attitude and practice towards black workers on the one hand, and the sponsored forms of black representation on the other, when faced with racism and racial discrimination black workers are forced to look for support towards militant black organisations which are neighbourhood- rather than work-based and which adopt the practice of defensive confrontation. Rex is therefore emphasising, as we do, that any consideration of black political action in Britain must move from the conventional to the unconventional spheres of politics if significant developments in black politics are to be appreciated.

This evidence is gathered from different locales and at different points in time but all locate their research in a 'race relations' problematic. We believe that such a perspective leads them to place considerable explanatory importance on the impact of racism and racial discrimination on black political action and inaction. Our theoretical approach leads us to begin our analysis by considering in a more systematic way the economic and social context of black political action. Drawing upon the theoretical approach outlined in the previous chapter, we argue that the political action of black migrant labour in Britain (i.e. which of the three strategies we have outlined is followed) has to be evaluated in the context of four factors.

First, from our argument that black migrant labour constitutes a fraction of the working class, it follows that the black working class share in many important respects the same relationship to capital and the political institutions of the bourgeois state as the indigenous working class. This means that we must take care at all stages of analysis to compare the political action of the black working class with that of the indigenous working class in order to identify continuities in belief and behaviour which might then be explained in terms of their shared position in class relations.

The potential significance of such a comparision lies in the fact that the available evidence suggests that the level of working class participation in the formal political process is low, usually being restricted to electoral participation and trade union membership. Where direct action in the informal sphere of politics does occur, it can be seen as a reaction to specific situational factors or the inability (or unwillingness) of established working class organisations to adequately represent the interests of certain class fractions.

Second, we must acknowledge that the black workers are migrants. They have entered the British social formation with the intention of 'bettering themselves' and of eventually returning to the country and village or town of origin. That this notion of return may be an important element of the migrant ideology (Philpott, 1973) but not be realised in practice may still be relevant to political action (or inaction) in Britain, particularly if the ideology is expressed in the continued meeting of remittance obligations and other facets of expressed commitment to the country and region of origin. Indeed, migrants may have direct material investments in the country of origin, interests that they will wish to retain (and defend) for so long as there is a belief in an eventual return. A continuing emotional, familial and material relationship to the country of origin can serve to constrain the extent of commitment to the social formation in which the migrant is 'temporarily' resident, including the commitment to involvement in political action. Recognition of this makes it difficult to argue that heightened levels of openly-expressed racism and discrimination, along with an increase in racially-motivated physical violence, must necessarily result in black workers becoming directly involved in the political process. Such a scenario might equally convince the migrant that he or she can no longer pursue the aim of migration (i.e. self-betterment) and that a return to the country of origin is therefore the most rational solution. Lawrence (1974, pp. 35–9, 196–7) places considerable emphasis on the importance of migrant status but it seems not to enter into Rex's analysis (1979).

Once having taken account of the factors that define the structural position of black migrant labour in British capitalism, one can, third, take account of the relevance of racism and discrimination. Processes of racial exclusion can have three related effects on political action. Their occurrence in various spheres of social life could serve to persuade black workers that they should withdraw from participation in British society as much as possible, including the political sphere (cf. Lawrence, 1974). More specifically, racism and discrimination could actively prevent participation in existing political institutions by ensuring that black workers are not admitted to membership of existing political organisations or, if admitted, excluded from holding office or exercising membership functions. This has a particularly important impact if it occurs within the traditional institutions of the working class (see Miles and Phizacklea, 1977b, 1978). Alternatively, such experiences could serve to persuade black workers that their position as a racialised fraction of the working class should serve as the basis for independent political action (i.e. the strategies of ethnic organisations and/or class unity). Such a development would be paralleled by the development of a particular form of political consciousness (see chapter 7) which we discuss below and call *racial consciousness*.

Finally, it is important to take account of the particular social and cultural characteristics of the migrants because these might encourage or inhibit participation in the British political process quite independently of processes of racial exclusion. Lawrence acknowledges this when he refers to 'Asians' being 'more willing to think in communal terms' (1974, p. 157) in order to explain why ethnic organisation is more likely amongst Indians and Pakistanis. However, as we have already argued, much finer distinctions than these are necessary if we are to grasp the dynamics of 'internal' social organisation of 'Asian' ethnic minorities and their relevance to participation in the British political process (cf. Le Lohé, 1979). Moreover, there may be features of social and cultural organisation amongst migrants from the Caribbean which encourage their supposed low level of participation in the British political process (see Pearson, 1977).

With these points in mind, we now turn to consideration of the evidence additional to that in the studies already reported of participation in the British political process on the part of black migrant labour. This summarises our previously published analysis (Miles and Phizacklea 1977a), but is updated to take account of developments in the past two years.

Class unity or ethnic organisation?

We must begin by saying that we have little reason for revising our agreement with Lawrence that, despite their common position as a racially excluded class fraction, migrant workers from the Caribbean and from the Indian sub-continent are unlikely to organise together on any significant scale in the immediate future, specific situational exceptions being noted (as in the case of the march in London in May 1979 to protest against the 'virginity' tests on black women seeking to exercise their legal right to enter Britain). The crucial factors here are the cultural distinctiveness both within and between these two groups of migrants and the mutual suspicion and hostility that seems to exist between them. Having ruled out the black unity strategy, what of class unity and ethnic organisation?

Concerning the former, black workers are just as likely as white workers, or more so, to vote Labour (Lawrence, 1974; Community

Relations Commission, 1975; Foner, 1979) and to join a trade union (Smith, 1977). There is no evidence to show that black workers are any less willing than white workers to join strikes or other forms of industrial action (Brooks, 1975a; Smith, 1977). However, we have very little evidence on the meaning that black workers attach to voting Labour (Lawrence, 1974, and Foner, 1979, excepted), joining a trade union and participating in industrial action, an important omission because only with such data can we seriously consider the extent of class consciousness amongst black workers. Our study attempts to at least partly fill this gap as far as West Indian workers are concerned. We know of no extant data on Labour Party membership amongst black workers, nor is there published data on the extent to which black workers are occupying lay and full-time positions in the trade unions, although our own research also partly fills this gap.

Evidence of class unity in action is perhaps more important than electoral support for the Labour Party and joining a trade union, because these are often only expedient forms of action in the circumstances and may not, in themselves, express class consciousness. Nevertheless, one can conclude from this data that the political action of black workers certainly does not prevent the development of class unity. However, class unity, given the existence of practices of racial exclusion, must be a two-way process, and can only develop when the political institutions of the working class both acknowledge and organise against the especially disadvantaged position of black workers. As we shall show in chapter 5, the re-emergence of fascism as an active political force, in the form of the National Front (Walker, 1977), served to jolt both the Labour Party and the Trades Union Congress in 1976 into campaigning against racism in their own ranks, but while such campaigns are vitally important (although the inactivity of the Labour movement since 1977 on this matter would not suggest so), they bring little if any material improvement in the position of black workers. In addition, there are plenty of examples of trade unions having been involved in discriminatory practices and/or having failed to give support to strike or other industrial action by black workers. The result is that ethnic organisation has, in a number of cases, been forced upon black workers as the only means of attaining their ends (the strikes at Mansfield Hosiery Ltd, and Imperial Typewriters are good examples).

At the level of informal politics, the situation is often more fluid and positive. While revolutionary groups have gained no significant membership from black workers (nor in fact from white workers), they are often quick to react to local situations affecting black residents and workers, giving necessary support and, perhaps more importantly, showing unreserved solidarity. But the clearest indicator of class unity often arises in relation to campaigns and organisations which are formed in response to a specific issue or problem at the local level. For example, Wallman (1975/6) and Ward (1979) both give evidence of unity in action over local authority clearance and redevelopment plans.

Hence we conclude that, while there is clear evidence to show that racial exclusion does not operate in all situations, the persistence of racist belief and practice amongst the white working class and its institutions and its legitimation by government policy and practice, fascist political parties and prominent politicians, produces situations where black people must organise along ethnic lines to improve and defend their position in the British social formation. So far, this response by black workers has been ad hoc and localised and we have no way of knowing whether a more formalised and national response would occur if discrimination became more widespread and was accompanied by a much more open racist political campaign, involving the existing major political parties and the fascist parties. We would also note that the developments we have described do not mean that the action that has been taken does not also include a class perspective.

It is also important to recognise that ethnic organisation need not necessarily be a response to racial exclusion because the migrants' cultural distinctiveness may give rise to demands for changes in existing administrative practices in order to accommodate different values and patterns of behaviour, although such demands may, in turn, stimulate a racist response. One can refer to the dispute over the wearing of turbans as a substitute for a crash helmet and the legitimacy of sending teenage Muslim girls to co-educational schools as examples here.

But is there scope for ethnic organisation within the British political process, and, if so, can it be successful? The size and geographical distribution of the migrant population in Britain rule out the election of candidates of ethnic political parties, such as exist (see Le Lohé, 1979), while the apparently increasing practice of Labour and Liberal parties of choosing black candidates to stand in predominantly black wards in local elections has to take account of the possibilities that the loss of white votes (based on racist sentiment) may not compensate for the gain in black votes, and that inter-ethnic hostility may overcome the appeal of a 'black' candidate to black voters. This practice is far less common during parliamentary elections, presumably because the possibility of a white backlash is considered to have more serious implications.

However, there are instances of the electoral machinery being used to publicise a specifically ethnic issue and, for the group concerned, this has the advantage of publicising the issue, despite the impossibility of a candidate being elected to office. But it is the numerical strength of black voters in some constituencies which has caused most attention and all three major political parties are now conscious of this fact, even if they are uncertain how they should act as a consequence. It has been argued (Community Relations Commission, 1975) that the black vote had a substantial influence on the outcome of the 1974 General Elections, and while the evidence produced to support this assertion can hardly be called conclusive, the results of the 1979 General Election would seem to confirm that assertion in so far as constituencies with a high proportion of black voters showed a much lower swing to the Conservative Party than otherwise similar constituencies. Given the Conservative Party's record on immigration control and Mrs Thatcher's reference in early 1978 to British people feeling 'swamped' by people of a different colour, such a vote may well have indicated a vote against the resurrection of 'Powellism' rather than a positive vote for the Labour Party. The empirical validity of this assertion awaits consideration of a more detailed analysis of the 1979 results, but it does serve to show the ultimate weakness of an electoral strategy as a means by which black workers may seek to improve their disadvantaged position. If the black vote can be organised or withdrawn on a block basis (as some black leaders have claimed), to whom can it be delivered other than to the Labour Party? But then is the Labour Party a suitable vehicle for the effective representation of these specific interests? The opening paragraphs of this chapter have already argued that it is not.

Our evidence and argument lead us back to the view that it is within the informal sphere of politics that one should expect to see black workers organising in response to racial exclusion. West Indian parents have organised on the issues of the treatment of their children in schools and by the police. West Indians, Indians and Pakistanis have taken to the streets to show that they will not tolerate the presence of National Front activists in the areas where they live. Bengalis and Sikhs have formed self-defence groups because they believe that they cannot rely on the police to protect them from violent attacks by racists. Black women have organised marches to register their opposition to immigration control and its mode of administration. In short, ethnic organisation remains a necessity for black migrant labour in Britain. We also expect that this necessity is and will continue to be accompanied by the development of a racial consciousness.

Racial consciousness and the West Indian migrant worker

In chapter 1 we argued a case for conceiving of black migrant labour as a racialised fraction of the working class. This was premised on the fact that black migrant labour occupies a subordinate role in economic, political and legal relations. This role is a structural one, independent of the consciousness of the black workers themselves, although we expect that at least a proportion of this fraction of the working class will be conscious, to some degree, of this position. In so far as this subordinate role is a function of racial categorisation and a supporting ideology of racism, and of racial discrimination, then it follows that those black workers who become conscious of their structural position are likely to assess this position in racial terms, although simultaneously rejecting or even reversing the negative evaluation implicit in racism and racial discrimination. In short, they are likely to develop a racial consciousness, and ethnic organisation, particularly in the informal sphere of politics, is likely to be its mode of political expression. In other words, a racial consciousness is an ideological concomitant of the structural position of black migrant labour as a racialised fraction of the working class.

As far as West Indian migrants are concerned, this process has very particular implications which do not necessarily apply in the case of migrants from the Indian sub-continent but which must be drawn out here because our own research was amongst West Indian (and English) workers. Above, we noted that racism and discrimination have been important factors in the development of a West Indian identity, overriding in at least some circumstances the island identities which the immigrants brought with them. This identity is an expression of racial consciousness but it is also a recognition of common cultural characteristics. That is to say, the sense of 'us' that is implied by the West Indian identity takes account of both their common blackness (whereas in the Caribbean, subtle differences in colour and other phenotypical variations are attributed with social significance) and the sharing of certain cultural traits (cf. Foner, 1979, p. 144). Hence, as we have argued elsewhere:

> It is the unique experience of blacks of racial exclusion that is the essence of black ethnicity ... it is the struggle against racial

exclusion by West Indians that has both stimulated and reinforced ethnic attributes which may not have been recognized as
such prior to migration. We would define this as emergent
ethnicity ... (Miles and Phizacklea, 1977a, p. 495).

However, because we are defining West Indian workers as a
fraction of the working class, it logically follows that these workers
may also be conscious of their class position. It is therefore possible
for black migrant labour to develop both a class and a racial
consciousness, the extent to which one rather than the other
predominates depending upon conjunctural features. In the present
conjuncture, with racial discrimination still widespread and political
violence motivated by racism not uncommon (Miles and Phizacklea, 1979), we would expect to find a racial consciousness amongst at
least a significant minority of West Indian workers. But this would
not be to the exclusion of class consciousness because political
violence is the practice of only a small minority and is not openly
sanctioned by the state (if such circumstances did apply, the return
of the migrants to the West Indies is at least as likely a possibility as
an active political response in Britain, based on a racial consciousness).

Moreover, because the ongoing economic and political crisis of
British capitalism necessitates a containment of the economic and
political aspirations of the working class, a containment that at
times borders on open class struggle, and, in so far as their presence
in Britain as migrants is materially inspired, so making them
particularly concerned about wages and prices, we believe that
levels of class consciousness amongst West Indian workers are
unlikely to be vastly different from those of English workers.

It might be objected that this claim is contradicted by the extant
evidence. Lawrence (1974) has shown that West Indian workers are
much less likely to explain their support for the Labour Party in
class terms while Foner, who produces evidence to the contrary,
argues that a class identity is of much less importance to Jamaicans
than colour (1979, pp. 143–4). Concerning Lawrence's findings, it
may be relevant that his data was collected in 1966–7, at a time
when West Indian workers' consciousness of themselves as short-stay
migrants was much more prominent and when their knowledge and
interest in the British political process was accordingly low. Ten
years later the migrant ideology remains, but, for most migrants, so
does the task of self-betterment, with the result that their immediate
prospect is that of continuing to live in Britain as wage labourers.
The realities of wage labour in a capitalist formation must now be

much clearer to them than was the case in the mid 1960s and their experience and knowledge of the political process must now be more detailed. Whether or not this argument is valid is not easy to prove in a clear-cut way, and might seem to be contradicted by Foner's findings about political consciousness amongst a sample of Jamaicans in London. However, as she herself admits (1979, p. 143), she has only very limited grounds for claiming that Jamaicans are more likely to identify themselves in racial than in class terms. We hope that our more detailed investigation of the political consciousness of both West Indian and English workers allows us to make a more considered judgment on this matter. Such a judgment will have the additional advantage of being based on data collected ten years after that of Lawrence.

West Indian workers and the political process: a summary

As a result of drawing out the implications of the theoretical approach outlined in chapter 1, in conjunction with the available empirical evidence, we have argued that black migrant labour in general, and West Indians in particular, although having themselves come to meet the initial preconditions for a strategy of class unity in order to rectify their disadvantaged position as a racialised fraction of the working class, have been forced for a number of reasons to adopt the strategy of ethnic organisation. We have also argued that the adoption of forms of formal political action which are class inspired, when considered in relation to the necessity for ethnic organisation, means that West Indian workers are likely to adopt a political practice and consciousness which is similar to that of the white working class because of their common class position, but that this practice and consciousness will be overlaid by recognition of their position as a racially categorised fraction. But in case we have given the impression that West Indian workers exhibit a high level of political action in both the formal and informal spheres of politics, we must draw attention to our references to the fact that much of the ethnic organisation that has occurred has been ad hoc and situational and that action in the formal sphere of politics is limited to voting and trade union membership. Lawrence has referred to this apparently low level of political practice as 'withdrawal' (1974, p. 197), arguing that it is the consequence of racial exclusion and migrant status. However, despite the fact that racism and discrimination are widespread and that West Indian workers do seem to demonstrate a low level of political practice, we do not believe that the relationship between these two factors is as clear-cut as he suggests, not least because political action amongst the working class generally is low, and West Indian workers do share this same class position (as well as because there may be characteristics particular to West Indians which discourage political organisation). Consequently, in the chapters that follow, we shall examine the extent to which a group of West Indian workers demonstrate class and racial consciousness and whether these are translated into and/or expressed by specific types of political action in both the formal and informal spheres of politics, but we shall do so in the context of a study of the political consciousness and action of the white, British working class. The location of our study was North West London and in the next chapter we will consider the economic and social characteristics of this part of the so-called 'inner city'.

CHAPTER 3

'Inner city' or declining centre of capitalist production

We begin this chapter by considering whether contemporary urban decay warrants analysis within a framework established by the concept of the 'inner city'. This serves as a prelude to describing the socio-economic characteristics of our research area, the now abolished (under local government reorganisation in 1965) Borough of Willesden, in the context of its position in London. It is our intention to show that Willesden has undergone a process of development and decline which is explicable in terms of the cyclical nature of the capitalist mode of production and that the decline which has occurred has coincided with the movement into the area of black migrant labour.

The 'inner city': old wine in a new bottle?

The 'inner city' label, in so far as it is new (it came into public prominence in Britain in the early 1970s), suggests that the phenomenon to which it applies is without precedent in the past. The phenomenon would seem to include poor housing, declining work opportunities, a depressed and depressing physical environment, and limited social facilities; the implied social correlates are poverty, unemployment, street crime, vandalism and violence: in short, the new phenomenon is urban decay. But, as Paris (1978) has argued, there is nothing new about urban decay, as acquaintance with the writings of Engels (1969 edn) indicates. What, then, are we to make of the 'inner city' label?

Use of the concept might be defended on the grounds that the circumstances described by Engels were extreme and that the extent of decay, poverty and oppression in the English cities of the 1840s can no longer be found. Moreover, it could be argued that the slums were an unfortunate side-effect of the initial phase of unrestrained capitalist industrialisation and urbanisation and that a more regulated and mature capitalism has contained the problem, the 'slums' that remain constituting a legacy of the past which has yet to be eliminated. What is required, it might be concluded, is a final injection of capital to complete the task. Finally, it might be argued that what is new about urban decay in the late twentieth century is 'the race factor'; that is to say, it might be conceded that urban decay has been with us since industrialisation and urbanisation but that the contemporary manifestation is different from the past in that black 'immigrants' are in some way intimately bound up in the process.

It is not denied that the particularity of Engels' description could not be reproduced for the 1970s: there have, indeed, been vast improvements in building standards and levels of income, and successive governments have passed social welfare legislation which has improved health and sanitation, etc. It can also be conceded that the 'inner city' slums of the 1840s were a direct effect of unplanned industrialisation and consequent urbanisation, while, as we shall argue, the contemporary 'inner city' problem is a product of, inter alia, industrial decline. But what is common to the 1840s and to the 1970s is that one can nevertheless explain urban decay by reference to the nature of the capitalist mode of production; that is to say, industrial and urban development is structured by the demands of capital so that, in the early phase of industrialisation, capital demanded a concentration of labour in expanding towns but was unable to supply housing, while new capital development usually demands or results in the decline of earlier development. We are not denying, then, that urban decay in the 1970s is different in certain respects from urban decay in the 1840s, but we are wanting to suggest that both can be explained by reference to the operation of the capitalist mode of production.

The Irish yesterday: 'race' today

But what of the so-called 'race factor'? On the face of it, this should constitute a crucial difference between the 1840s and 1970s because there were very few black people in England in the earlier period. But the issue is not so much the presence or absence of black people as of what is to be understood by 'the race factor'. In our opening chapter we have argued that the presence of black workers in England is to be explained in terms of the demand of capital for labour, and when the supply cannot be met from within the boundaries of a nation state, then the migration of labour from outside those boundaries can occur. Elsewhere we have argued that what differentiates the migration from the Caribbean and the Indian sub-continent in the 1950s from previous migrations to England is that the notion of 'race' was threaded into the subsequent political debate: in other words, the migrants were racialised (Miles and Phizacklea, 1979). Thus, although the migrants were physically distinct from the majority of the indigenous population (as well as from each other), this only had economic and social repercussions because the indigenous population, or at least sections of it, attributed significance to some of the differences that were perceived and thereby used the label of 'race' to refer to the migrants. Hence, 'race' is not a factor *in itself*, but is a label applied by one social group to another. What is of interest to us is the economic and social repercussions of this process of labelling.

It is true that the concept of 'race' is not threaded into Engels' description of the slums in the English cities of the 1840s. But Engels does have this to say about the slum inhabitants:

> The worst quarters of all the large towns are inhabited by Irishmen. Whenever a district is distinguished for especial filth and especial ruinousness, the explorer may safely count upon meeting those Celtic faces which one recognizes at the first glance as different from the Saxon physiognomy of the native, and the singing aspirate brogue which the Irishman never loses (1969, p. 123).

In other words, the urban slums of the 1840s were populated not only by the indigenous and recently emergent working class but also by migrant workers who were distinguished from the former by both physical and cultural characteristics. The intimate relationship between the demand for labour by certain sections of English (and Scottish) capitalism and migration from Ireland is now well established (e.g. Handley, 1943; Redford, 1976; Jackson, 1963) and permits comparison with the post-Second-World-War migration (again accepting that there are also major differences between the two periods). One can add to this parallel the claim that both the Irish and New Commonwealth migrations brought together, in a context of urban decay, populations which were able to distinguish each other by reference to physical and cultural criteria. So, although there was no 'race factor' in the slums of the 1840s in so far as the Irish migrants were not so labelled (although it has been argued that they were labelled *as if* they were a 'race': see Curtis, 1968, but also Gilley, 1978), they were identified, at least by Engels, as a distinct element in the urban decay that he described.

But is 'race' a factor in the contemporary 'inner city' crisis? At least for the Labour Government of 1974–9 it would seem to have been, although its reasoning was, at times, very obscure. For example, in a White Paper, *Policy for the Inner Cities*, it suggested that the contemporary problem had a number of different dimensions which were separately identified as economic decline, physical decay, social disadvantage and ethnic minorities (Department of the Environment, 1977, pp. 2–5). Ethnic minorities were identified as a separate dimension of the 'inner city problem', it was argued, because, like previous immigrants, they have tended to settle in the central areas of the major conurbations and, consequently, share with the other residents the disadvantages of living in these areas. But if disadvantage is shared in common with these other residents (who, one assumes, cannot be ethnic minorities), why should the ethnic minorities be identified as a separate dimension of the 'inner city' problem. The justification must lie in the White Paper's subsequent reference to 'their special needs' which it was recommended be taken into account when planning and implementing 'inner city' policies. Unfortunately the White Paper did not identify what these special needs are.

Neither was clarification forthcoming in the House of Commons debate on the Labour government's 'inner city' policy on 6 April 1977. In his opening speech, Peter Shore (Secretary of State for the Environment) claimed that

> the extent and the changed character of the inner city is only now becoming fully understood … During the past decade inner cities have suffered a massive and disproportionate loss of jobs and a major exodus of population. Substantial ethnic minorities in some cities have added an extra dimension (Parliamentary Debates, 1977, Cols. 1226–7).

What constituted the 'extra dimension' was not clarified by Peter Shore, nor by the subsequent debate. For example, when Mr Alex Lyon asked why Bradford had not been included in the list of areas to be assisted by planned improvements 'when it is third in the list of census deprivation indicators and third in the number of New Commonwealth immigrants who live there', Mr Shore replied: 'My purpose is to deal, regardless of whether there are black or white populations, with aggravated problems of poverty and deprivation in our major urban centres' (Parliamentary Debates, 1977, Cols. 1235–6).

But if the Labour Government of 1974–9 was coy about justifying why 'ethnic minorities' are a special dimension of the 'inner city problem', others were not. Indeed, some have gone so far as to imply that the presence of 'ethnic minorities' is *the* urban problem and that the only alternative to escalating urban conflict and violence is repatriation. We think it likely that the possibility, indeed reality, of urban conflict and violence is in fact a key concern of the state in its deliberations about the place of 'ethnic minorities' in the 'inner city problem' (although it is not the actual presence of black migrants which causes this conflict but rather the reaction of the indigenous population to their presence). This is clearly articulated by Sivanandan (1976, p. 350): 'the forced concentration of immigrants in the deprivated and decaying areas of the big cities highlighted (and reinforced) existing social deprivation; racism defined them as its cause.'

However, when racism becomes articulated through social conflict and political action, the state is faced with what it defines as a 'law and order' problem, as, for example, in Notting Hill (1958), Lewisham (1977) and Southall (1979). The immediate response is the use of the police and the legal system to restore 'law and order' while, in the longer term, it is deemed necessary to solve the 'inner city' crisis, defined in terms of economic decline, physical decay and racial disadvantage. So, although Paris may be formally correct when he argues that 'race is a crucial issue at the heart of the government concern' about the 'inner city' (1978, p. 165) (that is to say, the government believes 'race' to be a factor in the 'inner city' problem because of the violence involving blacks as both victims and aggressors), we believe that it is more accurate to argue that the real issues which, along with economic decline etc., constitute the parameters of the 'inner city' problem are racism and racial discrimination.

Two comments are required to clarify this claim. First, why should racism and racial discrimination be elevated to the position of a major parameter? The reasoning is that, as we shall argue in a later chapter, racism serves to produce an ideological and political dimension to the economic division between the migrant and indigenous working class, a division that is to be partly explained by the extent of racial discrimination. In other words, racism and racial discrimination compound the economic and social disadvantage facing the working class living in the 'inner city', and by adding to the internal stratification of the working class lead to further political cleavages which are then reproduced through social conflict. Second, it does not follow that racism and racial discrimination are synonymous with the 'inner city'. Both are evident and have effects throughout the English social formation: they are not confined to specific urban locations (e.g. Smith, 1977). Moreover, 'inner city' circumstances are not necessarily compounded by racism and racial discrimination because the processes that result in urban decay operate independently of the presence of black workers and the reaction to them.

'Race' neither is nor has been in itself a factor in the 'inner city' problem. We do not deny that the presence of black migrant labour in major English conurbations in the 1950s has led to the typification of the 'rediscovery' of urban decline in terms of 'race', but it does not follow that because Engels and other nineteenth-century commentators did not also utilise such a conceptualisation in relation to the 1840s, the presence or absence of the 'race factor' must constitute a significant difference between the two periods. The attribution of a racial label is not without significant effects but this social process of labelling must not be confused with the more fundamental material similarities (and differences) between the English cities of the 1840s and the 1970s: one important parallel is to be found in the extent to which migrant labour has taken up residence in areas which are characterised by urban decay, although in neither case can the urban decay be explained by the migrant presence. Moreover, the absence of the racial label in the 1840s should not hide the fact that the Irish migrants were the object of considerable hostility from the indigenous working class, as have been the more recent migrants from the New Commonwealth.

Beyond the myth

So far it has been argued that there is, historically speaking, nothing fundamentally new about the 'inner city'. Rather, it is a new name applied to a long-established phenomenon: economic decline, physical decay and social disadvantage (taking three of the four parameters advanced by the Labour Government's White Paper) have always characterised parts of urban areas. This is the first reason why we object to the use of the 'inner city' as an analytic concept.

At the same time we must recognise that there is a difference between urban decay and poverty being the result of unrestrained and uneven development such that even poor quality housing is insufficient to meet the demand of workers responding to the demands of an expanding industrial centre, and being the result of such a centre subsequently experiencing crisis and decline. The 'inner city' concept has in the 1970s been applied to the latter case rather than the former. Yet this designation is inappropriate because the dynamic behind the decline of such an area is not located within the 'inner city' itself: there is not an 'inner city' problem but an economic problem which has a national, even international, origin, but which manifests itself in different urban locations. In other words, the 'inner city' is not in itself a problem or an isolated phenomenon but a symptom of wider economic processes.

The initial phase of industrialisation in Britain was dominated by domestic production but with the development of transport and the establishment of capital goods industries in England went the widespread development of factory production. This second phase of industrialisation was characterised by the establishment and expansion of new factories and the building of adjacent housing in which the workers lived. However, as this phase of development expanded and matured, not only was capital developing new methods of production and new products but elsewhere in the world other nations were developing their own industries in competition with those in England. Hence foreign competition, combined with capital investment in new industries in other locations within the country, resulted in the declining profitability and decline of what were initially centres of capitalist production. And with industrial decline went social decline as certain sectors of labour moved from the geographical area of initial development to new areas, leaving behind those with fewer or inappropriate skills. Housing which was old and in need of repair was not maintained because of the cost of so doing. A declining manufacturing base, movement of labour away from the area and unemployment meant that there was less money to spend in the area and commercial and retail services went into decline (see Community Development Project, 1977).

This account is crudely simplified but is presented to indicate that the underlying causes of the 'inner city' crisis are not geographically limited to the areas themselves but are inherent in the competitive process of capital accumulation. Hence, second, we reject the 'inner city' as an analytic concept in so far as it implies that the phenomenon to be explained is both structurally and geographically isolated.

Finally, to talk of the 'inner city' is to imply that economic decline, physical decay and social disadvantage are only found in the inner area of conurbations, at the centre. It follows from the above analysis that there is no necessary reason why industrial and social decline should occur only at the centre of urban areas if initial industrial development was not limited to such an area. One survey included, for example, an analysis of the decline of Batley and

North Shields which are distinct industrial towns rather than small areas of a single town or city (CDP, 1977, p. 5). And, as we shall show later in this chapter, it is difficult to argue that the old Borough of Willesden is part of London's geographical 'inner city', but rather, that it is part of one of three concentric rings (see Lomas, 1975, p. 5). So, third, we reject the 'inner city' concept because it implies a coincidence of industrial decline and spatial location which is not necessarily found in reality.

It follows from these arguments that our interest is not the 'inner city' but urban areas which have been centres of capitalist manufacturing production which are now undergoing socio-economic decline due to, *inter alia*, the declining profitability of capital in that area and the establishment of new locations of capital investment elsewhere. From this perspective the 'inner city' concept is limited and misleading in that, in so far as it does have any precise theoretical meaning, it directs attention away from a long-term socio-economic process by focusing upon a static, spatial form. We hesitate to claim that the concept is theoretically defined: its use in government circles, for example, is without formal justification. There is no attempt to define the 'inner city' in *Policy for the Inner Cities* for instance (DOE, 1977, p. 2), where we are told only that 'economic decline, physical decay and adverse social conditions' are spatially located at the centre of major cities and differ only in scale and intensity from urban decay elsewhere. Similarly, those who claim a 'race' or ethnic dimension to the 'inner city' problem use the 'inner city' concept indiscriminately and without theoretical defence (e.g. Cross, 1978). In our view the 'inner city' concept is an excellent example of a notion in everyday usage which, because it *appears* so self-explanatory, is deemed not to require theoretical justification and so slips unobtrusively into academic and political analysis.

What we now wish to do is examine the bases of and evidence for industrial decline in London and the coincidence of that decline with both inadequate housing and the settlement pattern of New Commonwealth migrants. This will serve as a general framework to a more detailed consideration of just one area of London, the old Borough of Willesden.

London: a declining centre of capitalist manufacturing production?

There is no doubt that there is a process of industrial decline occurring in London, although it is a process that is not confined to

London as it has been shown that the central areas of all British cities have similar industrial structures and that these structures are undergoing a similar transformation (Cameron and Evans, 1973). There has been a decline in the working population in all the central urban areas as a consequence of a reduction in the number of persons employed in both manufacturing industry and the distributive trades. These changes reflect a general shift to tertiary employment in the national economy as well as a decentralisation of manufacturing industry. This process of decline is of fairly recent origin, and has to be understood in relation to changes in the outer areas, the metropolitan ring, of the cities (Drewett et al., 1976). The central areas had both an increasing population and employment growth in the 1950s but both trends went into reverse in the 1960s, showing a striking contrast with the outer rings which experienced a continuous increase in both population and employment in the 1950s and 1960s. However, although these processes characterise all urban areas, they are not of the same magnitude, nor are they proceeding at the same pace and, of all the British urban areas, it is London which seems to show the most dramatic contrast. For example, in the 1950s the inner area of London showed the largest absolute increase in employment, and in the 1960s the largest absolute decrease, while its surrounding metropolitan ring exhibited the largest absolute growth in both decades.

What are the specific dimensions of this decline? Between 1966 and 1974 London's total population fell by 9.4 per cent although the decline in the inner boroughs was far greater at 17.3 per cent than in the outer boroughs. In the same period there was a decline in manufacturing employment of 27 per cent (Dennis, 1978). Both Dennis (1978) and Gripaios (1977) argue that the industrial decline cannot be explained by London having an industrial structure in which generally declining industries and trades are unduly represented. They also agree that permanent factory closure is a more important explanatory factor than relocation: Dennis shows that 27 per cent of total industrial decline in London can be explained by the latter and 44 per cent by the former factor. There are a number of reasons advanced for factory closure and relocation, although most of them imply a declining profitability of production in London. The available evidence suggests that industrial production faces a lack of space for both the expansion and reconstruction of production (often vital if the firm is to remain competitive), large increases in costs in the form of rates and rent, and high wage costs and a related shortage of certain types of labour. Also important has been the impact of the rationalisation of capital at both a national and international level, leading to mergers and factory closures in order to maintain or improve profitability. Finally, government policy (both national and local) seems likely to have done more to encourage closure and relocation than to have retarded or even reversed it (Foreman-Peck and Gripaios, 1977; Dennis, 1978).

The major point of contention concerns the extent to which these processes characterise only the central boroughs of London. On the one hand it is argued (Foreman-Peck and Gripaios, 1977; Gripaios 1977; also Lomas 1975) that the decline is limited to central London, although it has had an impact throughout the city, while on the other it is argued (Dennis, 1978) that the industrial decline is occurring throughout London, although there is a different dynamic operating in each area. The evidence does not permit a clear-cut answer but there is no dispute over the implications of decline for unemployment.

On initial reflection, it might be first anticipated that London must have experienced a substantial and relative increase in the level of unemployment compared to elsewhere in Britain. One study (Foster and Richardson, 1973) has concluded to the contrary:

> Although the number of employees in manufacturing in the GLC fell substantially in the sixties, the unemployment rate in GLC manufacturing was always *lower* than the unemployment rate in other GLC sectors. The unemployment rate in GLC manufacturing was also consistently *lower* than the GB rate in manufacturing (p. 110).

Lomas (1975), using data for 1973, notes that '48,000 men were registered unemployed in mid-1973, a figure which, though large in itself, is perhaps surprisingly small in relation to the scale on which the employment structure of London has been changing' (p. 6).

Moreover, he claims that the proportional distribution of unemployment between manufacturing and services exactly reflects the employment structure of London, despite the fact that the bulk of redundancies between 1966 and 1973 have been in manufacturing (Lomas estimates that they constitute 75 per cent of the total – p. 2). Those that remained unemployed were predominantly unskilled workers, labourers or routine clerks, and few skilled or semi-skilled workers remained on the unemployment register for any length of time. Whether this is still the case as unemployment nationally has continued to rise since the mid 1970s is a matter for future investigation.

A number of factors have probably been operating to bring this about, the most obvious being out-migration of labour from

London, although other factors might include an increase in reverse commuting or a drop in the number of people commuting to work in London. It is also relevant to note that these figures may hide other disproportionate patterns of unemployment: for example, Lomas (1973, 1975) has shown that both black workers in general and black youth in particular have significantly higher rates of unemployment than white workers and white youth.

London's decline as a centre of capitalist manufacturing production has been accompanied by the development of both a shortage of housing and a decline in its quality. The origin of the problem has been well described by the Greater London Council:

> London's present housing problems stem from its rapid growth during the 19th and 20th centuries as a metropolitan capital of commercial, financial and political importance. From early in the 19th century the East End was developed with small two-storey cottages to house London's working class while, north and west of the centre, large solidly built houses arose for the middle and upper classes (1969, p. 3).

House building followed largely in the wake of the demand for labour by financial and commercial enterprise and by expanding industries in the nineteenth and early twentieth centuries. The contemporary pattern and quality of housing in London reflects this, particularly so in the case of the housing built in the mid and late Victorian period. On the one hand 'jerry-built' small houses were constructed whose physical condition has since deteriorated badly and which continue to lack basic amenities, while on the other more substantial, larger houses were built, usually for white-collar and professional workers. The latter have since become unecomonic for single families, having been deserted by their original inhabitants, and have been divided into flats and bedsitters, often becoming overcrowded as a result.

A Greater London Council survey of 1967 (GLC, 1969) concluded that 72 per cent of properties in its areas were in good condition, that 23 per cent were only in fair condition and that 5 per cent were unfit for human habitation or were in poor structural condition. Concerning basic amenities, 11 per cent of dwellings had no bath and a further 11 per cent had no inside toilet, with 7 per cent of dwellings having neither. Housing in poor structural condition and lacking basic amenities is not evenly spread throughout London but is concentrated in certain areas.

But London's housing problem is not simply the extent of poor physical condition and lack of basic amenities. Between 1951 and

966 the population of London declined by about 300,000 but in
he same period the number of households increased by 70,000, most
f the increase being in one- to two-person households. Given the
ailure of supply to meet demand, there was a significant increase in
he ratio of households to dwellings. Greve *et al.* elaborate:

> The main reason for this increase in sharing is that the reduction
> in the number of dwellings has far outstripped the rate of
> population decline – and the increased pressure on housing space
> has concentrated heavily on the private rented sector. But the
> supply of rented housing in this sector is falling because of
> demolition and transfer to owner-occupation. Council building is
> replacing much of the privately-rented housing on demolition
> but there is generally a net loss in dwellings owing to reduced
> densities as renewal proceeds (1971, pp. 12–13).

ut sharing is not a characteristic of small households alone. In a
umber of central boroughs, as well as in Brent, an increasing number
f medium and large households were found by Greve *et al.* to be
nared dwellings. There is, too, a correlation between shared dwellings
nd poor or absent basic amenities and standards of repair.

Finally, there was in the 1960s a decline in the overall number of
wellings in London: although the outer London boroughs showed
net gain, the net loss in the central boroughs was far greater. The
nportance of the pattern of building in the past is again indicated
y Greve *et al.*: 'Typically, it is the boroughs with large quantities of
ineteenth-century housing that are losing stock, and at the same
me face continuing problems of replacement, urban renewal and a
uge unsatisfied demand' (1971, p. 23).

The combination of crowding and sharing by large households in
nted, furnished accommodation has been referred to as housing
ress and Lomas has shown that the areas of most intensive housing
ress are to be found in the inner ring of London, surrounding
ntral London, areas which are inhabited by mainly less-skilled
orkers (1975, pp. 10–11). Lomas argues that these areas are not
ose of greatest employment stress, these being the middle East End
nd inner south London:

> to some extent therefore we have two situations – where one part
> of London is suffering restricted job opportunities, but where
> housing chances are more favourable (including the incidence of
> council housing); whereas over much of the rest of inner London,
> though job prospects are better, they are accompanied by
> difficult housing problems (1975, p. 14).

However, it does not follow that there is no coincidence of housing stress with a decline in manufacturing. Lomas's measurement o employment stress utilises a number of factors and the differences h distinguishes between different areas of London are differences o degree on a number of variables. Some of the differences betweer areas are not as great as Lomas's overall and apparently clear-cu conclusion might indicate, for both north and west inner Londor have an adverse ratio of vacancies to employment, adverse labou demand and quite high average redundancy sizes, and these ar areas clearly characterised by housing stress. Nevertheless, on th basis of the data he does assemble, Lomas is correct in pointing ou that it is in inner, south London that both housing and employmen stress are at their most severe.

Is, then, London a declining centre of manufacturing production The evidence we have assembled suggests an answer in th affirmative, and that there is a degree of overlap between industria decline and housing stress, although only in south inner Londo are both employment and housing stress equally extremely serious However, our argument is in need of some brief additiona comments because it should not be concluded that because th *industrial* base of London is in decline, its *economic* base is equally i decline. The first point is that London's industrial base has been, i one sense, in decline since the end of the First World War: even ir 1921 less than half of the male workforce was employed ir manufacturing and this was down to 29 per cent in 1966 (Lomas 1975). The obverse of this is that London is predominantly a city o services and its economic strength and role is very dependent on thi sector of production as much as on industrial manufacturing. But i does not follow that because the proportion of persons employed i manufacturing has been in decline, for some forty years or more, th most recent overall decline since 1960 is not without considerabl significance. Its immediate significance is for those areas which hav been the traditional location of manufacturing industry in Londor that is, the Victorian manufacturing belt which runs to the north o the central city of London; the Lea valley in north and east London the industrial belt running east along the banks of the Thames; th west and north from Cricklewood round to Hayes; and the Wandl valley in south London. In other words, large areas of London ar involved in what can be understood as a cyclical process o development and decline, a process which involves not simply jobs but housing and people's quality of life. Moreover, the cycle o decline in London is closely linked to new capital investment outsid London, as the movement of young, skilled workers to New Town i.e. new jobs and houses – see Deakin and Ungerson, 1977) and the relocation of industry from London in the same areas testifies. But before describing in more detail the cyclical process of capitalist development and decline in one part of one of these manufacturing areas of London, we want to briefly locate the place of black labour in the broad pattern of decline.

The place of black labour in socio-economic decline

The Caribbean migration to Britain created a black working class resident in major urban areas, and in certain sections of those areas; moreover, it was a black working class which was largely serving as replacement labour in those sectors which indigenous labour had vacated. By entering and by having their entry structured by racial discrimination, black workers have unwittingly become entangled in the process of socio-economic decline previously outlined.

Nationally, compared with white labour, black workers constitute a much larger proportion of employees in manufacturing industry, largely because they are concentrated in semi- and unskilled employment (Smith, 1977, p. 80). This pattern is clearly apparent in London (Lomas, 1975, p. 21), yet it is this sector of London's economy which is in decline, the obvious corollary being that a continued decline is, other things being equal, likely to have a proportionately greater impact on black workers than on white. There are countervailing tendencies (see Lomas, 1975, p. 21) for it is the case that a majority of black workers in London are already in the service sector of its economy (although often in low-paid employment with unsocial hours) but one might logically predict that where closure and redundancy do occur, then black workers will be disproportionately affected and will face greater difficulties in re-entering employment due to the continued prevalence of discrimination.

The extent to which black workers are disproportionately represented amongst the unemployed (Smith, 1977, pp. 66–72) in a national recession is not encouraging in this connection, although it is important to note that this pattern does not reflect only unemployment following redundancy from manufacturing industry. Indeed, Lomas indicates (1975, p. 28) that in the inner part of South London the most common previous occupations of the unemployed were routine clerks, lorry drivers, painters and decorators, kitchen assistants, etc., none of which are manufacturing occupations and all of which have tended to predominate amongst the unemployed in this area long before the beginning of industrial decline. But what is certain is that in London black workers have higher rates of unemployment than white workers and that, in the early 1970s, although the total number of unemployed fell, the number of West Indian unemployed rose (Lomas, 1975, p. 18).

Not only are West Indian workers occupying a more disadvantageous position in the London labour market but they are also disproportionately disadvantaged in the housing market. Housing stress in London tends to be concentrated in inner London and 67 per cent of the New Commonwealth migrants, compared with 40 per cent of the British population, in London in the mid 1960s lived in boroughs with housing stress. Within these boroughs nearly half of the New Commonwealth migrants lived in wards which were described as areas of housing stress (Lomas, 1975, p.9). Another analysis based on data for the mid 1960s has shown that West Indians were highly overrepresented in furnished accommodation; that the West Indian tenure pattern was not a reflection of the general tenure pattern in inner London and differed in important respects from the tenure pattern for English residents; and that West Indians live at higher occupancy rates, particularly in areas of greatest West Indian concentration and amongst those living in furnished accommodation (Haddon, 1970, pp. 96–106).

It might be objected that this presents too negative a picture and that there is also evidence available which shows that about 30 per cent of West Indians are owner-occupiers (Haddon, 1970, p. 96; Lomas, 1975, p.9). Compared with white English workers at the same occupational level, this is a high proportion, but this has to be evaluated in the context of both the type and condition of the property that is owned and the source of finance for the purchase. Haddon pointed out in 1970 that levels of owner-occupation amongst West Indians tended to be higher in areas of high, West Indian concentration and suggests that this means that the West Indian entry into the house purchase market in London is limited by a number of factors, including discrimination (see also Lee, 1977, pp. 91–2), and the property purchased tends to be of low quality (Haddon, 1970, pp. 114–15; see also Karn, 1979). Although the data is from a national survey and not specifically from London alone Smith has confirmed these speculations (1977, pp. 222–8; 234–5).

It might also be objected that much of the raw data upon which these arguments depend was collected in the mid 1960s and that there have since been important changes in the pattern described for example, a recent study based on the 1961 and 1971 censuses ha shown that West Indians have become more dispersed throughou

London in that decade (see also Peach, 1975). However, the author additionally comments that the extent of dispersal is very limited and that 'in 1971 almost two-thirds of London's West Indians were still living in wards of relatively high ethnic concentration, where the West Indian population was more than double that expected from a proportional distribution' (Lee, 1977, p. 156).

Lee also shows that the areas of greatest West Indian concentration remained areas of housing stress (ibid., p. 156), although where dispersal has occurred, the housing conditions of those who have moved have improved (p. 159).

Two points emerge from this analysis and argument. The first is that migrant labour from the Caribbean, in so far as it has settled in areas of housing stress and taken jobs in manufacturing and certain other industries, has become inextricably bound up in the process of urban decay in London. It has been argued that the fact that West Indians are concentrated in such areas can be explained by their 'social class' characteristics (e.g. Lee, 1977, p. 157) but the facts of the extent of racial discrimination in Britain as a whole (see Smith, 1977) imply that the disadvantage experienced as a result of being working class in a declining urban context is, for black migrant labour, both partly reinforced and even brought about by racial discrimination, for there is *no* reason to believe that discrimination stops at the edges of urban decline.

But, second, the preconditions and, in the case of housing, the actuality of urban decline were in evidence before New Commonwealth migration began. In so far as the capitalist mode of production ensures a cyclical productive process, by means of which centres of production eventually go into decline, the working population employed in those centres at the time of decline, irrespective of their physical characteristics, must face redundancy and unemployment. The origin of manufacturing decline in London (and elsewhere) is therefore material and does not reside in the specific social characteristics of the working population: the latter may or may not have an impact on the nature and course of the decline, but cannot set it in motion. This can be made particularly clear by a case study of urban decline in one area of London, Willesden.

The cyclical nature of capitalist production: the case of Willesden

Willesden has, since 1965, been part of the London Borough of

Brent: the formation of the new borough brought together, for administrative purposes, two areas (Willesden and Wembley) which were vastly different in socio-economic characteristics. The former was (and is) an area of socio-economic decline while the latter was and is clearly more prosperous and suburban in character. But a little more than a century earlier, both areas were well beyond the boundary of London, extending as it did in 1851 only as far as Paddington. The area which was to become known as the Borough of Willesden then contained a number of small rural villages (Kilburn, Cricklewood, Willesden, Harlesden and Kensal Green) which were separated from each other by farmland. However, there were connections between Willesden and London, for in the eighteenth century the area contained the houses of London bankers and financiers, the owners of which were able to travel to work by coach. The first real development and change to occur in the area coincided with the building of the railway in the middle of the nineteenth century, Willesden Junction quickly becoming an important railway centre.

At first the improvement of transport was accompanied only by the building of more large houses around Willesden Green and Brondesbury but the commercial and industrial development of Central London was increasing the demand both for labour and residential space. The solution to what was a joint problem was to build houses on the edge of London and, consequently, Willesden became a dormitory suburb for city workers after 1875. By 1885 there were 3,800 people living in Willesden and new estates were being developed at Willesden Green and Kensal Green. For the next thirty years there was a continuous growth of population which was encouraged by continued improvements in transport, notably the extension of the Metropolitan Railway from Baker Street. By 1905 the population had reached about 140,000, having grown faster than any other part of London (with only one exception) in the preceding decade, the main concentrations of population being at Kilburn, Willesden Green, Kensal Green and Harlesden. But despite this fast and extensive development of housing, and despite the fact that Willesden had been given the administrative status of an Urban District Council in 1894, the area retained a rural character, these concentrations of population being separated by meadow and woodland (Leff and Blunden, n.d., Morris, 1950).

The improvement in transport brought about the first major change to Willesden (Prince, 1964, p. 126; also Olsen, 1976, pp. 308–19), but its significance appears rather limited in the light of the impact of the second development, the movement of industry into the area. The initial phase of industrialisation occurred between 1900 and 1910 and was usually dependent upon access to the railway or canal (Martin, 1966, pp. 29–30). A smaller number of firms in Kilburn, a foundry at Stonebridge and a biscuit factory in Park Royal predated this first phase which, by the beginning of the First World War, had led to the establishment of light engineering, printing and foundries at various places in Willesden. The war itself brought munition factories to the area and established an industrial estate at Park Royal on the southern edge of Willesden but, although this passed into private ownership after the war, it was not developed until the late 1920s. However, when development did begin, it was both substantial and fast and many small manufacturing firms established themselves on the Park Royal industrial estate. This industrial development was not limited to Park Royal: large areas of what was then West Middlesex were the location for the development and expansion of new industries, many of which were (luxury) consumer goods industries (e.g. cars, food and drink), dependent upon the large London market (Smith, 1933; Hall, 1962; Martin, 1966). For a period between the wars this was the fastest expanding area in London.

By the mid 1930s Willesden was dominated industrially by four major industries. The first was car production which, in turn, had important links with the developing aircraft industry in the form of Handley Page, although the latter firm was forced to leave Willesden in the 1930s because of lack of space. Car production was dependent upon the manufacture of components and a number of factories were established to supply the former, notably Smiths Industries. Second, there was both general and electrical engineering, some aspects of which (e.g. machine tools), were related to car production. Third, there were a number of chemical industries established and, finally, food and drink manufacture, including the movement of Food Co. (see pp. 69, 234) to Park Royal from Southwark in the mid 1920s (Smith, 1933; Martin 1966).

The immediate post-war period, before industrial expansion really began after the mid 1920s, was a period of slow but continuing population growth and very few houses were built: 'When the second great wave of Metropolitan expansion hit Willesden there was already an acute housing shortage in the area, and industry was firmly established in nine of the twelve districts which make up the Borough' (Morris, 1950, p. 10).

The industrial development of the 1930s saw the final disappearance of open space, the movement of large numbers of workers into the area and, despite the movement away of older residents, a substantial net increase in population, the total reaching 198,000 in 1938. House building lagged behind this development and increasing population, and the obvious consequence was overcrowding and deteriorating housing standards. Morris, writing in 1950 about this period, commented:

> The street upon street of 'desirable villas' of the Edwardian period, although structurally sound, lacked the convenience, warmth and sanitary arrangements of later suburban universal plan houses and the former were too large for the modern family without servants. Most of these Edwardian villas are now shared by two or more families and the greater part of the population lives in this type of house today (1950, p. 12).

The Housing Act, 1935, required the newly-formed (i.e. in 1933) Borough of Willesden to report on the extent of overcrowding:

> More than 44,000 dwellings were surveyed. Just over 1,000 were owned by the Council; the remainder belonged to private landlords or owner-occupiers. It was found that about 2,000 families living in shared houses, or even in their own small houses, were so cramped for space that they were 'overcrowded' even according to the very low standard laid down (Leff and Blunden, n.d., p. 31).

In sum, the interaction between industrialisation and the growth of population in the context of a failure of private enterprise to build sufficient housing, led to overcrowding and low living standards in the Borough.

It was a problem that the Second World War did nothing to solve. Despite the fact that over 60,000 people left Willesden during the war, the population rapidly increased again afterwards and had reached over 180,000 by 1948. The demand for accommodation increased and it is perhaps therefore not surprising that the 1,300 houses in Kensal Rise and Harlesden which had been declared unfit for human habitation before 1939 had even more people living in them after the war than before (Leff and Blunden, n.d.). Slum clearance and council building began but had little impact and by the early 1950s it was recognised that Willesden had worse housing and sanitary conditions than anywhere else in Middlesex. The decline in standards was not reversed in the subsequent decade: between 1961 and 1966 the proportion of households in shared dwellings increased from 28.2 per cent to 35.8 per cent, while in 1966 46.7 per cent of households lacked exclusive use of hot water, a fixed bath and inside toilet (Greve et al., 1971, pp. 12, 32). Using

966 census data, the Greater London Council identified eight
ards in Brent which were characterised by housing stress (Round-
ood, Harlesden, Kensal Rise, Kilburn, Willesden Green, Stone-
ridge, Queens Park and Cricklewood) and more detailed studies,
sing additional census data, have shown that these wards tend to
e dominated by private renting of both furnished and unfurnished
ousing and a population which consists both of large numbers of
mi- and unskilled workers and of persons born in Ireland and the
ew Commonwealth (Greve *et al.*, 1971, pp. 37, 292; Daly, 1971).

The increasing rate of council building during the 1960s and
970s, along with rehabilitation and improvement, may have
meliorated the situation somewhat: the 1971 Census showed that
1.4 per cent of Brent's occupied dwellings contained two or more
ouseholds, this proportion containing 23.4 per cent of all house-
olds in Brent. Moreover, in Brent as a whole, there has been a
eady increase since 1961 in the proportion of the population living
both local authority property and rented furnished accommoda-
on, and a decline in the proportion living in rented unfurnished
roperty, although the Borough Council believes that this shift in
nure pattern has done much to contribute to homelessness in the
rea. In addition, there has been a decline in the proportion of
ouseholds in Brent lacking or sharing basic amenities, although the
roportions remain relatively high; for example, nearly a quarter of
ll households in Brent lacked or shared a bath in 1971. Finally, a
rent Council survey completed in 1972 concluded that about 27
er cent of dwellings in Brent were below the standards laid down in
e Housing Act, 1969 (Borough of Brent, 1977). In the late 1970s
ve areas of the Borough had been declared General Improvement
reas and three others Housing Action Areas; all of these were in
e southern half of the Borough, within the previous boundary of
e Borough of Willesden. Despite these limited changes and council
tivity aimed at improvement, the Council believes that the
orough will continue to face a severe housing problem for years to
me (Borough of Brent, 1977).

Our argument is, then, that the current housing problem in
illesden is not a recent creation but has existed for at least fifty
ears and has been caused in the final analysis by the inability of
rivate capital to meet the demand for accommodation occasioned.
y the movement of labour in the borough to take up jobs in what
as, until the mid 1960s, an expanding industrial area. The latter is,
owever, no longer the case and since the 1960s Willesden has
xperienced a considerable decline in manufacturing industry. By
940, the major industrial development of Willesden was virtually

complete, although there was further limited expansion between 1945 and 1948 and again between 1950 and 1960 (Keeble, 1968, pp. 23–5), but none of this fundamentally altered the industrial structure that had developed in the 1930s.

The available evidence does not make it easy to precisely date the commencement of industrial decline in Willesden. The Borough of Brent noted in 1971 that there had been a gradual increase in vacant industrial floorspace over the preceding three years, while Keeble suggests that a major movement of industry out of North West London began in the early 1960s (ibid., p. 25). However, the number of Brent residents actually employed in manufacturing industry has been declining since 1951, from 77,975 to 54,960 between 1951 and 1966 (despite an increase in the total number of persons employed), and then to 45,630 in 1971 (Borough of Brent, 1977). Manufacturing industry in Willesden was certainly in decline by the early 1970s and information supplied by the Borough of Brent indicates that this decline was in the food and drink, engineering and vehicle production industries, all of which came to prominence in the 1930s and provided the industrial basis to the growth of Willesden.

Although the data for London as a whole suggests that the closure of manufacturing firms is a more important factor in the decline of manufacturing than relocation, we have no means of knowing whether this applies specifically to Willesden, and the one relevant study deals only with industrial migration from North West London for the period 1940 to 1964 (Keeble, 1968). This suggested that those manufacturing industries moving away from the area were, in fact, expanding, and were moving precisely because their present location was restricting further growth and because they were experiencing a shortage of labour, particularly skilled male labour and unskilled female labour. Further growth was restricted by two factors. First, post-war factory construction had not been possible after 1945 because pre-war expansion, both industrial and residential, had utilised almost all available land, and this restriction in supply in the context of continuing demand had increased factory costs and had made new large-scale factory construction impossible. Yet second, the increasing capital intensity of manufacturing production (that is, the need for larger units of production and more productive machinery) necessitated by competition meant that further space was required by existing firms if production was to be expanded, particularly if the original factory site was based on design principles of the 1920s and 1930s and was not therefore easily restructured to accept new machinery. In other words, continued capital investment was a necessity if profitability was to be maintained in a competitive market, and by the 1960s there were major barriers to this investment being made in North West London. The advantages to capital of the region in the 1930s and the nature of the expansion, using up all available land, became disadvantages to continued investment in the 1960s.

A related factor, referred to by the Borough of Brent, had been the rationalisation of capital on a national and international scale, in the interests of capturing a greater share of the market and maintaining profitability by creating a larger unit of production. Electrical engineering was one of the dominant industries that was established in the 1930s and this was affected by the major GEC – English Electric – AEI merger of the late 1960s (see Counter Information Services, n.d.).

The effect of this decline in manufacturing industry has to be evaluated in the context of several factors (Borough of Brent, 1977). First, census data shows that the total population and the working population of Brent has been steadily falling since 1951. Second, some of the floor space vacated by industrial users has been reoccupied by the wholesale distributive and service trades, although these new firms do not employ as many workers as the manufacturing firms they have replaced. There has therefore been a shift in the employment structure. Third, it has to be remembered that there is considerable mobility of labour across Borough boundaries and workers made redundant in Brent may seek and obtain work in other parts of London: in 1971, about 55 per cent of Brent male and 49 per cent of Brent female residents travelled out of the Borough to work, while 55 per cent of all male and 35 per cent of all female workers in the Borough travelled in. Fourth, it was, until the mid 1970s, Borough and GLC policy to encourage labour to move to New Towns and Development Areas and this will have contributed to the decline in the working population, although it should be remembered that a study of such movement in another London Borough showed that the majority of such movers were young, skilled workers (Deakin and Ungerson, 1977). If the same were true for Brent, it should be recalled that it is skilled labour that has been in short supply in the Borough for some long time and that the majority of redundancies are likely to have been of semi- and unskilled workers.

Nevertheless, these factors must go at least some way to explaining why the decline in the manufacturing base has not led to substantial unemployment. The rate of unemployment in Brent was lower than that for Great Britain as a whole from the mid 1960s,

although it increased substantially after 1973 when the number o
vacancies declined. This increase was a function of the nationa
economic recession, although the fact that the local employmen
structure is still more dependent upon manufacturing industry tha
the national economy may mean that a national economic recessio
may have a disproportionate local impact. It should also be note
that black workers in Brent have constituted, since the mid 1970s
well over a third of the number of registered unemployed (Boroug
of Brent, 1977).

We are arguing, therefore, that it is possible to trace a process o
industrial development and decline in Willesden which is similar t
that identified in other parts of Britain, despite the fact that many o
the latter areas were originally dominated by heavy capital good
industries, whereas the development of Willesden was based upo
new consumer goods industries and related electrical and mechani
cal engineering (see CDP, 1977). Indeed, what is perhaps s
remarkable about the Willesden case, and no doubt other areas too
is the short time-span between development and decline (less tha
fifty years). This process of industrial development and decline ha
been intimately related to what might be described as a permanen
housing problem because, since industrial development began, the
has never been a time when the supply has kept pace with th
demand consequent upon industrial development.

Willesden and migration

Throughout its history as a part of urban London, Willesden ha
always been characterised by considerable movements of populatio
in and out of the Borough (see Morris, 1950, p. 10). This movemen
has included not only English manual workers but also worker
from Wales, Scotland and Ireland, as well as non-manual Jewis
workers. Jewish residence in Willesden can be dated back to the las
three decades of the nineteenth century – Brondesbury Synagogu
was in existence in 1870 (Newman, 1977, p. 227) – but it was aroun
the turn of the century that the Jewish population grew mos
substantially (Lipman, 1954). Brondesbury has remained an area o
Jewish residence, although we have no means of knowing wha
proportion of the estimated 20,000 Jews living in the Borough o
Brent in 1970 (Prais, 1972) live in this particular ward. What is clea
is that this ward is quite distinct in terms of its character and qualit
of housing compared with much of the rest of Willesden.

The movement of a Jewish population into Willesden wa

primarily for purposes of residence but the other movements have all been for the purpose of work. During the economic depression of the 1930s, Welshmen and Scots moved into Willesden in search of employment, and after 1945 both Jewish refugees and Irish workers moved into the area for the same purpose (Weintraub, 1972, p. 44). But by far the largest migration has been of workers from the New Commonwealth, primarily from the Caribbean. Despite the fact that the absolute total number of jobs was declining in Willesden, the decline of the 'established' resident population was even greater, with the result that from the mid 1950s to the late 1960s there was a shortage of labour in the area. These jobs were taken up by mainly West Indian workers who also sought residence in the Borough (Weintraub, 1972, pp. 46–52). Thus, in 1951 0.1 per cent of Brent's population had been born in the Caribbean, while in 1961 it was 5.5 per cent and in 1971 it was 6.5 per cent. The numbers of migrants from the Indian sub-continent and East Africa increased only after 1966, and in 1971 4 per cent of the population of Brent had been born in these areas. Brent is now the London borough with the second highest proportion of residents with both parents born in the New Commonwealth (17.4 per cent). But these figures should not lead us to ignore the size of the Irish population: in 1971 8.6 per cent of Brent's population had been born in Ireland (Borough of Brent, 1977).

The fact that we wish to draw attention to, on the basis of this evidence, is that the movement of black migrant labour into Willesden (as into London as a whole) post-dated both the shortage of housing and the emergence of the preconditions of industrial decline. Far from being the cause of the housing problem and industrial decline, black migrant workers have been the victims of economic and social processes over which they have little or no influence. This becomes clearly apparent if one's analytical framework has an historical perspective, focusing on the development and decline of centres of capitalist production.

Black migrants in Brent: the political response

The Labour Party has held office during the development of these processes since 1945. The old Willesden Council was Labour dominated as befits an area that contains a predominantly manual working-class population, and pursued policies which were of benefit to the working class as a whole (e.g. an emphasis on the building of council housing), but, with an eye on the newly arrived

West Indian migrants, it also pursued an independent 'race relations' programme. In 1959 the Willesden International Friendship Council (WIFC) was founded with Reg Freeson as chairman. He later became Labour MP for Willesden East (afterwards Brent East) and Minister for Housing and Construction in the 1974-9 Labour Government. The WIFC was succeeded by the Willesden International Friendship Council and Brent Friendship Society, which in turn was succeeded by the Brent Community Relations Council.

The local Labour Party also remained critical of the national party's growing support of immigration control (Weintraub, 1972, p. 152), at least up until 1965. But the merger of Wembley and Willesden in 1965 greatly reduced the Labour majority on the new Council and the party became increasingly preoccupied with maintaining itself in office and, hence, pursued policies that were unlikely to lose white working-class votes. This did not prevent the Conservative opposition from attacking policies aimed at benefiting the working class as a whole, as particularly favouring the black population (Weintraub, 1972, p. 194). The Labour Party lost their control of the Council in 1968 but subsequently regained it, and while their policies could in no way be said to 'favour' Brent's black population this had not absolved them from criticism, particularly over the housing of Ugandan Asians, and since 1974 over lettings and the formation of black estates in the southern half of the borough.

The emergence of the National Front as an electoral force in the 1974 General Election was met by a ban on its using any council-controlled property for meetings, following the formation of an action committee by the local Trades Council to organise opposition to the National Front's activity in the area. This opposition to the National Front was stepped up in 1976 with the organisation of the Brent Campaign against Racialism supported by the Trades Council, constituency Labour parties and the Brent Federation of Tenants and Residents Associations, amongst others. The aim was to 'weld together forces representing the overwhelming majority of working men and women and their families in Brent' in the fight against racism. The campaign organisers also recognised that

> Where black people feel the need to organise separately to
> achieve their rights, they will have the full support of our
> Campaign. In the same way, we welcome the initiative of groups
> such as the Brent Defence Campaign, which represents West

Indian people fighting against the harassment of their youth by the local police (From the leaflet 'What we stand for', Brent Campaign Against Racialism, 1977).

The Brent Defence Committee, originally known as the Campaign Against Racialism in Brent (CARIB), was organised in July 1976 following the arrest and alleged assault by the police of four West Indian girls. CARIB initially represented an alliance of black and white radical interests: local young blacks, the Socialist Workers' Party and black radicals from outside the area. They had taken the initiative in the fight against racism locally, to be quickly followed by the formation of the Brent Campaign Against Racialism. While there was therefore competition for the leadership of opposition to racism, all parties were at least agreed that any National Front presence in the area should be strenuously opposed.

The National Front has remained electorally weak in the area (compared to other parts of London), capturing 6.3 per cent and 4.6 per cent of the votes cast in Brent South and East respectively in the May 1977 GLC elections, and faring even worse in the council elections a year later with about 2 per cent of the total vote.

The Labour Party maintained their majority on the council in May 1978 because, according to the deputy leader, the Labour Party, by constantly stressing the need to fight the 'Nazi National Front' had impressed many Jews who might otherwise have voted Tory or not voted at all. 'Our campaign also reached the many immigrants in Brent who were apprehensive about the Front and also about what they regarded as the sympathy shown by Mrs Thatcher to racist views' (Willesden and Brent Chronicle, 12 May 1978). In reply, the leader of the Tory opposition accused the Labour Party of bribing the 'immigrant' vote with taxpayers' money. The Labour Party was for once not on the defensive.

At the parliamentary level Brent is split into three constituencies, Brent North which at the time of our presence in the area was held by Rhodes Boyson, Brent East by Reg Freeson and Brent South by Laurie Pavitt. Prior to selection as a parliamentary candidate, Freeson had been critical of national Labour Party policies on immigration but, during the 1964 election campaign, he indicated his acceptance of the policy of immigration control. Freeson won the seat (then Willesden East) from the Conservatives (who had held it only since 1959) and has retained it ever since. By comparison Brent South (formerly Willesden West) has been a safe seat, Labour having lost it only once to the Conservatives since 1923. Apart from a Communist Party candidate in Brent South, parliamentary elections tended to be two-way fights up until 1974 when the Liberals and National Front entered the arena, though both remain electorally weak in the area.

The 'official' channelling of black migrant interests is, of course, through the local Community Relations Council, though the extent to which this is true in practice is questionable given the fact that the majority of black migrants questioned in one study conducted in Brent had never heard of it (Morrison, 1976, p. 102). During our presence in the area the Council was in some disarray, culminating in its executive committee asking for the Principal Community Relations Officer's (PCRO) resignation, claiming that he was not working within the guidelines laid down by them. The PCRO strenuously fought back, but the issue raised a wider question within the parent body, the Commission for Racial Equality, over how much autonomy should be allowed to local community relations councils (Willesden and Brent Chronicle, 17 November 1978). The PCRO, a West Indian, became a Labour councillor in May 1978.

To conclude this very brief summary of local politics, we will reiterate two points. Firstly, the predominantly working-class nature of Willesden is reflected in the Labour electoral domination, while the arrival of black migrant labourers has forced the Labour Party to respond to white hostility, particularly on the issue of housing which, as we have shown in the previous section, is in poor condition and short supply. Secondly, the Labour Party has also had to adopt a position on racism, though the initiative on the issue had come from black and white groups operating within the informal sphere of politics.

Against this socio-economic and political picture of the area, we will go on to present a profile of the English and West Indian men and women whom we interviewed there.

CHAPTER 4

Some facts about our sample

In the methodological appendix we describe briefly how, through a combination of observational work and in-depth interviewing, we collected our data for this study. In this chapter we want to give our readers some facts about the men and women whom we interviewed.

The sample is divided into two parts which we will call the *factory sample* and the *residential sample*. The factory sample is composed of 72 men all of whom are engaged in semi-skilled manual jobs: 36 of the men are English and 36 West Indian. They were all interviewed at their place of work, a large food processing plant which we will call Food Co., which is situated on the Park Royal Estate. The estate is adjacent to the Harlesden area, the area from which we drew our residential sample. The latter sample is composed of 37 women of whom 17 are English and 20 West Indian and 40 men of whom 19 are English and 21 are West Indian. Occupationally the residential

Table 4.1 *Birthplace of sample*

English	Residential			Factory	Total
	Men (N = 19)	Women (N = 17)	Total (N = 36)	Men (N = 36)	(N = 72)
Local	13	8	21 (58%)	8 (22%)	29 (40%)
London	1	7	8 (22%)	18 (50%)	26 (36%)
Elsewhere in UK	5	2	7 (19%)	10 (28%)	17 (24%)

West Indian	Residential			Factory	Total
	Men (N = 21)	Women (N = 20)	Total (N = 41)	Men (N = 36)	(N = 77)
Jamaica	17	14	31 (76%)	20 (56%)	51 (66%)
Elsewhere in West Indies	4	6	10 (24%)	16 (44%)	26 (34%)

sample is more diverse than the factory sample with 55 per cent
engaged in semi- or unskilled manual work, 22 per cent skilled work
and the remainder made up of routine white-collar workers (9 per
cent), unemployed manual workers (5 per cent) and full-time
houseworkers (9 per cent).

As far as birthplace is concerned, there is greater uniformity in the
residential sample as compared to the factory sample. In the former
case 58 per cent of the English reported being born in the Harlesden
area and 76 per cent of the West Indians in Jamaica, compared to
22 per cent and 56 per cent respectively of the factory sample (see
Table 4.1).

Age and family structure

We were keen to ensure that all of our respondents had a relatively
long period of work experience, even if they were not currently wage
labourers. We were also keen to ensure that our West Indians came
to this country at an age which would facilitate, in most cases,
consideration of the effects of prior socialisation in the West Indies.

Thus all of the respondents in the factory sample are aged
between 25 and 40 years and those in the residential sample between
25 and 50 years. While it was possible to be precise about age in the
factory sample because we had access to factory records, we had to
rely on the respondents' information concerning age in the residential sample. In the case of the latter, we gave every potential
interviewee an introductory letter outlining who we were and what
we wanted to talk to them about. We made clear in this letter that
we were concerned to interview only men and women aged between
25 and 45 years. Even though we further asked the interviewee
whether he or she fell into this age group, on analysis of the data we
worked out that two men were nearer 50 than 45 years of age. In the
factory, the sample of English men had a much larger proportion
aged between 24 and 30 years (44 per cent), whereas 33 per cent of
the West Indians were aged between 24 and 30 years and 61 per cent
were aged between 36 and 40 years. Thus the English sample had a
younger average age.

Of the West Indians, over 80 per cent of the men and 82 per cent
of the women were married, the majority with children to support
Of the English 74 per cent of the men and 88 per cent of the women
in the residential sample were married, compared to only half of the
men in the factory sample. In the residential sample, half of the
respondents who were single had children to support, while in the

factory it was only amongst the West Indian men that we found a small proportion of one-parent families.

Accommodation

In the methodological appendix we explain why the majority of our West Indians in the residential sample were located in the private sector of housing and were predominantly owner-occupiers, while the majority of English were council tenants. The variance in this context must be seen in relation to our different sampling methods, but it also reflects the national pattern which indicates that, controlling for occupation, West Indians are nationally over-represented as owner-occupiers and under-represented as council tenants when compared to their indigenous counterparts (Smith, 1977, pp. 210–16). This is also reflected in the tenure patterns of the factory sample as illustrated in Table 4.2.

Table 4.2 Type of accommodation of the factory sample (%)

	Private furnished	Rented unfurnished	Council	Owner-occupied	Other
English (N = 35)	29.0 (10)	17.0 (6)	31.0 (11)	17.0 (6)	6.0 (2)
West Indian (N = 35)	17.0 (6)	3.0 (1)	23.0 (8)	51.0 (18)	6.0 (2)

We asked all the owner occupiers in the residential sample whether they had ever registered on the waiting list for council accommodation, why they had chosen to buy a house and whether they had encountered any difficulties in obtaining a mortgage. We asked our council tenants how long they had been on the waiting list prior to being housed in council accommodation and whether or not they had ever considered obtaining a mortgage to buy a house. Taking the West Indian owner-occupiers first (N = 25) we found that a quarter had registered on the waiting list before obtaining a mortgage to buy their house. Most of these said they had simply got fed up with waiting and set about saving or raising the money for a deposit on a house; two faced with eviction borrowed money from relatives for the deposit. The rest explained their reasons for buying either in terms of preference or necessity. The latter were the largest group, though the West Indian women were more likely than the men to say that they preferred to own their own house than to rent.

As one woman explained:

> 'Well, we were in rented accommodation and when I became pregnant with Alan we decided we weren't really free in this position, I mean you can just do as you please in your own place. There were too many restrictions, don't do this and don't do that and really the children need room to run about in and develop, that's the main reason'. (West Indian female: residential sample)

But for the majority there appeared to have been little choice:

> 'I was desperate because I had my children so I just struggled my own way through and went to the building society for a mortgage.' (West Indian male: residential sample)

> 'Well speaking as a West Indian, when I came here first there was no accommodation for immigrants in that time, you might find people like Jews who have houses and will let you a room. But back in the 50s I find that I have got to get a house. Then you set out saving for it.' (West Indian male: residential sample)

A few had bought their house outright, and a small proportion reported having had real difficulties in obtaining a mortgage, eventually resorting to finance companies. But the majority said that getting a mortgage had been relatively easy.

Turning to the council tenants (fourteen West Indian and thirty English), the question of necessity is more pronounced. Many indicated that they would like to own their own house or had tried to do so, but were prevented by financial limitations. All the council tenants were asked if they thought the allocatory system for council housing was fair. The majority of English believed that the system was unfair, half believing that the 'coloured' or 'coloured immigrants' got preference. In contrast, the majority of West Indians either thought the system fair or professed complete ignorance of how the allocatory system worked: as one woman suggested, 'Well it's their system.'

Accommodation is therefore an area where the position of our West Indians as a racialised fraction of the working class is of obvious relevance, owner-occupation being seen as a necessity by many.

Education

In an economic system increasingly dependent upon qualification, skill and training, those who lack such things tend to be restricted to a certain sector of the economy. The bulk of our respondents are not very well qualified, the majority having left school at fifteen or sixteen years of age, some earlier, and only a small proportion had sat an examination successfully prior to leaving.

Economic pressures were most commonly mentioned as the reason for early school leaving, lack of examination success and job qualifications:

'There was nothing like that when I was at school. It was out of school and into a job.' (English male: factory sample)

'I had to leave school to look after my smaller brothers and sisters while my parents worked.' (West Indian female: residential sample)

'The family situation didn't warrant that I could stay on. If I'd come from a rich family I could have afforded it.' (English male: residential sample)

Although a quarter of our English male respondents claimed that they had had some form of further education, mainly in connection with apprenticeship schemes and undertaken at technical college, only a small proportion had completed their period of education and training and only one was now using the skills that he had originally learnt. As one lorry driver explained:

'Well, I've got a two-year City and Guild Carpentry and Joinery, but in my opinion there's no such thing as a carpenter and joiner now, you're just a glorified fitter.'

But the majority of English men did not even begin or attempt any further education and those that did have some desire were held back for financial reasons, as the following quote illustrates:

'I was going to stay on but we didn't have much money. So from school to a £4 a week job was good to me then so I took it. I liked school but it was just one of those things that I had to get out.'

Three English women claimed to have had some form of further education or training, having undertaken secretarial courses. All three were currently using the skills they had learnt.

A third of the West Indian men reported having undertaken further education or training in the West Indies: many described this as 'learning a trade'. In some cases this would have been a fairly informal process, in others it was formal training, as one man explained:

'I left school at fifteen but I started to learn a trade when I was about fourteen. In Jamaica in the school holidays we used to go and learn some trade or other. Then when I left school I studied and became an apprentice electrician. Then when I came to England at the age of nineteen I found that it wasn't worth doing it because I wasn't getting enough money. The bloke I worked with who did the driving was getting more money than I was for doing all the electrical work. So I left that trade and went into industry where I did mechanical engineering, then I worked for the Transport people and now I'm working in a factory.'

None of the West Indian men were currently using the skills they had learnt in the West Indies. A further eight men (four of whom had come to Britain straight from school or had finished their secondary education here) had undertaken, though not all completed, further education or training in Britain. Four were currently using the skills they had learnt, but one man was less fortunate:

'I did a government training course in sheet metal work and I found it difficult to get work when I had done the course, so I got this job (assembly line worker). I couldn't find a job in the trade at all.'

Seven West Indian women reported further training, three in dressmaking in Jamaica and four in secretarial work in Britain. One woman was still dressmaking and two of the four who had secretarial training were currently using those skills.

Thus, while there are some exceptions in the residential sample, the majority of our English respondents entered the labour market as semi- or unskilled manual workers and had few other options open unless they undertook some further training. They were joined by the West Indian migrants who possessed skills which were not always deemed adequate to the demands made of skilled labour in a more developed capitalist economy, or who had few skills at all (we will discuss this topic in more detail later in the chapter). In this sense, both shared a similar position in the labour market, although if employers discriminated against the West Indian worker, the latter would be disadvantaged in that market, unable to compete equally with white workers otherwise equally poorly qualified.

Occupation

As indicated earlier, all the respondents in the factory were engaged in semi- or unskilled manual jobs. An occupational classification of the residential sample is given in Table 4.3. The higher proportion of skilled workers amongst the English, as compared to West Indian men in the residential sample, is attributable to the fact that over a quarter of the English were employed as lorry drivers.

Table 4.3 Occupational classification of residential sample

| | West Indian | | English | |
	Men	*Women*	*Men*	*Women*
Semi- and unskilled manual	13 (62%)	14 (70%)	9 (47%)	6 (35%)
Skilled manual	5 (24%)	3 (15%)	9 (47%) (5 lorry drivers)	—
Routine white-collar	2 (9%)	2 (10%)	—	3 (18%)
Unemployed	1 (5%)	1 (5%)	1 (6%)	1 (6%)
Houseworker	—	—	—	7 (41%)

Two English men originally interviewed were not included in the study for theoretical reasons: one was a student, the other a quantity surveyor. Five of the English women who were currently full-time houseworkers had been engaged in semi- or unskilled manual work prior to giving birth to their first child, two had continued to work intermittently since then. The other two English women not actively seeking work had previously been employed in routine white-collar work.

Taking the two samples together it is only amongst the small proportion of routine white-collar workers that there is some evidence of a 'settled' work history. The occupational histories of the majority of our English and West Indian respondents, male and female, are very similar, reflecting their shared position in the labour market as the following quotes illustrate:

'Well, the first job I did was a porter in a restaurant. Then I left there and went to work for Scholls. From there I went to work in a bakery and that's the hardest job I've ever done. I was there for about five months and I left and went back to Scholls and from there I went onto the buses. From the buses to Standard Telephone and from there I came here.'

'I've had a lot of jobs. I had that one before this on the printed circuits. Hotels, cafes, restaurants, mental hospital, a research place in Beckenham: really I've been moving about, I've had a lot of jobs.'

'I've had different jobs. The last job I was doing was a builder's merchant. I've worked in a big store up Queensway, various jobs. I always give these jobs a go and then if I find I don't like it, I go.'

'I used to work in a factory sewing. I did that for about nine years and then I was made redundant. I was unemployed for about six weeks and then I went into another job and I was made redundant again. I was only there a few weeks and they closed down, I don't think the business was doing well enough. Then I went to another factory. I'm enjoying this work I'm doing now though, with those old people. I'm sorry I didn't go into it earlier.'

Only eight of the manual workers in our sample had been employed in a non-manual job at some point in their lives. Although they were not specifically asked, many respondents indicated their reasons for having changed jobs so often. Low pay and poor conditions was a very common reason, though the attitude of the employer and prospects were also mentioned.

But these men and women did not always change their jobs by choice. Given the loss of semi- and unskilled jobs, particularly in manufacturing, in London in general and in the old borough of Willesden in particular, it is not surprising that a fairly large proportion of the sample had had some experience of redundancy. Although there were no specific questions on redundancy, the men and women recounted this event as yet another feature of their work history and did not express any undue concern or annoyance about it. One man said:

'Well, I didn't like it at the time because I was planning to get married and the money was coming in useful and if I was still at Walls I could have bought my own place, there is no doubt about that. The thought of having to go on the dole or finding another job wasn't very pleasing but it comes to us all at some time or other.'

We have not bothered to differentiate between our Englishmen's and West Indians' own account of their experiences and problems in the context of work histories, because those accounts are so similar. But on the basis of national evidence one possible line of difference would relate to the disproportionate number of black, as compared to white, workers employed on shift work (Smith, 1976, p. 78). At Food Co. there was no obvious disproportionate representation of black workers on the permanent night shift and a consideration of the reasons given by the English and West Indian men for working this shift suggests that they do so for somewhat similar reasons. Several spoke of the advantages for family organisation where the wife was working: the husband would be getting out of bed to prepare for work when the children were coming home from school. Other workers said that they found it difficult to get up in the morning and so found it more convenient to work nights. Further reasons included the higher wages that could be earned by working nights and the greater flexibility for leisure at the weekend through working four consecutive nights. In the residential sample 50 per cent of the West Indian men worked over 40 hours a week, compared to a quarter of the English men.

But the most pronounced difference between our English and West Indian work patterns is amongst the women. Firstly, except for one West Indian woman off sick, all were currently engaged in full-time work. Of the English women, only five worked over 35 hours a week and 41 per cent were not actively seeking work. Secondly, while a proportion of the English women give child care as their reason for not working or only working part-time, almost the same proportion of West Indian women said that child care governed the location and hours of their work as the following quotes illustrate:

'My little boy will be seven next Wednesday and he is the reason why I chose this place to live because he is able to keep the same nanny and go to the same school, plus I can also keep my job. I work for — they make books, I do 8 till 5 five days a week, next year I will be three years there.' (West Indian female: residential sample)

'I work at a school as a general assistant, I help to cook the meals and dish them up and I have a couple of part-time jobs as well … I work 32 hours a week at the school and 3 hours every afternoon in a hospital.'

What did you do before that?

'I worked in a factory for seven years but when my little boy started school it was difficult to get someone to take him to school in the mornings because I had to start at 7.30 a.m. Then during the holidays I had to pay so much money to keep him in the play centre I thought I'd get something that would be more convenient.' (West Indian female: residential sample)

A number of West Indian women did several jobs: one (Jean) had six children. She got up every weekday at 6 o'clock in the morning to make the family's breakfast. By 8.30 a.m. two small children would have been brought to the house by their mothers for Jean to look after along with her own two pre-school children. After feeding the family and her husband's return from work in the late afternoon, she would set off to work the 'twilight' shift at a local biscuit factory. She returned at 10.30 p.m. Her husband worked all day on Sundays as well as during the week.

As we have no information on incomes we cannot posit financial reasons for the difference between the number of West Indian, as compared to English, women who work full-time in our sample. But other evidence suggests that West Indian women work from necessity (Smith, 1977, pp. 65–6), as the following quote illustrates:

'If you look into it you'll see that the working-class people aren't getting anything, we can just barely make it. My husband isn't working, I have to pay for everything and they still take so much in tax from me. Everything keeps rising and I'm straining, I can't even buy anything for myself ... there are lots of men out of work and the poor women have to strain.' (West Indian female: residential sample)

In the next section we will discuss other factors which we believe to be relevant to West Indian women's role as wage labourers in Britain. The point to be made here is that women's acceptance of the responsibilities of child care further forecloses what we have identified as the limited employment options open to the majority of our sample.

The West Indians' migration

The nature and causes of New Commonwealth migration to Britain, of which migration from the Caribbean was a part, is now well established (Glass, 1961; Davison, 1962; Davison, 1966; Peach, 1968; Castles and Kosack 1973; Smith, 1976), and the information obtained from the West Indian sample does not contradict this literature in any substantial way. It is generally agreed that the bulk of West Indian migration preceded the migration from the Indian sub-continent and from East Africa (cf. Smith, 1976, pp. 24–5) and that a very substantial proportion of West Indian migration preceded and, indeed, was encouraged by the 1962 Immigration Act (e.g. Peach, 1968; Smith, 1976). The vast majority of West Indian men and women in our sample came before 1962, and the remainder after the imposition of immigration control from the New Commonwealth (cf. Smith, 1976, p. 24).

Because we have precise information on the age of our factory sample workers it is possible to establish that those who came by or before 1962, now aged between 31 and 40 years, would therefore have been born between 1936 and 1945 and could have been no older than between 17 and 26 years when migrating; this, too, corresponds with the facts established by other studies (e.g. Davison, 1962, p. 16; Smith, 1976, p. 27).

As stated previously, a third of our West Indian male respondents reported having been trained in the West Indies for a particular job. As can be seen from Table 4.4, just over a third claim to have been

Table 4.4 Occupation of West Indian men prior to migration

	N = 57
Agriculture	9 (16%)
Unskilled/semi-skilled manual	7 (12%)
Skilled manual	20 (35%)
Service industry	5 (9%)
Manufacturing industry	1 (2%)
Unemployed	4 (7%)
Came to England straight from school or finished secondary education in England	8 (14%)
Routine white-collar	1 (2%)
No answer	2 (3%)

in some form of skilled manual job prior to migration, the majority of this group referring to their work as a trade. The most commonly mentioned trade was in connection with building and included builders, masons, plasterers and carpenters. The other trades mentioned were tailor, shoemaker, baker, butcher, mechanic and electrical engineer. Only one man had been employed, prior to migration, in any form of manufacturing industry (he worked in a sugar factory). Those identifying themselves as having a 'trade' were not employed in any manufacturing enterprise, nor were those employed in services or in unskilled or semi-skilled jobs: the latter jobs were shop assistant, taxi-driver, lorry driver, labourer, etc.

These two points warrant some comment in the context of extant findings. It is recognised that the nature of the economies of the Caribbean islands produce a different definition of 'skilled' when compared to Britain, where there is a tradition of formal apprenticeship and craft unionism which defines and defends the skilled worker. Thus, 'learning a trade' in the Caribbean is a fairly informal process:

> 'My uncle used to do tailoring and before and after school I used to go and help him to do some buttons and hemmings and things from when I was about eight years old. When I left school about 15–16, I bought a new Singer sewing machine and I used to do tailoring in the town and teach some guys as well.' (West Indian male: factory sample)

A movement of self-defined and, in the Caribbean, socio-economically defined skilled workers into the English economy might therefore be expected to produce discrepancies between occupational status before and after migration. This is well illustrated by one of the West Indian respondents who identified himself as a mason by trade before migration but, having come to England with his tools, was unable to continue in this work. He explained why:

> 'When I came to England I went to the Exchange and the man asked me what I used to do. I told him and he said it was different in this country so I explained what I used to do in detail. He then said that I could go to the school here and catch up. I said all right but when I went home and thought about it, I ignored it. And now I regret it.' (West Indian male: factory sample)

Another described his disillusionment about applying his trade as a cabinet maker in England:

> 'I tried cabinet making over here for one month but I didn't like

it. It's not what you've learnt, you know, it's just fitting. Just everything on a conveyor belt as it passes along, to me that's not cabinet making, that's not a trade.' (West Indian male: residential sample)

However limited, the empirical evidence on this matter is confusing (cf. Wright, 1968, pp. 31–8; Patterson, 1969, pp. 146–7). The analysis by Glass of previous occupations of migrants in the Caribbean emphasises most strongly the proportion of skilled workers amongst West Indian migrants, but Wright is very critical of this analysis (1968, pp. 34–7) and Glass has certainly played down the argument of Davison (1962, p. 21) that the migrants have good reason to exaggerate their attained skill. What this small sample does illustrate, nevertheless, is that Caribbean migration has brought to England a substantial proportion of individuals who, in the context of their island of origin, were (or are still) skilled, although an almost equal proportion were engaged in unskilled manual work, agriculture or in some service industry, those in the latter probably also being unskilled, at least in English terms. What is also clear is that irrespective of this argument about skill the majority of the men in the residential sample and all the men in the factory sample are now all classified as semi- or unskilled labourers in the English economy, being engaged in a type of factory work or service industry of which they had no experience prior to migration. Five of the seven men in the residential sample who now occupy skilled or non-manual occupations completed their secondary education in Britain.

While we have detailed information on occupation prior to migration for only 75 per cent of the West Indian women in our sample, only four of the fifteen had worked regularly prior to migration. The fact that few had worked prior to migration is in line with Foner's evidence (1979, p. 64). The opportunities for earning a regular wage are very limited for women in the West Indies, but this is not to suggest that as a result they occupy a legally or economically dependent position in those societies, for two main reasons. Firstly, legal marriage is not entered into in the Caribbean until the male partner is reasonably secure economically. This means that a legal marriage often comes late in life for West Indian women (Smith, 1956). Secondly, West Indian women have therefore a history of self-reliance, earning money through doing sewing or selling excess vegetable produce, to name a couple of ways in which they manage to subsist.

Thus while the majority of men in our sample were wage

labourers prior to migration, few of the women were. Foner argues that this ability to earn a regular wage in England represents a real improvement in the lives of the women she interviewed (1979, pp. 63–70). Foner also argues that domestic work was avoided by women in Jamaica because 'they did not like to place themselves in a subordinate position to higher status persons' (1979, p. 64). Yet the majority of the wage-earning women in Foner's sample and many of the women in our sample (see Table 4.5) were involved in what

Table 4.5 Occupation of West Indian women in London

	N=20
Factory worker	10
Cleaner/laundry worker	3
Canteen assistant	1
Cook	1
Ward orderly	1
Typist	1
Clerical worker	1
Cashier	1
Off sick	1

might be described as industrialised housework. West Indian women may not, like the men, suffer occupational status discrepancy before and after migration, but we certainly did not get the impression that the opportunity of becoming a wage labourer, and the control over labour power which the wage relation imposes, was seen to represent any kind of improvement by the women we interviewed.

Thus the majority of our West Indian men and women are employed in semi- or unskilled factory work in England. Whether the migrants, male and female, were aware that they would fill such jobs is difficult to say: it would seem from the interviews that they did not have any detailed knowledge of life and work in Britain. Ignorance in such matters as the cost of living relative to income can lead to disappointment, as was the case with this Jamaican migrant:

'I suppose I came to England looking for riches but all I got was work. You have to travel to know things. I didn't leave a good position to come here but I know lots of people who did. Some of them had small businesses that would turn them over nicely and they came here and now they have to struggle. When I was home earning £4 a week, I was living all right and then I heard that I could earn £16 a week here in England so I thought if I could earn that much I would be able to save about £10 a week. But then you have to pay the rent, and pay for heating, and buy winter clothes: all these things you aren't used to and you don't think of.' (West Indian male: factory sample)

Another explained:

'Well you are in Jamaica and you don't know what England is like, you see everyone going crazy about coming to London and when they talk about London you can imagine streets of pure gold. It's the truth because I had absolutely no reason at all to leave Jamaica and come here. I suppose I just followed everyone else.' (West Indian female: residential sample)

Another Jamaican argued that the information he received was incomplete:

'Well, I saw my mates leaving and also other people so I decided to come as well. The information we got from people already here was so good in the 1960s. They would write back and say they are earning £25 per week but they don't tell you that they have to work nearly two weeks with the overtime to get that amount of money. They don't tell you about the cold or anything bad. They only tell you the good parts. So I thought I would come and see but when I came it was something different.'

But information, its absence or its partial nature, does not in itself explain Caribbean migration. It is now well established that Caribbean migration to England was economically motivated, and the debate has tended to focus on the relative importance of 'push' and 'pull' factors (e.g. Davison, 1962; Peach, 1968). But acceptance of the fact that a shortage of labour in certain sectors of the English economy was the crucial factor in stimulating immigration can blind us to other facets of the migration process and may seem to make it difficult to explain why only 31 per cent of the West Indian men in our sample mentioned work as a reason for migration to England. The crucial analytical point is that once a social process is set in motion, it can be maintained by secondary or quite separate factors from those which initially motivated it. In the case of Caribbean migration, the early migrants certainly did set out for England in search of work, but once they had arrived and settled, if only temporarily, kin and friends would follow partly because of the previous migration. MacDonald and MacDonald have defined this as *chain migration*, 'that movement in which prospective migrants learn of opportunities, are provided with transportation, and have initial accommodation and employment arranged *by means of primary social relationships with previous migrants*' (1964, p. 82; see also Price, 1968, pp. 210–12). This is not to say that chain migration, once established, is not structured by economic factors: kin and friends may only act upon the link established by primary social relationships if economic opportunities continue to exist. But it is to argue that the individual explanation for migration may be in terms of familial connections, the economic factor thereby seeming to be irrelevant, although, in fact, still being important to the establishment and maintenance of the chain.

A further factor has to be considered when dealing with Caribbean migration. The colonial relationship between Britain and a number of the Caribbean islands had resulted in a perception of England as the Mother Country, a perception encouraged not least by the colonial education system. Thus, one Jamaican said of his migration:

> 'Well, I didn't mind really because I was told that it was our Mother Country and I knew one day that I would come to know her'. (West Indian male: factory sample)

And another:

> 'Well, the impression they paint of Britain as the Mother Country was so beautiful out there that you want to come.' (West Indian male: residential sample)

Such maternal symbolism can develop in a number of different ways and probably lies behind the idea that England is, or at least was in the 1950s and early 1960s, a country of opportunity, to which one could legitimately migrate.

The argument is, then, that when considering the reasons given by the West Indians in our sample for their migration, a number of factors need to be considered in addition to (but also in relation to) the shortage of labour in England in the 1950s. When they were asked why they had migrated, the West Indians did not always give a single explanation. All of the women who explained their reasons for coming to Britain said that it was to join either a husband, parents or relatives. The reasons given by the men are set out in Table 4.6.

Table 4.6 Male West Indians' explanations for migration to England

	N=57
Family reasons/connections	22 (42%)
Economic motivation	16 (31%)
Friends were migrating	13 (25%)
Broaden my experience/travel	11 (21%)

Sub-Ns total more than 57 because some respondents gave more than one reason.

The following quotes from interviews are illustrative of these explanations:

'Well, in my country, we don't have as big an industrial set-up as in England so we have to go to different countries to look for work. I couldn't find any other work at home so I decided to come somewhere else and try to find some.' (West Indian male: factory sample)

'People from the London Transport were recruiting people from Barbados to work on the system so I thought I would give it a try.' (West Indian male: factory sample)

'I saw everyone else coming so I decided to come along as well.' (West Indian male: factory sample)

'Well I came here to make a living because there wasn't enough work in my country for everyone.' (West Indian male: residential sample)

'Well most of my friends had travelled about and they were all coming to England so I thought I'd come too.' (West Indian male: residential sample)

'My husband came first and he said things could be better and he asked me to come, so I came over to join him.'

Did you find things better or not?

'At first it was a little better, but not now, it's terrible.' (West Indian female: residential sample)

The argument is, then, that for the West Indians in our sample the individual motivation for migration was often multi-dimensional and dependent upon the prior migration of family and close friends, although the economic motive, at least for some men, was far from being irrelevant. These individual motivations have to be explained, in turn, in the wider context of the colonial connection with the Caribbean and labour shortage in the 'metropolitan centre'.

A further important aspect of migration concerns the possibility of a return 'home'. Philpott has argued that all migrants possess a cognitive model about the nature and goals of migration, a model which he calls the *migrant ideology* in which 'the migration is perceived as a temporary state, mainly to gain money, which will ultimately result in a return to the home society' (1973, p. 188). Whether a return is actually achieved depends upon a number of factors but the myth of return (Ballard and Ballard, 1977, p. 40) can still have important effects on the migrants' behaviour in England. The West Indian men in the factory sample were therefore asked whether they were going to stay in England or whether they were going to return to their island of origin. Their answers show that the large majority claim that they do plan to return: 72 per cent (26) responded in this way, with 14 per cent (5) saying that they planned to stay in England and an identical proportion saying they did not know.

However, they were also asked whether they thought that they would actually return to the Caribbean. A much smaller proportion, 29 per cent (10) believed they would definitely return, while a further 20 per cent (7) said that they probably would return; of the remainder, 29 per cent (10) were doubtful and 5 per cent (2) believed they never would return, with 17 per cent (6) saying they did not know. When the responses to the two questions were correlated, it was found that 49 per cent (17) planned to return and believed that they definitely or probably would return while 26 per cent (9) planned to return but were pessimistic about the actuality of return. Thus, only about half of the West Indians had clear plans to return and felt certain or very certain that they would do so, while for the other half, some planned to return and others planned to stay, but all were uncertain about the actual possibility of return.

None of the sample were actively preparing to return in the immediate future and those who said they both planned to return and believed they would return were of the view that this would happen when they were older:

'I think I will, not now, may be some years to come when I'm getting older.'

'Well I came to this country and there is nothing to say I won't die here but I do have the intention of going back and settling down when I get a bit older ... When I do go back home, maybe I will just sit down and do a little cultivation until the time comes for me to die. Just a little piece of land.'

For some it was because they saw almost no chance of owning 'a little piece of land', of being independent, which made them feel uncertain about whether they would return, even if they wanted to:

'When you leave an island like that, your ambition is that if you go back, then you go back with some money so that you don't have to work for anyone else. That's my idea anyway. Right now I'm not in the position to go.'

'I can go back when I want to really. I could go back now because my dad has quite a lot out there but I don't want to go out there and work for him. I am a man of my own now. I got my wife and kids so I have to make my own foundations. If I need any help then I would ask him but I want to try my own thing first.'

In these cases, the migrants are probably concerned that if they return without evidence of material success (i.e. being 'independent' of an employer), then they will lose the status they would otherwise have as returned migrants (cf. Philpott, 1973, pp. 190–1).

A similar concern may lie behind other specific reasons given for believing that a return is unlikely. There were references to the actual cost of returning, air fares for a complete family being very expensive relative to income, to the increased or high cost of living at home, to the difficulty of finding employment and to the need to 'start again':

'Well, at the moment in my present situation I'm happy: I've got a wife and a couple of kids and I can more or less afford to keep them going. Back home I would have to more or less start all over again. I would have to try to get a job, try to settle down and it would take time. But I suppose one day I will go back.'

'I learn that it is rather expensive now and I don't see any way in which I could go back and settle now. I'm not saying I wouldn't like to but I've got a few young children and with the fares to go out there and settle down plus all the relatives out there who are looking for something from here, I don't think it's worth it. I'd rather go on holiday.'

These material concerns were mixed with a vaguer worry about

coping with the changes that they know or feel will have occurred
since leaving:

> 'Well, at the time I was there I knew the place when I was
> growing up with my parents. But in the last ten or twelve years
> this place has changed and it would be the same over there as
> well. For me to go back home I would have to be independent.
> First of all, I didn't have any kids when I left there and now I've
> got five so I would have to make way for them. Then I would
> have to make way for my wife and I would have to have money
> to go ... Also back home things are more expensive than they are
> here, also jobs are scarce.'

The importance of material concerns is matched by the obligations brought about by marriage and children. As already mentioned, over three-quarters of the West Indians were married and
had families, and this constituted a major constraint upon return,
not only because of the cost but also because it was felt that England
was 'their children's country' and that they should choose where
they wanted to live:

> 'I said I'd stop here and let the kids grow up here. Maybe later I'll
> go if they want to come and if they don't want to they can stop
> here because this is their country really: they were born and bred
> here and when they get about eighteen or twenty and they say
> they don't want to leave, then I can't force them. But I think
> about it all the while.'

> 'I suppose I'll go back to live one of these days. But I'll have to
> wait to give my kids their choice. If they want to come back home
> with me then they can but if they choose to stay here but not
> come back then they have to be old enough to look after
> themselves.'

But in spite of these material, practical and moral obligations and
constraints, the 'myth' of return remains, maintained in the
following instance by religious belief. In response to a question
asking him whether he would like to return to Jamaica, one
Jamaican said:

> 'Yes. But my family comes first. I came over here alone and land
> up with a large family. If I had a proper foundation to take them
> back to then it would be lovely to go back but I haven't. I
> couldn't go now.'

He was then asked whether he would actually return:

'Yes. I had a dream and I know am going to go back home and I pray to Allah that my life is spared to go back home because I am a Muslim.'

Thus, for these West Indians, the act of migration has led them to an ambivalence about their future in England. Ideally a large majority plan to return to the Caribbean, yet when faced with the practical realities of both leaving England and returning to the Caribbean, only half of those interviewed were still adamant that they actually would return. As to how many of these will eventually return, one cannot be certain, because they still have much the same set of obligations in England as those who are less convinced.

The residential sample were not asked if they planned to return home, though many of our respondents volunteered information relevant to this subject. The women in particular seemed to express the view that because their children had been born and brought up in Britain the idea of going back was ruled out. It was more often the men who wistfully referred to some future return. One man described at length how he dreamt frequently about Jamaica, but how on waking he would face the reality of five children and no savings. Others explained that however long they stayed in Britain, they continued to feel like foreigners. When one man said that he still planned to return he was asked:

What would you like to do if you went there?

That's the thing that I'm thinking about now, I suppose I could go in for motor body repairs, I'd probably have to go back to the government training school again for some time and then when I'd finished I could do that. You see whatever happens to me in this country I still feel like a foreigner.

Do you want to go back because of Jamaica itself or is this because living in England you still feel like a foreigner?

Yes, I still feel different.

What are the main reasons that make you feel like a foreigner here?

I look at myself for a start, I'm black and I don't fit in at all.

Having described the characteristics of our sample, we go on to analyse our interview and observational data.

CHAPTER 5

The working class and trade unionism

Within a capitalist social formation, trade unions are defensive an[d] reformist organisations, their aim being to both defend and improv[e] the conditions under which labour power is sold to capital (e.[g] Hyman, 1971; Anderson, 1967). Although their origins lie in th[e] conflict within the place of work between worker and employer ove[r] wages and conditions of work, trade unions have developed t[o] become large bureaucratic organisations which have negotiate[d] access to involvement in state decision-making over a wide range [o]f issues, generally all related to the management of the capitali[st] economy. There is, therefore, a certain institutional duality abou[t] the form of trade unions: on the one hand the trade union is [a] workplace organisation, consisting of members, shop stewards an[d] lay branch officials, while on the other it is an administrativ[e] hierarchy of full-time officials, paid to negotiate with employers an[d] the government. This duality is reflected in union member[ship] consciousness which indicates a close attachment to the workplac[e] organisation, yet tends to reject a broader 'political' role of trad[e] unions, believing that trade unions have 'too much power' as well [a]s asserting that the union bureaucracy fails to adequately represent i[ts] membership (e.g. Goldthorpe *et al.*, 1968, pp. 107–14; Hill, 197[6] pp. 132, 140–1).

In this chapter we are concerned with the former aspect of th[is] duality, but from a very specific perspective. The vast bulk of th[e] literature on trade unionism and industrial relations tends not t[o] recognise that black workers have become union members; whe[re] interest has been shown, it has been structured by somewhat limite[d] concerns, such as whether black workers, by joining unions, ar[e] adopting white working-class norms (e.g. Brooks, 1975a) or whethe[r] racial discrimination prevents or prohibits unionisation (e.g. Smit[h] 1977). Consistent with our earlier theoretical starting-point, that [o]f the capitalist mode of production and not 'race relations', we wish t[o] pose a somewhat different question, although it is a question whic[h] does not ignore these other two issues. Can black workers' unio[n] membership be explained, at least in part, by their relationship to capital *qua* wage labour?

This question forces us to consider to what extent the capital/ labour contradiction is manifested in the consciousness of the working class regarding the nature of trade unionism. Our analysis therefore develops against the background of, first, explanations of union membership amongst the working class. The more recent sociological debate has tended to centre on the claim by Goldthorpe *et al.* that the unionisation of semi- and unskilled workers is best explained by the notion of 'instrumental collectivism', that is, collectivism which 'is directed to the achievement of individuals' private goals, outside the workplace' (1968, p. 106), with Westergaard (1970) being one of the critics of the more general interpretations and implications of this 'Affluent Worker' study (see also Blackburn, 1967; Nichols and Armstrong, 1976). We shall refer to this debate at the end of the chapter.

But, second, we must also consider whether there are processes occurring which have a direct and independent effect upon black workers' union membership and ideological approach to trade unionism. We suggest that there are two distinct sources of influence to be considered in this context. On the one hand, the policy adopted by, and the practice of, British trade unions towards black workers may, by its reproduction of racist ideas, have led black workers to reject union membership. The possibility of such a development has been voiced (with a certain amount of alarm) in the past by the Commission on Industrial Relations (1974) in the light of its investigation of the Mansfield Hosiery Mills Ltd dispute, the Commission's report warning that black workers may form their own unions. On the other hand, the black workers in our study migrated from the Caribbean and may therefore have come to an industrial context and to trade unionism with experiences faced and attitudes formed in a different context which serves to distance them from trade unionism in England. Hence we are concerned to consider whether the position of male and female black workers as part of a racially categorised class fraction and as migrant labour has an effect on their membership of and attitude towards trade unions in England.

We begin this chapter by presenting evidence which suggests that the latter is a defensible consideration, after which we show how women are also disadvantaged by union policy and practice. Then, from our own research, we shall present evidence on the level of trade union membership and the reasons given for membership and attitudes towards the trade unions amongst our male and female, white and black workers, the implications of which will be drawn out in the context of the previously mentioned debates about trade unionism and the basis of union membership.

Trade unions and black workers: the historical context

Although trade unions principally exist to represent the working class in the workplace, this role is conducted within the context of certain collectivist (even socialist) principles. Other things being equal, one would expect that the trade union's representative role would mean that it would encourage black workers to join and participate in its activities, not least because black workers *are workers*. Moreover, given the principles of internationalism and solidarity, one might also expect further union initiatives in response to the experiences and circumstances of black workers in England. For instance, if worker solidarity is both an important end in itself, as well as a means to an end (in the sense of 'united we stand, divided we fall'), one might expect trade unions to attempt to combat those processes which most clearly exist as obstacles to a united struggle. These factors include racism and racialist practices within the white working class and in British society as a whole. In addition, and following from the previous point, one would expect trade unions to pursue policies directed towards the eradication of the material disadvantage specifically experienced by black workers in Britain.

We have documented at length elsewhere the policy and practice adopted and pursued by the Trades Union Congress towards the presence of black workers in the period 1954–73 (Miles and Phizacklea, 1977b). We have also commented on the qualified reappraisal of this policy and practice during the period 1974 to 1976 (Miles and Phizacklea, 1978). Although this work does not consider in any detail either the national policy and practice of individual unions (such a study would show interesting variations) or local workplace or area initiatives and activities, because the TUC claims a national union leadership role, its policy and practice is indicative of a general union expectation of an acceptable position and strategy.

Our examination of policy and practice between 1954 and 1973 has shown that the TUC's failure to act positively towards the issues raised by the presence of black workers from the New Commonwealth in Britain followed from the way in which it chose to define the situation in Britain. Although it had a principled policy of opposition to all forms of racial discrimination, the TUC did not believe it necessary to take any direct action to deal with the actuality of discrimination in Britain, partly because it denied that it was widespread. For the General Council of the TUC, the more serious problem was what was seen as the unwillingness of black immigrants to 'integrate', thus transferring the onus for an initiative from the indigenous working class to black workers. Additionally, the largest unions representing manual workers, and thereby a large proportion of black workers (see Smith, 1977), did not contribute to debates on the 'race issue' and failed to speak in support of anti-discrimination motions. Finally, the General Council was, with varying degrees of emphasis, more concerned with immigration or, more precisely, with immigration from the New Commonwealth, and although it regularly declared itself opposed to any form of immigration control that was racially biased, it nevertheless failed to oppose both the Commonwealth Immigrants Act 1968 and the Immigration Act 1971 on these grounds (although a motion of opposition to the 1971 Act was passed at the 1973 Congress).

During the subsequent two years, a coincidence of three developments forced a re-evaluation of policy and practice. First, during the early 1970s a number of industrial disputes occurred during which black workers alleged discrimination on the part of white workers and trade union officials, the most notable of which were at Mansfield Hosiery Mills Ltd (CIR, 1974), and Imperial Typewriters Ltd (see Moore, 1975). Although neither of these disputes (nor the others involving black workers) had any immediate impact on TUC policy, there is little doubt that they did serve to force the issues of racism and discrimination within the trade union movement towards the front of at least some TUC leaders' minds.

Second, there was a growing level of criticism amongst a minority of delegates at the Trades Union Congress and at the grass-roots level. Many locally based committees were set up by trade unionists in London, the Midlands and the North of England in the 1970s to combat discrimination and to attempt to change the policy of their respective unions and the TUC. In addition, Trades Councils organised conferences and campaigns, expressing concern about racist ideology and racial discrimination within the Labour Movement. Thus within the trade union movement there existed a small but concerned minority of trade unionists who desired a more positive policy from the TUC.

Third, there was the apparent growth and increasing public awareness of the National Front. By the end of 1974 street demonstrations and a substantial electoral intervention had established the National Front as a real political threat in the eyes of trade union leaders. Having drawn parallels between Germany in the 1930s and Britain in the 1970s, the General Council of the TUC came to the conclusion that some new initiative was required.

Our argument is, then, that coincidence of these developments led the General Council of the TUC to reorganise itself internally to deal with 'race relations' and to produce anti-racist leaflets for distribution by constituent unions on the shop floor. In addition, an anti-racist campaign was jointly organised with the Labour Party, culminating in a demonstration attended by some 30,000 people. However, this flurry of positive action (as of writing, there is little evidence of any continuing sustained action) did not arise from a positive decision to implement resolutions accepted at previous conferences, but from a perceived threat posed by the National Front. The emphasis of the initiative in the mid 1970s was therefore upon providing a counter to racist belief within the white membership rather than upon eradicating material disadvantage amongst black workers. As far as the latter is concerned, the TUC's stated policy has been to press all affiliated unions to negotiate acceptance by employers of equal opportunity policies, and to press both Government and the CBI to pursue such policies. How effective this has been is a matter for investigation.

We began this section by arguing that, given certain principles of trade unionism, one might expect trade unions to take initiatives in at least three areas. In conclusion it could be argued that the General Council of the TUC has shown itself more willing than in the past to face openly the reality of racism among trade union members and has campaigned against it, and that to a lesser extent it has recognised the reality of material disadvantage among black workers and is committed by pressing for certain measures directed towards eliminating that disadvantage. However, these initiatives have to be weighed against past policy and practice, for it is this which could more obviously (although this should not be read to mean that present policy and practice could not also warrant a similar conclusion) provide a justification for black workers refusing to join trade unions or, having joined, deciding not to participate in union activities. We shall take up this issue and refer to the extant evidence later in this chapter. What we now want to consider is whether the position of black workers as migrants and as part of a racially categorised class fraction is likely to influence their commitment to trade unionism.

The relevance of racial categorisation and migrant status

It is not only within the trade union movement that black workers have had to face racism and racial discrimination: indeed, it is arguable that racial categorisation has had its greatest impact when black workers have been seeking employment and accommodation (e.g. Smith, 1977). Lawrence has argued that this experience of racism and racial discrimination has had a profound effect upon migrants' (and particularly Caribbean migrants) appraisal of England and has been a central factor in encouraging them to withdraw from participation in English institutions (1974, pp. 196–7). To the extent that black workers do withdraw from institutional participation in general, one might expect them to remain outside the trade union movment or to refrain from active participation within it.

This possible tendency could be encouraged by their status as migrants, two dimensions of which are relevant in this context. First, as has already been explained in chapter 4, the economic migrant justifies and plans his/her migration, that is to say, the migrant has an ideology about migration (Philpott, 1973). In so far as this migrant ideology includes the notion that the migration is a temporary phenomenon, the intention being to return 'home' when the earnings 'target' (see Bohning, 1972) has been achieved, then one might expect that the migrant, because there is no long-term commitment to the social formation in which he/she has taken up 'temporary' residence, may abstain from membership of or involvement in indigenous institutions. This ideology may, over a period of time, become little more than a 'myth', but, nevertheless, an important one for the individual who continues to experience racial exclusion.

Second, one should take account of both the original class position of the migrants before migration and the nature of the political and labour tradition of the countries from which the black workers originate. Although the evidence is not completely unambiguous (see Davison, 1962, 1966; Glass, 1961; Deakin, 1970), it would seem that most migrants from the Caribbean were either petit-bourgeois, peasants or part of an emergent wage-labouring working class, and few have had previous experience of trade unionism as we shall see. Hence, the individual who was originally a cane cropper or a seamstress in rural Jamaica and who is now an assembly-line worker in London has experienced a substantial change in class position but, again, this new position is not defined as a permanent one. To use the words of the men and women we interviewed, migration was for 'advancement', to gain sufficient money to return 'home' to a 'better position'; in short, the aim was to leave the ranks of the poor peasantry or the working class, both in the Caribbean and in England, forever. How far such an intention is realistic depends not only upon the effort of the migrant but also upon structural constraints, such as the nature and extent of discrimination and the scope for the reproduction and/or expansion of, say, the skilled manual or non-manual sections of the working class or the petit-bourgeoisie in the country of origin. Even though this 'target' may never be realised, to repeat an earlier point, it is important to the individual and will inevitably influence the migrant's appraisal of and approach to trade unionism in England.

However, although we are arguing that, objectively, black workers in England are migrants and are a racially categorised fraction of the working class, in so far as we are concerned with their attitude towards and action with regard to trade unions, we must take account of their own perceptions of their socio-economic position in England. We cannot therefore assume that black workers see themselves as migrants and as part of a racial category for all, or even some, of the time. A black worker may see himself or herself as a migrant and/or part of a racial category in some situations and as a wage labourer in others. Beyond this, there will be instances when being a skilled worker, or a woman, or a rate-payer will be the most important basis for identity and action. At the same time, the fact that the black worker is a migrant and part of a racially categorised fraction of the working class does structure (in the sense of set limits to) the possibilities for identity and action; for example, it is because black workers are wage labourers that trade unionism is an institution that they must come to terms with.

But before we can take up some of these issues in relation to our own data we must, finally, consider the policy and practice of the trade unions towards women. For the same reason as given earlier, our focus will be upon the Trades Union Congress, although not to the exclusion of individual unions where necessary.

Trade unions and women

The neglect of women's issues and interests by the trade unions is perhaps most remarkable given that over a quarter of their current membership is female and that women constitute 60 per cent of the new membership since 1962. It could be argued that, by issuing a model equal-opportunity clause with the recommmendation that it be written into all relevant union agreements with employers, and having supported the demand of equal pay for women since 1882, the TUC has recognised and acted to combat the disadvantaged position of women workers. We have already suggested that the signing of such agreements should be treated with some scepticism, a warning which is supported by the conclusions of the Equal Pay and Opportunities Campaign (1976) and the fact that the gap between men and women's pay had, in 1979, once more begun to widen.

But even when Equal Pay is negotiated it does little to eradicate either the ghettos of 'women's' work which exist throughout the British economy, or women's dual role in production which makes them a most vulnerable section of the workforce. The TUC itself recommends that employers recognise that women must work the hours that allow them to fulfil their domestic responsibilities, a view which may reflect reality but which also condones a crucial aspect of the situation that perpetuates women's disadvantaged position as wage labourers. Of course, the TUC set up a Women's Conference in 1931, which was at least a recognition of the fact that women workers have special interests, but its overall effectiveness is doubtful. At best it can pass on resolutions to the General Council which may choose to ignore them: it is, after all, nearly a hundred years since the TUC first declared itself in favour of Equal Pay.

In the mid 1970s well over half the male workforce in Britain was unionised, but only a quarter of the female workforce. At the same time women have constituted the majority of new members in the last eighteen years and those unions which have benefited most from this growth are in the public sector. White-collar unions are active in both the public and private sector and while female membership still lags behind male, women are joining these unions in increasing numbers. It is therefore not surprising that they are now more willing to recognise the way in which trade unions have failed women in the past. A statement from the Technical, Administrative and Supervisory Section of the Amalgamated Union of Engineering Workers is illustrative of this recognition:

> It would be easy but not very constructive to dwell on the singular lack of progress we have made. What is important is that, belated though it is, unions do now recognise that their women members have been shamefully neglected and many of them are genuinely trying to make up for lost time, their new-found interest is not merely altruistic. Women constitute a majority in several large unions and there are increasing signs

that they are questioning why the goods haven't been delivered (quoted in Mackie and Pattullo, 1977, p. 170).

As with black workers, women are less likely to attend branch meetings than men, the most usual explanation being that the times of meetings conflict with women's domestic responsibilities. Given the number of obstacles which exist to obstruct women's full participation in union activities, it is not surprising to find that they are severely under-represented as lay and full-time union officials (McCarthy, 1977, pp. 166–8). Moreover, if women workers only have the experience of seeing men in these positions, it can only reinforce the perception of unions being run by men for the benefit of male members.

This low level of representation cannot be explained in terms of the failure of women to engage in union struggle, despite their low level of formal participation. Although women tend not to be employed in those industries which have a high level of industrial struggle but in sectors of the economy which are less well organised by trade unions, the fact remains that thousands of women are engaged in industrial action every year, not just over Equal Pay (as at Trico, Wheway Watson and Newmark in 1976, to name but a few), but also over issues which affect men and women together (e.g. NUPE, 1979). Black migrant women too have a history of industrial struggle in England, as evidenced by the disputes at Imperial Typewriters, Grunwick, and within the Health Service (see Phizacklea and Miles, 1978 and *Race Today,* May 1975). The evidence and argument in this and the preceding two sections could be interpreted to mean that black workers and women must therefore have a lower level of commitment to trade unionism than white working-class men. For instance, it could be argued that because trade unions have neglected both black workers' and women's interests, both black workers and women will be less likely to join trade unions. We are not predisposed to accept this hypothesis because it over-emphasises what can be shown to be a less important determinant of, certainly, trade union membership and, perhaps, trade union participation. Hence, the emphasis of our argument in the following sections will be, as we indicated at the outset, upon the essentially defensive role of trade unions, mediating the relationship between capital and wage labour (which includes both women's and black migrant labour).

Union membership in South Brent

Our findings with regard to union membership are summarised in

Table 5.1. The overall picture is that of a high level of union membership amongst all groups with the sole exception of the English women in the residential sample. However, the nature of the

Table 5.1 Union membership in factory and residential samples

	Factory sample		Residential sample			
	English men (N=36)	West Indian men (N=36)	English men (N=19)	women (N=17)	West Indian men (N=21)	women (N=20)
Union members	100% (36)	100% (36)	74% (14)	18% (3)	62% (13)	60% (12)
Not union members	—	—	21% (4)	35% (6)	33% (7)	35% (7)
N.A (i.e. not working)	—	—	5% (1)	47% (8)	5% (1)	5% (1)

differences between the two samples require that, beyond this very general statement, each should be analysed separately.

Concerning the factory sample, the data should be evaluated in the light of the fact that, at the time of interviewing, there was an informal closed-shop agreement in operation; that is to say, both management and the shop stewards' committee at Food Co. were in favour of all employees joining the relevant trade union. Moreover, there was a general recognition on the shop floor that in order to work at Food Co. it was necessary to join a union, and conversations with both shop stewards and shop-floor workers suggested that the majority of workers approved of this situation, considerable hostility being expressed towards those opposed to membership on the grounds that they were willing to accept the benefits of union membership while disapproving of paying the costs (such persons being described as 'cowboys' who 'rode on other people's backs'). There were, therefore, very strong normative pressures upon all employees to join the appropriate trade union, and hence our findings that all of the men in the factory sample were union members.

The data from the residential sample presents a slightly more complex picture. The English men show the highest level of unionisation, yet over three-fifths of the West Indian men and women were union members. This fairly small difference is, however, of limited significance in the face of the very low level of unionisation amongst the English women, although this is to be explained primarily by the very large number (47 per cent) of English women who are not currently employed as wage labourers. Additionally, of the 9 English women employed, 4 are employed only on a part-time basis and union membership amongst part-time workers is notoriously low. The differences between English women and West Indian women in terms of the proportion who are wage labourers and the proportion who are union members probably only reflects the national pattern of women's employment: Smith has shown, for example, that a much larger proportion of West Indian women of child-bearing age work, compared with all women (1977, p. 65).

In so far as it is legitimate to compare our findings with the national pattern (and there are great limitations due to the fact that our sample was drawn from a very specific type of area which is not necessarily representative of national trends), we would conclude that there is nothing in this data on union membership which would substantially contradict previous findings. Extant evidence shows that black workers are just as likely to join a trade union as white workers and, indeed, may be even more likely to join (Brooks, 1975a, p. 295; Smith, 1977, p. 191). This finding holds, according to Smith, even after controlling for job level, type of industry and pattern of union organisation (1976, pp. 116-17). Although our data from the residential sample indicates a slightly lower level of unionisation amongst both West Indian men and women when compared with English men, the difference is neither great nor significant when the size of the samples is taken into account. What is more significant is that with the exception of the English women, well over half of the residential sample are union members.

However, the level of union membership does not necessarily tell us very much about the reasons why people join trade unions. For example, the fact that an informal closed shop was in operation at Food Co. may explain 100 per cent membership amongst the factory sample, but it does not tell us very much about the workers' attitudes to unions. Hence, we asked our respondents why they were union members.

To join or not to join
First, very few respondents refer to principle or tradition in explaining their membership. The very small number who did made the following types of statement:

'I've always been in a union. Everywhere that I worked at I

joined the union there if they had one. It's been in the family. I think my grandfather was in the union and I know my father was in one.' (English male: factory sample)

'Because the trade union is the defensive mechanism for the working class.' (English male: factory sample)

Second, with the exception of the West Indian factory sample workers, about half of the sample said that they had joined the union under some form of compulsion, whether it took the form of a formal closed shop agreement or some more informal means. Again the following quotes are illustrative:

'I didn't have any choice. It was a closed shop.' (West Indian male: residential sample)

'I was compelled to. You have to be in the union.' (West Indian male: residential sample)

'You have to be. It's not a closed shop but if you don't join them you don't get the job.' (English male: factory sample)

'Yes, I belong to it but I couldn't say much about it, I had to join it. I don't have anything against it but I don't know anything about it.' (West Indian male: factory sample)

'They said I had to, to get the job.' (West Indian female: residential sample)

But it cannot be assumed from this alone that union membership for all of this group was viewed simply and solely as the function of external pressure, whether formal or informal. For example, half of the English men in the factory sample went on to qualify this explanation with reference either to some subsequent benefit that they saw arising from union membership or to some degree of support for trade unionism:

'Well, this was the first union I've joined: I've never been in a union before. It took me a long time and I was probably one of the last to join in the department where I worked. But then it was a case of having to join or the other fellows wouldn't want to work with you. Now I think they are a very good thing and they get things done for you. I think that they could be stronger in many ways from what I've heard from other factories but since they've been here they've done a lot.' (English male: factory sample)

'Well, you go to some places and as soon as you arrive, they bring the form round and say you have to join the union. It's the same here. Whether you have to join or not, I don't know. But I've always joined anyway ... the reason why I joined here was because I thought a big union like the TGWU should be all right so I joined.' (English male: factory sample)

The same was true for the West Indian respondents in the factory sample: about half of those who explained their membership in terms of compulsion went on to qualify their answer in similar ways:

'Well, when I started, they told me that I should join the union here and I suppose when you go to a factory and they have a union there that you join it because it speaks for you.' (West Indian male: factory sample)

'I was told that I had to be a member of the union to work here and I think it's right. If the unions took up a point for the workers here and they work for everyone, they would have to negotiate for me as well. If the unions are working on the workers' behalf, they would be working for me as well and I wouldn't be maintaining it. That's not right. This is now a world where you don't get anything for nothing, you have to pay for it. So I think every member of the workforce should be a member of the union and pay their dues.' (West Indian male: factory sample)

A similar pattern of response was found in the residential sample, particularly amongst West Indian men and women:

'When you go for a job in this firm you have to agree to become a union member or you can't work there. I think it's right because what the management would like to do to the workers is prevented by the unions, so we are protected.' (West Indian female: residential sample)

'It was compulsory to join but I don't resent the unions because they are the only weapons the working man has really, they have nothing or no one else to negotiate for them. It's a good thing as far as I'm concerned.' (West Indian male: residential sample)

'I had to join, but it's all right because it helps sometimes. If anyone tries to push you around they help us.' (West Indian female: residential sample)

Thus, although a substantial proportion of our two samples make reference to compulsion in explaining their union membership, far from all of them experience this 'compulsion' as illegitimate. Either their reference to 'compulsion' is to no more than a matter of fact, or they believe that union membership is legitimate or even necessary, or they have since come to appreciate the value and benefit of trade unionism.

Third, in addition to the references to compulsion, the other major explanation for union membership is instrumental and individualistic:

'Well, if I'm in the union and I was officially sick, I would get a better chance of getting my wages for the weeks that I was out.' (English male: factory sample)

'It's very good in case anything crops up inside here. They can help you out.' (West Indian male: factory sample)

'Well, from the driving point of view you never know. You can get yourself in a fix and need legal advice, etc. Something falls off a lorry say, and if it came to a court case you'd need a mouthpiece.' (English male: residential sample)

'At first I joined because I was introduced to it by a chap who I thought was a very genuine person and I liked his views on public life and politics. But now knowing more about it I think that if my bosses tried to tell me "Well Tom, please take a month's notice", I laugh at them. Now I know that personally in the union I am slightly more secure.' (West Indian male: residential sample)

'It meant more money.' (West Indian female: residential sample)

These attitudes approximate to what Goldthorpe *et al.* (1968) describe as instrumental collectivism.

But what of those twenty-four workers in our residential sample who are not members of trade unions? The most common response explaining their non-membership, particularly amongst the West Indians, was that they were employed at small non-union firms. But two West Indian and one Englishwoman said they would like to become members. In addition one West Indian woman told us of her own and fellow workers' attempts to unionise in their workplace, which had been met with redundancies. In this connection, it is interesting to note that the local Trades Council claimed a large increase in enquiries about trade union membership from black workers in small non-union firms as the dispute at Grunwick escalated in 1976–7. Significantly, only two of the twenty-four workers explained their non-membership in terms of principle. These responses suggest that for English and West Indian workers alike, non-membership is more likely to be explained in circumstantial terms rather than by reference to individual ideological objections. Certainly there is no evidence here to suggest that a large proportion of West Indian workers, or indeed English workers, have deep-seated objections to union membership as such, even if a minority object to being, as they see it, compelled to join, as is suggested by the evidence presented above.

The other evidence we have from our interviews bearing on union membership concerns the extent to which our respondents had a tradition of union membership, either within their own families or in terms of their own previous work experience. The West Indian respondents in the factory sample were asked whether they had had experience of union membership prior to their migration: only 8 per cent said that they had. Both the West Indians and the English were also asked whether their fathers or mothers had been union members. Again, only 8 per cent of the West Indians reported in the affirmative, as compared with 47 per cent of the English workers. Given the low level of trade union organisation in the Caribbean when these individuals would have been eligible for membership, this pattern of response is not particularly surprising and indicates that for our black migrants trade union organisation and membership is a new experience. However, working at Food Co. did not provide the majority of our West Indian workers with their first experience of union membership; only just over a third (39 per cent) of those interviewed said that they had not been union members before coming to work at the factory (the comparable figure for the English workers was 33 per cent). This implication is that a majority of the black workers at Food Co. brought some experience of trade union membership with them when they took up employment there and, in this respect, were little different from the English workers. None of these questions were directly asked of the residential sample, but only one of the West Indian individuals or families studied in detail had had any previous experience of trade unionism before arriving in England.

Up to this point, therefore, we suggest that our data supports the following conclusions. First, the level of union membership amongst English men, West Indian men and West Indian women is broadly similar, varying between about two-thirds and three-quarters. The lowest level of membership is amongst English women and this is explained by their low level of participation in the paid labour force at this point in their lives. There is no evidence here to support an argument that West Indian workers are less likely to join trade unions than English workers. Second, this is true despite the fact that, before their migration, the West Indian workers had had almost no experience of trade unionism, either directly or indirectly. Third, there are no consistent differences between our English and West Indian workers over their explanations for union membership, the vast majority of both groups referring to either instrumental and individualistic or external pressure as the major motivating force. The major difference in our data on this point concerns the West Indians in our residential sample as compared with those in our factory sample, the majority of the former, but not the latter, giving compulsion or external pressure as a reason for joining a trade union.

The role of trade unions
Although our question on the reason for trade union membership gave some indication of how our respondents viewed the role of trade unions, we also asked a direct question : 'In your opinion, what should a good trade union do?' The responses are coded in Table 5.2.

Table 5.2 Perceived role of a good trade union (%)

	English (N = 72)	West Indian (N= 77)
Improves working conditions/ helps/ protect workers	67	61
Go-between	8	18
Political role	4	1
Negative view of trade unions	8	6
Don't know	7	8
No answer	6	5

The majority of the sample defined the role of trade unions in instrumental and individualistic terms, saying that they should improve working conditions, or help or protect the workers:

'They should make sure that you don't get pushed around and if anything goes wrong they'll sort it out. They stick out for your rights.' (West Indian female: residential sample)

'Well, if there is anything that we want done or any trouble, then we would go and ask them and they would go and see one of the bosses and try and get things sorted out. Then they would come back and let us know what happened.' (English male: factory sample)

'It's there to speak for the workers. No union should be on the firm's side and some of them are, which is wrong. They should be on the side of the workers. If the factory gets too cold or something looks a bit dangerous, then you go to your shop steward and he'll see about it for you. Also, if you think you aren't getting enough money according to the way inflation is going, I think they should put in for a pay rise and stick out for it. They should also stop those foremen who pick on workers because they don't like them for personal reasons.' (West Indian male: factory sample)

Although this form of response was the most common one in both samples, the proportion making it was lower in the residential sample. However, this difference is mirrored by a larger proportion of respondents in the residential sample who gave 'don't know' responses to the question. All, except for one, who gave this type of response were women who were either non-union members or who were not engaged in wage labour: the lack of direct experience and a feeling of detachment from trade unions may partly explain this discrepancy.

What is of greater significance in this context is that there is no systematic difference between the proportion of West Indian as opposed to English workers who see the role of trade unions in these terms. Indeed, in so far as there is any difference at all between our English and West Indian respondents in their view of the role of trade unions, it is a minor and not completely clear-cut one. Overall, a larger proportion (18 per cent) of our West Indian workers identified the trade union role as that of a 'go-between':

'A good union should look after the rights of their members. But they have to work with the employers as well to try and get some sort of co-operation between the two.' (West Indian male: factory sample)

'The first thing is to look after the workers but I don't think the union should get too much hold on any firm because as soon as the people in charge can't manage the union then they just close the place down. The unions are good but I think they have taken away the right of the foremen to demand from a man to pull his weight. One time the foreman had the right to demand from any man a full day's work, but they can't do that any more. There's a few things happening that's preventing the employers from investing this money because if you don't think you will get a fair return then you won't invest will you?' (West Indian male: residential sample)

'It should be a good arbiter between management and workers.' (West Indian female: residential sample)

Thus, although many of these respondents saw the trade unions as representing and protecting the interests of their members, they believed that this was best achieved by mediating between worker and management (or, in some instances, between worker and government), accepting that management (and government) demands and problems were equally, if not more, legitimate than those of the workers that the unions were representing.

A small proportion of the sample had very negative views of the trade union role ('They're running and ruining the country') and an even smaller proportion believed that the trade unions had a broader political role in addition to directly representing their members' interests in the factory context over pay and conditions. One worker illustrated this broader role in the following way:

'Well I think to get a fair week's wage for the worker members and fair working conditions. Also other things it could do is to deal with unfair things like the Chilean takeover by the Colonels. At that takeover, about 40,000 trade unionists got killed and Food Co. wanted to buy Chilean beans and some good shop stewards stood up and said that they didn't want that sort of thing to happen.' (English male: factory sample)

Within the residential sample, West Indian women were more likely than our other respondents to expect trade unions to perform the role of representatives of the working class, for example:

'They should fight for better wages to bring the level up to the rise in prices and also fight for more jobs because there are a lot of unemployed.' (West Indian female: residential sample)

Perhaps the most distinctive aspect of the West Indian women's responses is their emphasis on the gap between rising prices in the shops and their take-home pay. In all probability this reflectects an increased awareness of declining working-class living standards during a recessionary period, an increased awareness which springs from their dual role in production.

The residential sample were also asked 'Do you think that the trade unions have a political role to play or that they should restrict themselves to industrial matters?' The majority of English men and women said that the trade unions had become 'too powerful' and that they should stay out of politics completely:

'I think they should restrict themselves to industrial matters. Once they start going into politics, it's a minority trying to foist their views on the majority as in the case of the miners. I don't think they used fair methods to get what they wanted. They brought the Conservative Government down which was an elected government of the people and they were brought down by a minority. Now you can't say that's fair.' (English female: residential sample)

'A line must be drawn somewhere. For instance, over this wage business. The trade unions can dictate to the government and I think that is all wrong. It's not their function. We elect a government to do it and I don't think the trade union people are qualified to do it.' (English male: residential sample)

Some of the West Indian men concurred with this view but a large proportion again suggested that the unions should play a role of 'go-between':

'I don't believe in the political role of the unions. I believe if they do play a political role they should do it on the basis of thinking seriously about the economy and not strictly political. If the Unions believe in the country, they should take the economy first.' (West Indian male: residential sample)

West Indian women were far less likely to endorse either of these views, half suggesting that the unions had a political role to play and a sizeable minority articulating something other than the 'consensus' view on this issue. Overall nearly half of the West Indians in the residential sample felt that the unions had a political role to play compared to only a quarter of the English.

Although this question was not asked of the factory sample, two other questions were asked of these respondents which have relevance to the perceived role of the trade unions. First, the respondents in the factory sample were asked 'Do you think that the trade unions should be involved in discussions with the government about wages, prices and the economy in general?' (see Table 5.3). More than three-quarters of the complete sample agreed with this statement. However, the proportion of West Indian workers concurring with it was much larger than the proportion of English workers (92 per cent as compared with 61 per cent), while almost half (47 per

Table 5.3 'Do you think that the trade unions should be involved in discussions with the government about wages, prices and the economy in general?'

	Factory Sample		
	English *% (N = 36)*	*West Indian* *%(N=36)*	*Total* *% (N = 72)*
Very favourable	8 (3)	47 (17)	27.5 (20)
Favourable	53 (19)	45 (16)	49.0 (35)
Unfavourable	6 (2)	0	3.0 (2)
Totally opposed	25 (9)	8 (3)	16.5 (12)
Don't know	8 (3)	0	4.0 (3)

cent) of the West Indians gave very favourable responses, compared with only 8 per cent of the English workers. It is therefore not surprising that the majority of those opposed to this focus of trade union activity were English workers, 25 per cent saying they were

Table 5.4 'What do you feel about the attempts of previous governments to limit the right to strike?'

	Factory sample		
	English *% (N = 36)*	*West Indian* *% (N=36)*	*Total* *% (N = 72)*
Very favourable	11 (4)	11 (4)	11.0 (8)
Favourable	6 (2)	33 (12)	19.5 (14)
Unfavourable	31 (11)	28 (10)	29.5 (21)
Totally opposed	36 (13)	19 (7)	27.5 (20)
Don't know	8 (3)	6 (2)	7.0 (5)
Other	8 (3)	0	4.0 (3)
No answer	0	3 (1)	1.5 (1)

totally opposed and a further 6 per cent saying that they were unfavourable. Second, the factory sample was asked: 'What do you feel about the attempts of previous governments to limit the right to strike?' (see Table 5.4). This question too brought a more favourable response from the West Indian workers, with 44 per cent, as compared with 17 per cent of the English, indicating their support; in contrast, 67 per cent of the English workers were opposed to limitations on the right to strike, compared with 47 per cent of the West Indian workers. This suggests that the West Indian workers at Food Co. were somewhat less likely to support the trade union shibboleths of 'free collective bargaining' and the 'right to strike', although at the same time it must not be forgotten that a majority of the English workers also supported the trade unions having discussions with the government about pay and conditions, while the West Indians were almost equally divided in their support for limitations on the right to strike. What this data does suggest (along with that in Table 5.2), and this must be both stated and interpreted with great care, is that there appears to be a tendency for a slightly larger proportion of West Indian workers to hold accommodationist or conservative views on the role of trade unions and trade unionism. We shall return to this point later in the chapter.

Levels of union participation and activity

It is nothing new to claim that workers' level of participation in union affairs is very low: this is certainly the conclusion from our data from South Brent. Of those interviewed at Food Co., 84.5 per cent reported that they never attended a union branch meeting; this total figure obscures a slight difference between the English and West Indian workers with 78 per cent of the former and 91 per cent of the latter reporting that they never attend. A large minority of non-attenders indicated that they felt an obligation to attend, but said that they found it very inconvenient to attend a union branch meeting when it is held on a Sunday morning, particularly if they did not live within walking distance of the meeting place. Most of the shop stewards who were interviewed at Food Co. confirmed that the timing and location of the meeting discouraged attendance, although one shop steward who was also a member of a revolutionary political party added that members saw little point in attending when decisions taken at branch meetings were regularly ignored or reversed by the shop stewards' committee. But no one suggested that there were special reasons for the non-attendance of black workers.

But although the affairs of the union branch, as well as the time and location of its meetings, may seem remote to the majority of our respondents, participation in union activities in the place of work is not as limited as the figures for attendance at union branch meetings might suggest. For example, 28 per cent of the English male workers at Food Co. and 35 per cent of the English male workers in the residential sample reported that they had been shop stewards at some time in the past. This is of interest in the light of what is known about the process by which union members become shop stewards. McCarthy and Parker (1968, p. 15) reported that 40 per cent of shop stewards had to be persuaded to take the job on and a further 36 per cent were happy to do the job but first had to be asked. Beynon (1973, pp. 189–92) stresses that union activism is always the outcome of a dialectical process: 'Men who become stewards have to recognise the potential in themselves and to have it recognised by others' (ibid., p. 192). Who becomes a shop steward and when is then not so much a function of individual personality as of a situation in which there is at least someone with at least some commitment to what Beynon calls humanistic collectivism (i.e. a desire to help one's fellow man). Most of those who had been shop stewards, as well as those who, when interviewed, were shop stewards, indicated that they took the job on because they were asked to by their fellow workers or because they were aware that if they did not do it, no one else would and the collective would suffer as a consequence. For example, one English shop steward at Food Co. (who, incidentally, was physically very well built) said:

'Well, I got asked. A lot of it was because I was big. I don't know! In some ways, I think it was because at that time if anyone said anything to me I wouldn't stand no trouble from anybody. Whether they think I was too big to argue with I don't know but that is how it started off. Well, I have been in it [i.e. the union] ever since it has been here.'

Another shop steward reported:

'Well, it came about by people on the floor actually approaching me. I never approached anyone. I didn't put my name up to be nominated. In fact, I refused at first because I was ignorant of the steward's role.'

Our point is that although the union *branch* may seem remote to the majority of workers, at least at Food Co., there are nevertheless a significant minority of workers who are prepared to become caught up in *workplace* union activity. This is not unrelated to the fact that a majority of our respondents in the factory justified their union membership and expressed a view of the role of the union in terms of the need to protect workers' interests, explaining this in terms of the day-to-day conflict in the factory between management and workers. It was the latter that mattered to all of those who had been or who were shop stewards, although some had wider orientations in addition. There is, therefore, a reservoir of previous and/or potential shopfloor activists amongst our male, English factory workers at Food Co. This argument can be supported by reference to the finding that although 28 per cent of the male English workers at Food Co. had been shop stewards, none had served on a trade union branch committee. Moreover, 39 per cent reported that they had at some time wanted to be a shop steward.

But does this actual or potential reservoir of *workplace* activists exist amongst the black workers? Only 8 per cent of the West Indian workers at Food Co. reported that they had been shop stewards, the same percentage stating that at some time they had wanted to be a shop steward. None of the West Indians in the residential sample reported that they had been a shop steward. Of course, this should not be read to mean that there were no black shop stewards at Food Co. or elsewhere in Brent, nor that the process by which West Indians become shop stewards is *necessarily* any different from that producing English shop stewards. There were, in fact, five West Indian shop stewards at Food Co. and we came into contact and interviewed a number of others who were working in other factories in the research area. All three of the shop stewards interviewed at Food Co. reported that they had become shop stewards primarily because members of their department had asked them to take the job on. For example:

'Well, the bloke who was shop steward before me was the same sort of bloke like me. He would stand up for the blokes and if he wanted something for them he would have to get it. The management didn't like that but the blokes were all behind him. In the end, he went for a "green collar" [i.e. foreman]. Now they are trying to get me out of the way but there is no way they can do it now. I have the experience of the management from my last place and I know I have to stand up for the blokes because I know what the management can get up to. The management didn't know that I was going to go for the job because they had a friend of theirs lined up for the job who is now a foreman. They knew that if he got the job, the shop steward's job, then people on the floor would have to do what they wanted. So when this other steward was going, the blokes said to me to go in for it because they needed someone to represent them because they knew that other bloke would be no good to them and only good to the management. So, to get him out of it was the reason I took it.'

This statement clearly indicates that the social dynamic underlying the assumption of the role of shop steward is rooted in the particularity of the conflict between capital and labour as expressed on the factory floor. Hence, at one level, the fact that this shop steward was black is irrelevant: the men in the department wanted a representative to defend and advance their interests against management and this particular man was prepared to 'stand up for the blokes'. However, at another level, the fact that this shop steward was black is relevant: the majority of the men in his department were black and this was true of the other black shop stewards interviewed at Food Co., while predominantly white departments were represented by white shop stewards. The implication is that black participation in workplace unionism may be structured and limited by racial categorisation. However, our evidence suggests that this is not the only reason. Rather, there are a number of processes operating together, reinforcing one another, and they can only be separated for analytical purposes.

Before we attempt to do this, let us summarise what has to be explained. Our data suggests that, first, there is a very low level of attendance at union branch meetings on the part of all workers, although the proportion of black workers not attending might be slightly higher (see Brooks, 1975a, pp. 295–6). Second, at the same time, about a third of the English male workers at Food Co. had, in the past, become involved in workplace union activity, while a third said that they had wanted to be a shop steward. Third, the proportions of West Indian workers reporting shop steward experience or intentions were much lower when compared with their English counterparts. However, and fourth, those West Indians who had become shop stewards reported that the reasons for taking on the job, and the process by which they did so, are the same as for the English shop stewards.

What processes are operating which might explain this apparent lower level of participation? It first has to be re-emphasised that participation is a minority phenomenon: even amongst the English workers at Food Co. two-thirds had no experience of workplace activism and the same proportion had no intention or desire to become active. Non-participation is a norm, in much the same way that actually joining the union is a norm at Food Co. For the majority of workers, the union is viewed on the one hand as a necessary and useful organisation but on the other hand as a force external to the member, an organisation whose support can be engaged when necessary:

> '*They* help *you* out with jobs, plus pay rises and things like that.'
> (English male: factory sample)

> 'Well, it's to fight for the workers. If there is an argument and you feel you aren't wrong, then you go to the unions and they should fight your case for you.' (West Indian male: factory sample)

In this sense the union, even at the place of work, is for a majority of workers, both black and white, an agent external to themselves: their obligation to it is based on a contract, in that they receive a service in return for payment, but their payment is the limit of their obligation.

Second, there is some evidence from our shop steward interviews which suggests that a proportion of black workers see the union as a 'white man's organisation' (see Brooks, 1975a, p. 298), a view which could obviously serve to limit participation in the union. A long-standing female shop steward argued that low turn-out at branch meetings and lack of interest in holding a shop steward's post was to be explained by the lack of representation above the shop steward level in the trade unions. This view was echoed by a black shop steward interviewed at Food Co.:

> 'There should be more black trade union officials. If black people can look up and see some black man in a position like Jack Jones or Hugh Scanlon then they will say "Yes, they are doing well." But every time they look at the trade union they see that it's always a white man who heads it even when there are a lot of black members and a lot of them with good education, good enough to do the job, they will be disillusioned.'

Additionally some, but by no means all, black shop stewards suggested that some white shop stewards were both racist and willing to discriminate against black members:

> 'I have heard though that some of the head people in the union here are a bit prejudiced, not about taking on workers but if there is an issue where someone's been involved, say in a fight or something like that. They will try for him but they wouldn't try as much as they would for a white man. I notice this in some of the cases and also how they talk about it. If a black man thumps someone they will say send him back to his jungle if he wants to

fight. That is not the way for the union to talk. If a white man did that, you wouldn't hear those remarks passed.'

'Well, it's [i.e. racial discrimination] done in such a concealed way that it would be hard to prove that it's done because of race. It's there, but you can't make a case out of it … But if I went to the senior shop stewards and complained, they wouldn't believe me. They would say that I had a chip on my shoulder. Maybe they would come up with some story as well that I didn't like white people.'

Moreover, the union is not defined as being sympathetic to allegations of discrimination in the factory. Another steward said:

How far these views are widespread amongst black workers is not easy to say. The bridging position of shop stewards between shop floor worker and trade union officials is significant in this context. But, as we shall show in the following section, those black workers who criticise the union do so in terms very similar to those used by white workers, and this is confirmed by the same black shop steward who claimed that some shop stewards discriminate against black members:

'Well, they [i.e. black workers] think about the same way as the white men think. If the white people think they [i.e. the union] are no bloody good, they think the same way.'

This implies that such views are held only by a minority, and this is supported by the English shop steward who is also active in revolutionary politics:

'Yes, there is a distrust of white organisations, in political senses in particular. There is a feeling that you can't trust these "honkeys" because they are going to take over the organisation for their own interest. Yes, that is there. I would say that was mostly amongst the guys who are better militants, the guys who are closer to us. That is the kind of thing that stops them joining us. We are seen as a white organisation. How far that feeling goes, I don't know.'

Those who were much closer to shop floor feelings at Food Co. than we could ever have been did not believe that a majority of black workers viewed the union as a 'white man's organisation', yet some of them were firmly of the opinion that there was evidence to justify holding such a view.

Third, it is relevant to take into account the fact that our black workers were migrants, with a clear intention of 'one day' returning to the Caribbean and this potentially could limit the extent of their commitment. This was suggested by a West Indian we met through our local network, who had himself been a shop steward:

> 'You tell them that it's a good thing to belong to the trade union because they protect the workers. They ask how much it will cost and when you tell them they say "All right" and that's it! They pay the money but they don't get involved. They won't attend any branch meetings or any other meetings. There are very few West Indians involved in union activities ... They have the belief that they are just here to work. If anything is going on they will become part of it but not an active part because they don't want to get involved in it. They believe that getting involved might prejudice something against them. Over here they are still regarded as foreigners and they regard themselves as foreigners so they say why should I get involved in other people's things. I think you'll find that well over half of the black people here have the idea in their heads that they will go back where they came from one day so why should they interfere in things here.'

We are stressing, then, that if it is the case that the level of black participation in workplace unionism is lower than it is for white workers, there is not one single explanation. Moreover, one must take care to specify the particular significance of racism and discrimination in explaining this lower level of participation. Our data suggests that only a minority of black workers would explain their non-participation and, as we shall shortly see, their criticism of unions, in these terms. It is here relevant to recall that a major national study concluded that black workers in England underestimate the extent of racial discrimination:

> West Indians are no more aware of discrimination than whites, and Asians are less aware of it; far from being over-sensitive to any signs of unfair treatment, resentful of their position in relation to the host community and militant for change, the minority groups are often the last to recognise an injustice that affects them most closely (Smith, 1977, p. 129).

In this context it is not surprising that the negative and passive record of the trade union movement regarding racism and discrimination is not a dominant factor in explaining the lower level of black participation. Additionally, if, as we shall shortly emphasise, workers' knowledge and understanding of unions is predominantly structured by local, factory experience, then black workers' awareness of this history is likely to be very limited.

Evaluation of trade unions

Membership of (and, indeed, participation in) a trade union should not necessarily be equated with a positive evaluation of the union. Our interviews revealed considerable dissatisfaction with trade unions amongst a substantial minority of both our English and West Indian workers, there being little difference between these two groups of workers in the source of their dissatisfaction. The most common reason for dissatisfaction was that the union was 'weak':

'This is a weak union here: the leader hasn't got the bottle for the job. He's got 1,800 members here and he don't know how to use them.' (English male: factory sample)

'No, it's diabolical. They are all "guvnor's men". They are all too old. They are sixty-five and seventy years old. They have been here for twenty-five and thirty years most of them and they are too old to get a job anywhere else. When they come from the meetings, they won't tell you anything.' (English male: factory sample)

'We had a strike there last year for more money and the whole factory was out so naturally we thought that the whole factory would benefit from the strike. But what they did was to give the engineers £6 a week and we got £1.34. And we were the lowest paid in the beginning.' (West Indian male: residential sample)

'Well, the unions are a good thing, although in this firm I don't think it's good enough. It was completely different in Walls when I was working there, from this one ... When all the workers came together, the union sticks up for them right to the end, no matter what happens. I remember one time at Walls when we asked for the roof of the factory to be fixed because the women working below were getting wet, or to give them some money for working in those conditions. The management refused so it was "All Out!" I think it would take a very long time for something like that to happen here.' (West Indian male: factory sample)

'In our place I think it's more for the company. If you have any complaint to make you don't get any satisfaction.' (West Indian female: residential sample)

But what is viewed as 'weakness' by some workers is viewed as 'strength' by others (although only one of our West Indian workers made this sort of reference):

> 'Well, when I first came here I was strongly advised to join the union and I don't think it's a militant union like Fords for instance. This one's fairly quiet. They do help you out if you need it and they've helped me out a couple of times.' (English male: factory sample)

Finally, a small group of workers expressed the view that the union was too strong and/or (for some other reason) was therefore unable to achieve its aim of protecting or advancing workers' interests:

> 'Sometimes you wonder if they are in your interests, management's, or just trying to destroy the country.' (West Indian male: residential sample)

> 'I think they have a bit too much power really.' (West Indian male: factory sample)

> 'If something goes wrong, they make a scapegoat, like striking for more wages. That's not doing any good. It's only good for the top people because they still get their money but the workers don't get any.' (English male: factory sample)

> 'When they become trade unionists, I think they're only after feathering their own nest, not to help anybody else. They're just trying to make themselves like little bloody dictators most of them.' (English male: residential sample)

What was *not* evident in the answers of our samples of West Indian respondents, apart from one black worker (although it was apparent in some of our interviews with West Indian shop stewards), was any reference to the union exhibiting racist sentiment or being responsible for or condoning racial discrimination. It might be argued that because we did not ask our black respondents specifically about racial exclusion they would not volunteer relevant information spontaneously. A few respondents in the residential sample were asked specific questions about black representation etc. in the follow-up probes. With one exception none of these indicated that they had any specific grievance about their trade union's representation of their interests *as black* workers rather than as workers. The exception (a West Indian car assembly worker) when asked about union membership said that there were times when he left the union because either he or a colleague had been treated unfairly. When asked about this he was rather vague. But when asked about his shop stewards he responded,

'Some of the people they treat all right, but others they treat almost like dogs.'

Whom do they represent better than others?

'Well, their own people. The Indians have a shop steward and he represents his own people and the whites look after their own problems.' (West Indian male: residential sample)

In so far as the rest of our black workers did criticise their union, it was in terms consistent with the dominant view of the role of trade unions (i.e. to improve working conditions: help/protect workers), the dominant criticism alleging that the union was not successfully fulfilling this role. In sum, what concerned both the English and West Indian critics of the unions was that the ends (i.e. 'good' wages and acceptable working conditions) which they hoped to gain by joining the union were being obstructed by the union itself, usually, but not always, personified by the shop stewards collectively, the union convenor or the national union leadership. The distinction here would seem important for some.

The residential sample were asked whether they thought their trade unions adequately represented their interests and also what they thought of their shop steward representation. Only half of the English were satisfied with their union representation, compared to around 60 per cent of the West Indians. Two of the West Indian women explained this in terms of the union's (successful) fight for Equal Pay. For both it was the only point in their reference to their trade unions when they became animated, identifying themselves as *part* of the union.

English men were more likely to express only a qualified satisfaction with their union. But it was on the question of shop steward representation that the longer and more varied experience of trade unionism among English men clearly differentiated their responses from the other respondents. It should be remembered that 5 per cent of the English men in the residential sample had been or were currently shop stewards. Their responses reflect this in both emphasising the difficulties of performing the role well and the necessity of educating stewards for the job. This type of response was obviously missing amongst the West Indians, particularly the women, some of whom believed that their stewards were 'management' men and women, for example:

'I think she's more for the management than the workers really, but I don't say anything because probably some of the other workers will be offended so I just close my mouth. But I feel she is on the management side.'

So you don't think your union protects your interests?

'No, not the union, the union don't trouble us, I haven't got anything to say against the union. But any little thing that you would say to her she will say that's not union business. It's as if she's a bit scared.' (West Indian female: residential sample)

Discussion

Our most general observation about our findings from data collected from south Brent is that there is a considerable degree of similarity between the level of unionisation and ideological orientation to unionism of white and black workers. Specifically, both white and black workers are equally likely to be union members, to explain their union membership either in terms of 'compulsion' or individualism or instrumentalism, to define the union's role in individualistic or instrumental terms, to view the union as an external agent and to criticise the union to which they belong in similar terms. We believe that this is to be explained by the fact that our focus is upon white and black *workers*. That is to say, what is most important in explaining our respondents' level of unionisation and ideological orientation to unionism is that they are *wage labourers*, while the effects of social significance being attached to physical differentiation (i.e. racial categorisation) have only a secondary impact (along with other factors).

Except for those temporarily not working due to child-bearing, sickness or unemployment, all of our respondents were wage labourers: their means of livelihood was dependent upon their continued ability to sell their labour power to an employer. Decisions about union membership and ideas about unions are decisively structured by this class position and, in turn, by the nature of the work situation which, amongst other things, is characterised by the exercise of control by management over the work process (i.e. for example, management determines, or attempts to determine, hours of work/overtime, integration of individual work activities etc.). The wage that the worker receives for the sale of labour power, and the conditions under which work is carried out, are of necessity the consequence of conflict and negotiation between worker and employer. Out of this conflict and negotiation have developed trade unions. Although the trade unions now have an institutional existence, with the consequence that they make strenuous efforts to reproduce themselves (e.g. maintain and increase membership, increase their financial reserves), the *raison d'être* for their existence is daily reproduced in the very nature of the capitalist relations of production. Hence, as we have shown, for the majority of workers the role of the union is to attain the best return on the sale of their labour power:

> 'Well, I think it's [i.e. the union] a good thing for groups of workers if they find their living standard dropping, or their take-home pay, or they have a grievance with the management here.' (English male: factory sample)

But it is also a means by which workers may resist management's control of the work process:

> 'I like to be in one [i.e. a union] because they will help you with the management. You may be working somewhere and the management victimises you and you then have the unions to fight for you, or you might have an accident and the unions will be behind you – things like that.' (West Indian male: factory sample)

And even those workers who are ideologically inclined to oppose unionisation, or at least the closed shop, often recognise these bases of union organisation. For example, one worker who explained her union membership in terms of 'compulsion' also claimed:

> 'If you look at past history in England when the old man could come up to you and say you are fired and that was it. That can't happen any more because of the unions. That's a good thing.' (West Indian female: residential sample)

This is not to deny that about two-fifths of our combined samples explained their own union membership in terms of 'compulsion', but it was also recognised by over 60 per cent of all our respondents (members and non-members) that the role of trade unions is to improve working conditions; help/protect workers'.

The importance of unions to a majority of our respondents is as a means of asserting a degree of autonomy in the work process and obtaining what they regard as an adequate material return, and this tends to be expressed in both individualistic and instrumental terms. Moreover, most of our workers tended to talk about unions in terms which implied that, like the business or service for which they worked, they were part of the exterior institutional world with which they had contact for very specfiic ends. There is little evidence in our data of a positive or active identification on the part of the majority of respondents with an organisation which is *ours/mine* and in and through which *we/I* can struggle (witness for example the low level of interest in the union branch and the vast majority of workers who have no desire to be a shop steward). Rather, the union struggles *for* me, on *my* behalf. Joining the union is therefore similar to taking out an insurance policy: an agent of the organisation collects a payment and the payee calls on the agent when a service is required in return. Finally, this contract is struck in relation to the workplace and is not viewed on the part of the majority as having repercussions in the wider economic and political arena. Indeed, where it is, it tends to be viewed in negative terms (e.g. 'the unions have too much power'), although it can be noted that this view is partially contradicted by that current of opinion which believes the union at the place of work to be weak and ineffective. In the same way both black and white respondents might suggest that 'strikes were ruining the country' yet report having been involved in industrial and strike action at the workplace, without appearing to see any contradiction between their beliefs and actions.

Much of the argument so far may seem to parallel the analysis advanced by Goldthorpe *et al.* (1968) who argued that the modern 'affluent worker' views union membership and activity in instrumental and local terms (although it should be noted that our sample of workers could hardly be called 'affluent' in the terms of this study). Subsequent argument and research has criticised this work and we can find evidence in our own data which supports some of this criticism (e.g. Blackburn 1967; Westergaard, 1970; Beynon, 1973). For example, Goldthorpe *et al* claim that 'the significance which unionism has for these workers is very largely confined to issues arising in their employment which are *economic* in nature and which are local in their origins and scope' (1968, p. 113).

As we have already emphasised, our own data clearly illustrates the 'local' (in the sense of workplace) orientation to trade unionism but we would not accept that the significance of unionism is predominantly economic, or that collectivism is 'directed to the achievement of individuals' private goals, *outside* the workplace' (1968, p. 106, our emphasis). Certainly, much of the instrumentalism and individualism of our respondents was expressed through their concern with their wages (i.e. the cash nexus: Westergaard, 1970) and wages are spent outside the place of work. But, as we have already shown, our respondents were also concerned about their conditions of work and, additionally, were aware that the issue of wages required union organisation *inside* the workplace. Those workers in the residential sample who worked for small, non-union firms are an interesting exception, although, as we have already pointed out, some of these believed that their position would be improved if they were members of a trade union.

The 'economistic' explanation of Goldthorpe *et al.* ignores the political dimension of both the cash nexus (Westergaard, 1970) and workshop union organisation. Beynon claims that this organisation is based upon a working-class factory consciousness and that

> it understands class relationships in terms of their direct manifes-
> tation in conflict between the bosses and the workers within the
> factory. It is rooted in the workplace where struggles are fought
> over the control of the job and the 'rights' of managers and
> workers. In as much as it concerns itself with exploitation and
> power it contains definite political elements. But it is a politics of
> the factory (1973, p. 98).

We believe that this argument embodies the keystone of our explanation of the majority of our respondents' ideological orienta-tion to trade unionism. More importantly, it applies to our white *and* black workers because they are all wage labourers involved in struggles in the workplace over the sale of their labour power and the conditions under which it is expended, whether or not the workplace is a factory.

This is not to say that struggles in the workplace never involve or are not structured by racial discrimination and racism: the indus-trial disputes at Mansfield Hosiery Mills Ltd and Imperial Type-writers Ltd (see Moore, 1975) constitute evidence to the contrary. But it is misleading to suggest that such disputes, or, indeed, the conditions that give rise to them, necessarily occur in every workplace. Just because *black* workers are to be found working in a factory or a hospital or driving tube trains then it does not follow that their attitudes and actions towards work and their union must necessarily be structured by racial discrimination and racism at all times. To return to one of our introductory comments, we must not assume that being part of a racially categorised fraction of the working class structures all possibilities for identity and action among black workers. It does set limits to those possibilities but there will be instances when being a woman or a migrant worker will structure perceptions as well.

The differences between our West Indian men and women are a clear example: their similar decisions about union membership are structured by their common class position as wage labourers. But as far as the role of the trade union is concerned West Indian women are more likely than their male counterparts to believe that the trade unions are failing to adequately represent and defend working-class interests. This was expressed many times by reference to the gap between wage and price rises, and by reference to unemployment levels. We have already commented that women's dual role in production heightens their awareness of the slide in working-class living standards in inflationary periods, a factor which dominates many of the interviews with women and situates much of the resentment towards the ineffectiveness of trade unions in a material reality.

But for West Indian women the role of their union was not seen simply as attaining the best return on the sale of their labour: they were equally concerned (and more than any other group) that their union should resist management's control of the work process and many complained that their shop stewards obstructed this goal. A recurrent theme was their refusal 'to be pushed around' at work, yet they felt that their efforts to resist this were hindered rather than helped by their shop stewards. One of our informants, a shop steward, told us that it was her persistent refusal to be 'pushed around' and resultant conflicts with management which led her black fellow-workers to ask her to become a shop steward. In short, being a female wage labourer structures belief and action towards work in a particular way. While there were no direct references to sexual discrimination within the union by any of the West Indian women, they appeared to have higher expectations of their union's performance than the West Indian men. What is most clear about the responses of the English women is their lack of direct experience of trade unionism. Some professed complete ignorance in relation to the attitudinal questions, while others drew heavily on media coverage of trade union activities in justifying their belief that the 'trade unions are too powerful' and irresponsible. West Indian women were, by contrast, less likely to draw on information from media sources.

What all of the West Indian women share with their male counterparts is migrant status. We have shown, for example, that most of our black workers had little or no experience of trade unionism prior to migration, that there was a slight tendency for black workers at Food Co. to hold more conservative views on the rights of trade unions to strike and to involve themselves in discussions with the government about an incomes policy, and that they had a lower rate of participation in workplace union activity. The fact that our black respondents were migrants is a relevant consideration in evaluating all three tendencies. The relevance of migrant status is obvious in the case of the first. The other two tendencies could be explained by the black workers' class position prior to migration and their ideology which is related to their migration. The migrant has a 'target' (i.e. a certain level of earnings and a return to the homeland to occupy a more economically and socially advantageous class position) which potentially binds him/her to the capitalist mode of production so long as it seems to have the potential of allowing these goals to be realised. Joining a union is not inconsistent with realising these goals (indeed, where union membership is a norm, joining is the epitome of instrumentalism) but there might be cause for concern about union policy and practice if it seems to threaten earning capacity. In such circumstances, migrant workers may be more likely to accept the consensus view of legitimate trade union activity and to avoid active involvement themselves for fear of obstructing their earnings potential. On the other hand this preoccupation with an earnings target can, in other circumstances, provide the catalyst for active trade unionism.

Having said this, our data does also suggest that awareness of racial discrimination and racism within the place of work and within the workplace union is a factor in explaining the lower level of black participation in workplace union activity. The fact that fewer of our black workers had had shop steward experience and were uninterested in becoming shop stewards cannot be explained solely by reference to their relative lack of experience of trade unionism consequent upon being 'strangers', because most of them have been in England for fifteen years or more and hence now have a considerable experience of work. We argue that there is considerable scope for racial discrimination and racism to have an important impact on the level of active participation by black workers in workplace unionism because the process by which shop stewards are selected and elected involves a considerable degree of informal persuasion within a work group and depends upon the willingness of an individual to make certain personal sacrifices for the collective good. Thus, if racial discrimination is practised and racist ideas are articulated within work groups containing both white and black workers, black workers may not be approached with a view to persuading them to become shop stewards, and/or black workers may decide that they do not wish to participate. Our observation that black shop stewards tended to represent work groups which were predominantly black is clearly relevant here. If our findings and explanation are repeated on a wider scale, there are considerable implications, not only in the fact that a feeling amongst black workers of inadequate representation in the workplace union structure was an important element leading to the dispute at Imperial Typewriters Ltd, but also because it is from the position of shop steward that individuals are able to enter and work their way up through the union organisation (e.g. Beynon, 1973, p. 74). It follows that there may be good reason to be sceptical about the possibility of a proportionate number of black workers moving up through the union bureaucracy to positions of national leadership.

CHAPTER 6

Class consciousness: the ideological dimension

In writing about class consciousness one is aware of an extensive literature and controversial theoretical debate. We wish to draw upon this literature and debate with the aim of considering a quite specific problem which is discussed in this and the following two chapters. This problem follows logically from our contention that black migrant labour constitutes a fraction of the British working class, from which one can argue that not only do black and white workers in the United States exhibit class consciousness, but also that black workers are more class conscious than white workers because of their marginal status (Leggett, 1968). On the other hand, it could be argued that the process of racial categorisation encourages the development of a racial consciousness amongst black workers, with the consequence that their political consciousness would differ in important respects from that of white workers. In order to evaluate the validity of these two possibilities it is necessary to evaluate the political consciousness of the white working class.

There is a second reason for being interested in the nature and extent of class consciousness amongst our English workers. Although we do not intend to enter the debate about the origins of racism, we do wish to argue that racism is not the ideological prerogative of the ruling class as some writers have suggested (e.g. Cox, 1970; for a critique see Gabriel and Ben-Tovim, 1978, and Miles, 1980). We shall show, particularly in chapter 7, that the racist ideas are articulated within the working class and this raises the question of whether and how such ideas coexist with ideas which can be described as exhibiting class consciousness.

Political consciousness and class consciousness

In talking of political consciousness, we are referring to people's ideas about the structure of power and the way in which it is exercised in economic and political relations. The concept is being used in a broad, generic sense and should be kept analytilly distinct from the concept of class consciousness. The latter is a form of political consciousness but it is only one form. For example, we have to consider the fact that bourgeois class interests or dominant beliefs are reproduced within working-class consciousness, especially when those beliefs are presented as being of universal validity (at least within the confines of the nation state) (cf. Parkin, 1971). Empirically, different forms of political consciousness are not easily distinguished.

A major problem in ascertaining the nature and extent of any form of political consciousness concerns the relationship between belief and action. We do not believe that there is any necessary or consistent relationship between the two; for example, much of the academic debate about class consciousness seems to assume that it can be measured by ascertaining whether workers articulate certain ideas, and in so far as they do not it is concluded that they have a low level of class consciousness. But ideas do not always precede the action. Indeed, the opposite can occur where workers suddenly become involved in political activity, the reason for the repercussions of which are only articulated during and after the action. In other words, class consciousness can be expressed in action. But it is also the case that the articulation of ideas constitutes action. For example, the articulation of ideas can have the effect of forming or reinforcing a sense of group solidarity or of creating or deepening a conflict within a group. For these reasons we shall approach the question of whether our respondents express class consciousness by considering both their ideas about certain issues (e.g. perceptions of class, the exercise of power) in this chapter and their record of political activity in chapter 8.

A second problem concerns the fact that most discussions of class consciousness usually refer only to the working class, yet all classes develop a class consciousness. This is important because, as we have already indicated, bourgeois class interests are usually presented as national interests and, on that basis, come to be articulated within the working class. The extent to which this is the case is in the final analysis an empirical question. Parkin argues that the working class will draw heavily on bourgeois, or what he calls 'dominant', values when faced with questions of a non-situational nature. But this assertion is challenged by Moorhouse and Chamberlain (1974; also Chamberlain, 1977) who produce evidence to show that the working class articulate oppositional as opposed to purely accommodative responses to both situational and non-situational questions. For reasons of brevity, all subsequent references to class consciousness are to the consciousness of the working class, except where specifically indicated otherwise.

A third problem evident in the literature is the failure of some authors to identify the parameters of class consciousness. For example, Goldthorpe *et al.* contrast the 'status' consciousness of the 'new' working class with class consciousness understood in a 'traditional' sense (1969, p. 155) but fail to specify what traditional class consciousness is and how it differs from status consciousness. Indeed, by phrasing their discussion in terms of 'social perspectives' (ibid., pp. 116–21), one could conclude that the authors have attempted to avoid defining class consciousness (cf. Westergaard, 1975). Subsequent research has also been much influenced by an earlier attempt by Lockwood to identify the bases of variations in working-class 'images of society' (1966) and although such 'images' are an important constitutive element of class consciousness, some of this work focuses on 'images' without confronting the class consciousness problematic (Bulmer, 1975; Davis, 1979).

Restricted and radical class consciousness

Within the Marxist tradition, proletarian class consciousness is a concept used broadly to refer to the articulation of beliefs within the working class about the existence of classes which have conflicting interests, giving rise to economic and political conflict. We develop our analysis by first drawing a distinction between restricted proletarian class consciousness and radical (or revolutionary) proletarian class consciousness. The distinction here is an empirical one, but it has theoretical status (see Meszaros, 1971). A *restricted class consciousness* is evident when the ideas and/or action of a working-class individual or group indicates:

(1) a belief in the existence of a class structure, in which classes have conflicting interests;

(2) that there is a self-identification in being a member of the working class;

(3) that, as a member of that class, there are material and social disadvantages in common which give rise to collective interests which have to be pursued collectively.

We define this form of class consciousness as *restricted* because, although it manifests an awareness of class division and conflict, it does not include any notion of an alternative socialist society, nor any strategy for attaining that alternative. Restricted class consciousness can therefore include or co-exist with the notion that the

resolution of class conflict can occur within the framework of bourgeois democracy. This is the crucial feature of the ideology of Labourism (see Nichols and Armstrong, 1976). Hence, a *radical proletarian class consciousness* is evident when ideas and/or action indicate:
(1) that the objective of class struggle is the attainment of a socialist society through revolutionary means;
(2) that the existence of common working-class interests requires organised class struggle through the medium of a revolutionary political party.

   This form of class consciousness takes a different form in different historical circumstances. As a mass phenomenon, it is only evident in revolutionary conjunctures (indeed, its existence is one of the defining characteristics of such a conjuncture) and is expressed through the mass support given to a revolutionary party rather than by a coherent articulation of revolutionary theory (cf. Moorhouse and Chamberlain, 1974, p. 398). In 'stable' capitalist formations it is evident amongst only a small minority of the working class and is expressed through the articulation of a 'coherent' political ideology and an associated political practice. Given that there was no *sustained* political challenge to capitalism from the working class in the mid 1970s, we did not expect to find evidence of a widespread radical class consciousness amongst our sample. These definitions do not differ greatly from those of Mann (1973, p. 13) or Westergaard (1975, p. 252) but we are making a more explicit distinction between levels of class consciousness when we distinguish between a restricted and a radical proletarian class consciousness.

Class consciousness and trade union consciousness

We now consider the relationship between class consciousness and trade union consciousness with the aim of establishing a theoretical link between the empirical content of this and the preceding chapter. That Lenin at one point drew a formal and dichotomous distinction between trade union and Social-Democratic (or revolutionary) consciousness is well known, although this distinction is not consistently maintained throughout his writings (Hyman, 1971, pp. 41–2). The point with which Lenin was concerned in 1905 was that trade union consciousness was an incomplete form of revolutionary consciousness which arises from and is ultimately limited by class struggle at the place of work (see also Anderson, 1967, pp. 343–4).

The significance of these distinctions lies in the fact that if, as we have argued in chapter 5, the conflict between capital and labour produces, of necessity, trade union organisation, this can be expected to be reproduced in some mediated form in the consciousness of the working class. In so far as this consciousness embodies an awareness of conflict with the employer and of the need for the combination of the working class in order to pursue common interests, one could conclude that this is compatible with our definition of restricted class consciousness. However, because this consciousness is limited to the factory context (cf. Beynon, 1973) and expresses itself in the need for trade union organisation only, there is a good reason for drawing an analytical distinction between trade union consciousness and restricted class consciousness. The latter is certainly implicit in the former but because ideas about the nature of the conflict between the employer and worker at the place of work may not necessarily be transferred to the wider context of capitalist society, there is good reason to analytically distinguish trade union consciousness as a mode of restricted class consciousness which is formed within and may be constrained by the place of work. In this and the subsequent two chapters, we are concerned with restricted (and radical) class consciousness in the wider sense.

Concerning consistency and class imagery

There are two final issues to be considered before presenting our data. The first follows from the fact that we speak of class consciousness being manifest in a *cluster* of ideas and actions, from which it follows that not all ideas may be consistent with one another and that ideas may not be consistent with action. In this connection, it is important to recognise that only the class consciousness of the revolutionary leadership is abstract and impersonal, and that that of the majority of the working class is expressed in personal terms and is very much bound up with the everyday circumstances of working-class life (Reich, 1971, p. 68). Hence, we are not searching for the articulation of abstract theories about surplus value. But if we are not searching for abstract theorisation, we need not assess the ideas articulated by the working class by criteria pertaining to abstract theorisation, criteria which include that of logical consistency. This is no new claim (see Westergaard, 1970; Moorhouse and Chamberlain, 1974, p. 198; Nichols and Armstrong, 1976, pp. 150 ff.) but is taken up here to argue that we do not conceive of class consciousness as some absolute, logical quality which is either present or absent. Rather we are interested in whether the varied and often half-formed complex of ideas and actions exhibited by the working class (which Gramsci called 'common sense': 1971, pp. 323–33) include ideas which can be considered to indicate class consciousness, and not whether these same ideas logically interrelate with all others.

The second concerns that vexed question of the sort of questions which legitimately elicit the expression of class consciousness. Goldthorpe *et al.* concluded that the 'affluent' working class was not class conscious because the majority of their sample failed to articulate a 'power' model of the class structure (1969, pp. 149–55). Moorhouse and Chamberlain (1974) have observed that it is an unnecessary constraint to be concerned only with responses to questions about images of class structure and that class consciousness can be expressed in ideas about other areas of socio-economic activity. Accordingly, we questioned our respondents about a range of issues (although not all questions were asked of both samples because we wanted to obtain data on a wide range of issues) and this data we now present.

Perceptions of class

Only the factory sample was asked direct questions about class and class structure. Just over 75 per cent of the sample identified and went on to describe a class structure in Britain, the West Indian workers being slightly less likely than the English workers to conceive of society in such terms. The sample was then asked to say how many classes there were (see Table 6.1). Over half identified two or three classes, with a small minority describing a more complex class structure, involving four, five or even more classes. Those who described four classes usually added an 'underclass' (e.g. the 'down-and-outs', the 'unfortunates') to an otherwise 'conventional' three-class model, whereas those who identified five or more classes either said there were too many classes to be able to count them or that the main three classes were further subdivided into 'upper' and 'lower'. The majority who identified a two- or three-class model tended to do so using terms such as the 'rich class' and the 'poor class' or 'upper/rich class', 'middle class' and 'lower/working class' respectively. Despite such variation in terminology, they all identified the structure as a hierarchy, this often being expressed in terms of wealth or money:

Table 6.1 Number of classes perceived by factory sample

	English % (N = 36)	West Indian % (N = 36)	Total % (N = 72)
2-class model	19 (7)	28 (10)	24 (17)
3-class model	39 (14)	28 (10)	33 (24)
4-class model	14 (5)	8 (3)	11 (8)
5 + -class model	8 (3)	8 (3)	8 (6)
Does not articulate a class model	19 (7)	28 (10)	24 (17)

Note Percentages do not total 100 in some cases due to rounding.

'You have the working class and the people with the money who don't work.' (West Indian male: factory sample)

'Well, it's whether you are a working man or in the middle classes like a lawyer or doctor, or whether you just sit down and watch the money roll in.' (English male: factory sample)

Table 6.2 Self-assigned class position of factory sample

	English % (N = 36)	West Indian % (N = 36)	Total % (N = 72)
Working class/lower class/ poor (as lowest class)	47 (17)	52 (19)	50 (36)
Working class (as intermediate class)	11 (4)	6 (2)	8 (6)
Middle class	8 (3)	6 (2)	7 (5)
N.A.	14 (5)	8 (3)	11 (8)
Does not articulate a class model	20 (7)	28 (10)	24 (17)

Note Percentages do not total 100 in some cases due to rounding.

There was a slight tendency for West Indian workers to be more likely to identify a two-class model as opposed to a three-class model.

Concerning self-assigned class position, about half of the factory sample (see Table 6.2) said they were in the lowest class of whatever number of classes they identified (that is, in the working, lower or poor class) while a further 8.5 per cent said they were working class but had identified a class below that of the working class. Only 7 per cent of the sample claimed they were middle class. Thus, of those identifying a class structure, a substantial majority see themselves as belonging to the working class.

The sample was then asked what they believe distinguished one class from another. Over half of the sample referred to money:

> 'Well, I think the rich ones have enough money to do what they want and they can actually do anything. The middle class man is the one who can just barely make himself independent. And the lower class person is the one that has to fight hard. He can't even take a day off work: you can't miss a day out.' (West Indian male: factory sample)

> 'It's the money. The poor class haven't got much and the one at the top must have plenty.' (English male: factory sample)

A much smaller proportion of the sample (11.5 per cent, and they were mostly West Indians) said that the basis of class differentiation was whether one worked for a living:

> 'Well, as long as you work, you are in the working classes.' (West Indian male: factory sample)

An equally small proportion (10 per cent, mainly English) made reference to some inherent characteristic or ability as the reason for class divisions:

> 'I think intelligence. If you have intelligence then you will be in the upper class because you're earning a lot of money. If you are of average intelligence, then you'll be in the middle class.' (English male: factory sample)

Education and/or the possession of qualifications was the only other characteristic mentioned by any significant number of respondents.

The fact that a majority of the factory sample perceives the class structure as a hierarchy of classes divided according to money might suggest that our findings are similar to those of Goldthorpe *et al.*

(1969) who argued that the majority of their sample held a pecuniary model of the class structure. However, as Moorhouse has pointed out, 'people do not neatly distinguish between money and power because they are so obviously related in social life as opposed to social analysis ... Statements about money are statements about power' (1976, p. 484).

With this in mind, the factory sample was asked 'Do some classes have more power than others?' Over half of the sample stated that the upper class or the rich have the most power and many of the responses additionally confirmed that there was a relationship between being rich and having power:

> 'The rich one. Because he has the money so he can do what he likes. Money talks.He could run you over in his Rolls and get away with it because he's got the money to pay his lawyer to get him off. It all comes back to money.' (West Indian male: factory sample)

> 'Well, obviously the upper class with the more money will have more power than I have. Money talks a lot everywhere.' (English male: factory sample)

Amongst the remainder of the sample, there was a variety of minority responses, the most significant being that which identified the latent and generally unrealised power of the working class:

> 'Well, I think if the crunch came, the working class have got the power because if they got together and decided to withdraw work, the rich wouldn't be able to get any richer. There would be nothing produced.' (English male: factory sample)

This data allows us to conclude that a majority of the factory sample both identifies a class structure and sees itself as a working class in a hierarchy in which the 'upper class' is identified by its wealth and its power. This conclusion applies almost equally to the English and West Indian workers in the sample.

Perceptions of the exercise of power

Separately from our questions on class, we asked both samples questions designed to obtain their perception of the exercise of power in Britain. The factory sample was asked 'What sorts of people or groups would you say have the biggest say over the way things are run in Britain?' (see Table 6.3). Apart from those who said that they did not know, the vast majority of respondents

Table 6.3 'What sorts of people or groups would you say have the biggest say over the way things are run in Britain?' (Factory sample)

	English % (N=36)	West Indian % (N=36)	Total % (N=72)
The government, MPs, Cabine., Prime Minister, etc.	25 (9)	53 (19)	39 (28)
The ruling class, the rich industrialists, bankers, etc.	22 (8)	19 (7)	20.5 (15)
Trade unions	17 (6)	17 (6)	17 (12)
The people, voters, everyone, etc.	8 (3)	—	4 (3)
The working class	6 (2)	—	3 (2)
Others	3 (1)	6 (2)	4.4 (3)
Don't know	22 (8)	17 (6)	19.5 (14)

Note Columns total more than 100 per cent because a small number of individuals gave more than one response to this question

Table 6.4 'Some people say it's not the government that makes the important decisions, but big business and financiers both at home and abroad, while others say that the government is able to control the most important things. What do you think?' (Factory sample)

	English % (N=36)	West Indian % (N=36)	Total % (N=72)
Government controls	14 (5)	53 (19)	33.5 (24)
Big business controls	44 (16)	39 (14)	41.5 (30)
Government and big bankers have equal control	14 (5)	—	7 (5)
Trade unions control	3 (1)	3 (1)	3 (2)
Others	8 (3)	—	4 (3)
Don't know	17 (6)	5 (2)	11 (8)

referred to the government (or MPs, etc.), the ruling class (or rich) or the trade unions. The English workers were more or less equally divided in their references to these three groups (although the lowest proportion referred to the trade unions) while a majority of the West Indian workers (compared to 25 per cent of the English) said that the government runs Britain. The sample was then asked specifically whether it was the government or big business which makes 'the important decisions'. Faced with this alternative, about three-quarters of the sample was prepared to choose between the two alternatives with 41.5 per cent saying that big business makes 'the important decisions' and 33.5 per cent saying that it is the government (see Table 6.4). A similar proportion of English and West Indian workers said that big business makes 'the important decisions' but a much larger proportion of West Indians said that the government does so (53 per cent compared with 14 per cent of the English). Reference to the trade unions was almost non-existent.

Finally, the factory sample was asked whether it was the government or the trade unions who made 'the important decisions'. Given that this followed two previous questions on the exercise of power, it is perhaps not surprising that this question produced a more complex pattern of responses (Table 6.5). However, the overall

Table 6.5 'Some people say it's not the government that makes the important decisions, but the trade unions, while others say that the government is able to control the most important things. What do you think?' (Factory sample)

	English % (N=36)	West Indian % (N=36)	Total % (N=72)
Government controls	28 (10)	47 (17)	37.5 (27)
Trade unions control	22 (8)	17 (6)	19.5 (14)
Government and trade unions have equal control	14 (5)	8 (3)	11 (8)
Big business controls	8 (3)	17 (6)	12.5 (9)
Trade unions and big business control	3 (1)	3 (1)	3 (2)
Government, trade unions and big business have equal control	8 (3)	—	4 (3)
Others	11 (4)	3 (1)	7 (5)
Don't know	6 (2)	5 (2)	5.5 (4)

picture is consistent with that arising from the previous questions. The proportion identifying the trade unions as making 'the important decisions' was only slightly larger than that obtained in response to the initial open-ended question. Although just under 20 per cent responded in this way it was far from being a majority view. A larger proportion of the sample (37.5 per cent) maintained that it is the government which is in control, although again it is the West Indian workers who are more likely to make this response. This difference is balanced by the larger proportion of English workers who perceived a 'corporatist' situation with the government, big business and/or trade unions all involved in decision-making:

> 'They [i.e. MPs] work side by side. I mean, half the government are on some kind of connection with these big firms aren't they? It's all fixed from the top.' (English male: factory sample)

The residential sample was asked a different question: 'Do you think that the government takes notice of some people's needs and demands more than others?' According to bourgeois democratic theory, power is dispersed and non-cumulative but only 20 per cent of the residential sample endorsed this view by replying in the negative. A range of responses were offered by the rest of the sample. Amongst the West Indians, 40 per cent of the women said that the government takes more notice of the rich or upper class, compared with 18 per cent of the men:

> 'They are concerned about the people who are all right already, the rich people. But they don't worry about the poor working class.' (West Indian female: residential sample)

> 'The government listens to the people with the money more so than they would someone like me who isn't worth their dinner.' (West Indian female: residential sample)

Slightly more English than West Indian men articulated this view, but none of the English women. But it was not only the rich who were perceived to have privileged access to the government. The West Indian respondents also referred to 'the Asians' and to the unemployed. For example:

> 'Well, the working-class people get the worst out of the government and the people who don't work get everything. The working class don't get anything, for everything that they do earn they will take three-quarters of it out in tax. I don't think it's fair when all those people that don't work get all that money each week.' (West Indian female: residential sample)

However, amongst the English workers, apart from reference to the rich, the other group considered most likely to have its needs taken into account by the government was 'the coloureds'. This response is considered in chapter 7.

What general conclusions can be drawn from these findings? If it is assumed that the legitimation of bourgeois democracy lies at least in part with the claim that power is dispersed, competitive and non-cumulative so that government does not favour particular groups, then the data from the residential sample suggests that only a minority support this claim. Diverse groups from the rich to the unemployed were identified as receiving privileged treatment, but what was common to the majority, both the English and West Indian, was the view that 'I'm not one of them'. It is a perception of national power and resource allocation shaped by the 'smaller societies in which they live out their daily lives' (Lockwood, 1975, p. 16). A sense of injustice is paramount, along with a feeling of powerlessness to do anything about it.

Given the more specific questions about the exercise and distribution of power asked of the factory sample, these inchoate perceptions were supplied with a framework which allowed more structured responses, so the picture which emerges is more detailed yet is somewhat similar. Only amongst the West Indian men do we find a majority stating consistently in response to all three questions that the government makes 'the important decisions', a belief that is consistent with the bourgeois defence of the existing political structure. Less than a quarter of the English men consistently made this response. This may partly reflect the fact that our West Indian respondents were socialised in a colonial context where the 'Mother Country' was portrayed as representing the quintessence of democracy, although this cannot constitute a complete explanation because it does not help to explain the more radical response of the West Indian women revealed in the residential sample.

Apart from this majority of the West Indian men and a minority of the English men, the remainder of the factory sample see the power to make 'the important decisions' as lying in the hands of either big business or trade unions, or some combination of these two groups along with the government. The relative proportion opting for each of these groups varies from one question to another, depending upon the parameters offered, but close inspection of Tables 6.5 to 6.7 shows that, for both English and West Indian men, it is more likely that they will say that big business makes 'the important decisions' rather than the trade unions.

Conversely this majority of the English workers and large

minority of the West Indian workers do not seem to believe that the power to influence events lies in the hands of the working class. By definition, big business cannot be open to working-class influence while we have already shown that the trade unions tend not to be perceived as working-class institutions in the representative sense but rather as dispensers of a service which is obtained by entering into a contract. As far as the government is concerned, we shall show in chapter 8 that over half of the English workers (compared to about a quarter of the West Indian workers) believe that voting does little to change things in Britain. Our assumption is confirmed by the fact that 92 per cent of the English workers and 84 per cent of the West Indian workers in the factory sample reported in response to a direct question that working-class people have little or no influence over what goes on in Britain. In sum, apart from the majority of the West Indian workers who believe that government has the power (along with a minority of the English workers), these questions reveal a general feeling of powerlessness which follows from a perception that the power to determine 'the important decisions' lies in institutions which are not open to the representation of working-class interests.

Perceptions of justice

We have already shown that one shibboleth of British bourgeois democracy does not receive widespread support from our working-class sample (the West Indian male workers constituting an exception). A second shibboleth concerns the operation of the British legal system, and we were interested to know whether our respondents accepted the view that all are equal before the law, especially given the fact that there is evidence available which suggests that the police discriminate against black migrants and, especially, young British-born blacks (e.g. Humphrey 1972; Pulle 1973; Demugh, 1978; Institute of Race Relations, 1979). No previous study has systematically attempted to relate this sort of data to arguments about class consciousness, with the possible exception of Goldthorpe *et al.* (1968, pp. 25–6). However, a Westergaard has noted (1970), Goldthorpe *et al.* play down the significance of their finding that 72 per cent of their working-class sample agreed with the statement that there is 'one law for the rich and another for the poor'. The rationale for asking questions about perceptions of police and legal practice lies with the possibility that this practice is seen to systematically favour one class in society

Hence, if it is believed that the police and legal system systematically discriminate in favour of 'the rich', we suggest that this implies not only a perception of a hierarchical class structure but also that the dominant class in that structure has life advantages which imply corresponding disadvantages for the working class. In short, such a belief is an indicator of class consciousness.

We asked the factory sample about the practice of both the police and the courts, in each case, beginning with a general question about police/legal practice which was followed by questions about their practice in relation to specific groups. Often the first question elicited responses relevant to either one or both of the two supplementary questions, but the data for all three questions for

Table 6.6 *'In carrying out their job, do the police treat everyone the same or do they treat some people differently from others?' (Factory sample)*

	English % (N=36)	West Indian % (N=36)	Total % (N=72)
Treat everyone the same	28 (10)	36 (13)	32 (23)
Treat some people differently	56 (20)	56 (20)	56 (40)
Depends on circumstances	11 (4)	—	5.5 (4)
Don't know	5 (2)	5 (2)	5 (4)
No answer	—	3 (1)	1.5 (1)

Table 6.7 *'Some people say that the police treat ordinary working people differently from rich people. What do you think?' (Factory sample)*

	English % (N=36)	West Indian % (N=36)	Total % (N=72)
Police favour rich people	58 (21)	58 (21)	58 (42)
Police favour working people	—	3 (1)	1.5 (1)
Depends on circumstances	—	3 (1)	1.5 (1)
Police treat all people the same	36 (13)	19 (7)	27.5 (20)
Don't know	6 (2)	14 (5)	10 (7)
No answer	—	3 (1)	1.5 (1)

both police and court practice is analysed separately for ease of practical presentation.

Table 6.6 shows that 56 per cent of the total sample believe that the police treat some people differently from others, a substantial minority volunteering the view that the rich receive much more favourable treatment when compared with 'us', the working class. There was no difference between the views of the English and West Indian workers on this, and the same applies to the responses to the second question (see Table 6.7), in reply to which 58 per cent of the sample reported that the police discriminate in favour of rich people. The following quotes are illustrative:

'It's the same in every walk of life. Money talks and it will always talk. There's a law for the rich and one for the poor.' (English male: factory sample)

'The working-class bloke would get a rougher treatment from the police than some rich bloke with his flashy car would. That bloke don't seem to worry. He probably just gives him a few quid to keep quiet. I think it's probably something like that that goes on.' (English male: factory sample)

'Well, most of the police have no choice really. I mean the majority of them are ordinary working men like myself, used to taking orders from the rich and I suppose it's difficult to approach someone in a Rolls Royce and say "Look, I think you have done so and so wrong" when you are used to this person telling you what to do. The rich will always be favoured more.' (West Indian male: factory sample)

'There is nothing in this world that money cannot buy and a rich man can afford to buy his freedom. Money is power and from the moment you can buy your freedom you can do anything.' (West Indian male: factory sample)

In all these responses there is a clear notion that those with money are able, by virtue of being rich, to 'purchase' favourable treatment from the police, the consequence of which is that there is 'one law for the rich and one for the poor'. As we shall see, the same picture is revealed by the questions on the practice of the courts.

The sample was then asked whether the police discriminate against black people and, by implication, in favour of whites. The sample was closely divided (Table 6.8) with 44.5 per cent expressing the view that whites receive preferential treatment and blacks are discriminated against, while 39 per cent said that both groups receive the same treatment. Moreover, there was almost no difference between the responses of the English and West Indian workers, although there was a small minority of English workers who claimed that it is West Indians who receive preferential treatment. For example:

> 'I think they are frightened of doing some things to a coloured person in case they shout racist. Like in this firm in my department, there is a coloured bloke who takes over one hour for his dinner and nothing is said to him. It's been pointed out to the foreman that someone else is having to do that man's job but the foreman's done nothing about it and we feel it's because he's coloured that the foreman's done nothing about it because he's frightened to. I think the police might be the same way.' (English male: factory sample)

Table 6.8 *'Some people feel that the police treat West Indian people differently from British people. What do you think?' (Factory sample)*

	English % (N=36)	West Indian % (N=36)	Total % (N=72)
Police favour English	42 (15)	47 (17)	44.5 (32)
Police favour West Indians	8 (3)	—	4 (3)
They treat everyone the same	39 (14)	39 (14)	39 (28)
Don't know	11 (4)	11 (4)	11 (8)
No answer	—	3 (1)	1.5 (1)

But there was a consensus among over 40 per cent of both black and white workers that the police discriminate against blacks:

> 'Well, white people get better treated than coloured people for one thing. People without criminal records are also far better treated than people with criminal records. I think the police have very strong opinions which they stick to. One is that white people are better than coloured people and they have you one side of the fence or the other.' (English male: factory sample)

> 'Well, I don't know about everywhere else but if a black bloke was walking down the road here in Harlesden and a couple of white blokes were coming the other way and one of them said

something to the black bloke and they developed an argument and punches were thrown, they would deal with the black bloke harder than they would the white blokes, even though there was two of them.' (West Indian male: factory sample)

Both English and West Indian workers supported this opinion by reference to their own personal experience or to the experience of their friends:

'They don't treat some of the people properly, especially coloured people. A friend and his father-in-law left work a couple of weeks ago and were on a bus stop waiting for a bus and a police officer came along and waited until they got on the bus, then took them off and accused them of loitering and he arrested them. These men had just left work and they showed the officer their pay packet to prove that they just came out of work that very minute but he wouldn't listen. In the end, the firm had to write to the police saying that the men had just left work but by that time it was too late and they are in court now. If the police carry on like that then you can't have any respect for them. People will carry a grudge against them over cases like that.' (West Indian male: factory sample)

'Well, I used to know a policeman in Reading and he was telling me that four of them were patrolling around the shopping centre one night and there was a coloured youth who came along and was causing a bit of trouble and apparently two of them just laid into him and started kicking him around. So I say it does happen.' (English male: factory sample)

A small majority of the English workers who said that blacks were discriminated against claimed that this was deserved because of their own behaviour:

'Well, in the few instances I've seen I would go along with that. They do take it out on them. But I must say a lot of the time it is them that is causing the trouble anyway.' (English male: factory sample)

But only one English worker was aware that 'mugging', supposedly a 'new' crime committed only or mainly by young blacks (Hall *et al.*, 1978), was not a new phenomenon requiring police attention:

'Well I think everyone who lives round here in this class will get it rough but they (i.e. West Indians) are getting some bad publicity now with this mugging thing. Our geezers used to do it and we called it rolling. They used to do it for the sake of doing it, not so much for the money. But that was never in the headlines. Now they really blow it up. If someone's found lying in the gutter he's been mugged but he could have fallen over. It's blown to pieces really, but they aren't doing anything new.' (English male: factory sample)

Although the proportions of English and West Indian workers who claimed that blacks were discriminated against were very similar, their emotional reactions were different. For many of the English workers, discrimination was reported in a matter-of-fact manner:

'I think they [i.e. the police] tend to discriminate against them [i.e. the coloureds]. The majority of people are prejudiced against coloured people and the police are no exception.' (English male: factory sample)

From a proportion of the West Indians we detected a sense of reluctance to believe that the police could behave in this way, but it was their own experience or the experience of family or close friends which was paramount in their forming the view that they were the subject of discrimination and that they had a reason to, as the West Indian quoted above said, 'carry a grudge'. A small proportion of West Indians said that young, British-born blacks were particularly vulnerable:

'To tell you the truth, I've never been involved with them. [i.e. the police] in any way but I think there are a lot of racialist policemen who pick on black people, especially the youths. Some of these youths, they can't help it. They have "A" levels, "O" levels, some of them are born here and it's their country so why should they do all the bum jobs that they are offering them. Us older men will do anything, cleaning the roads or toilets or things, but they don't want these jobs. They can't get the jobs they want and they walk about on the streets and the police pick on them.' (West Indian male: factory sample)

However, it would be incorrect to suggest that the resulting feelings of distrust and acrimony were common amongst all of the West Indians we interviewed. In the same way that many West Indians claimed that the police discriminated against them by reference to personal experience or to the experience of family and friends, others rejected this view also on the basis of personal experience, some adding that in so far as there was conflict between the police and black people it was due to the behaviour of blacks. For example:

> 'A lot of people say they treat black people different. But if you talk rude to the police, then you must expect punishment. The police have stopped me and asked me questions and I've answered them and they've let me go. But if I'd started saying what are you questioning me for, they would probably have bent my arm or beaten me up. One guy told me that he was carrying a ladder to a friend's at 2 a.m. and they stopped him and he didn't think they should have. Another person was carrying a suitcase in the early morning and they stopped him and asked what was in it so he didn't answer so they had to take him in.' (West Indian male: factory sample)

Thus, there was considerable diversity of opinion amongst the West Indians we interviewed, although there were slightly more who believed that they were the subject of discrimination than believed that they received the same treatment as the English. What was also apparent was that this was clearly an issue that was commonly discussed amongst West Indians and about which there was strong feeling on both sides. In so far as opinions were held and changed on the basis of personal experience or the experience of friends and family, then it only takes one negative incident to convince more West Indians that they receive different and unfair treatment at the hands of the police.

The pattern of response found in reply to questions on police practice was repeated in response to questions on the practice of the

Table 6.9 'Some people believe that in Britain everyone gets fair and equal treatment from the courts while others believe that the courts treat some people differently from others. What do you believe?' (Factory sample)

	English % (N=36)	West Indian % (N=36)	Total % (N=72)
Courts treat everyone the same	25 (9)	22 (8)	23.5 (17)
Courts treat some people differently	59 (21)	61 (22)	60 (43)
Depends	8 (3)	—	4 (3)
Don't know	8 (3)	17 (6)	12.5 (9)

courts: 60 per cent of the factory sample reported that the courts do treat some people differently from others (Table 6.9) and 64 per cent agreed that it was easier for a rich man to stay out of jail (Table 6.10). This was usually explained by reference to an ability to pay

Table 6.10 'Do you think that if a rich man breaks the law, he is just as likely to end up in jail, or do you think it's easier for a rich man to stay out of jail?' (Factory sample)

	English % (N=36)	West Indian % (N=36)	Total % (N=72)
Courts favour rich men	67 (24)	61 (22)	64 (46)
Courts favour working men	—	—	
Depends	3 (1)	6 (2)	4.5 (3)
Courts treat all the same	25 (9)	19 (7)	22 (16)
Don't know	5 (2)	14 (5)	9.5 (7)

for a good solicitor and barrister who would be able to put up a good defence, while the ordinary working man did not have the resources to purchase such a 'service'. Often implicit, and sometimes explicit, in these comments was a view that the law was not a sacred, universal code of right and wrong which was then fairly (or unfairly) applied, but was little more than a mundane text susceptible to unlimited manipulation. These views were equally common amongst both West Indian and English workers:

'No, I think the rich person is more in the position to wangle his way out of jail with all the top solicitors and people like that who know how to twist the law. The average man couldn't afford that kind of defence.' (English male: factory sample)

'I think money buys justice.' (English male: factory sample)

'Take John Stonehouse for instance. If he was a poor man he would get twenty-five years. Being as he's rich and well known, he only got seven years.' (West Indian male: factory sample)

'Well, I don't think they would try and put the rich man straight to jail but they would throw the poor man straight in. They always respect the rich man because the rich man could buy them.' (West Indian male: factory sample)

A somewhat different interpretation of differential treatment by the legal system was provided by a minority of West Indian although money remained a key element:

'Well, a rich and influential man can pay for his crime with money. The poor man has to go to prison. When he comes out he's had it because no one wants to know him. He can't even get a job. The rich man pays cash and it's all over.' (West Indian male: factory sample)

'You have two choices: usually you go to prison or you pay. If you are rich you pay. If you are poor and cannot pay, you go to prison.' (West Indian male: factory sample)

Finally, the factory sample was asked whether it was easier for a Englishman to stay out of jail when compared with a West Indian This question did produce a clear difference of opinion between ou English and West Indian respondents (see Table 6.11). A third o

Table 6.11 'Do you believe that if an English person breaks the law he is ju as likely to end up in jail as a West Indian or do you think it's easier for a English person to stay out of jail?' (Factory sample)

	English % (N=36)	West Indian % (N=36)	Tota % (N=72
Courts favour English person	25 (9)	42 (15)	33.5 (24
Courts favour West Indians	20 (7)	—	10 (7
Depends	11 (4)	3 (1)	7 (5
Courts treat all the same	33 (12)	33 (12)	33 (24
Don't know	11 (4)	22 (8)	16.5 (12

both groups said that the courts treat everyone the same way, but 4 per cent of the West Indians, compared with 25 per cent of th English workers, stated that the courts favour the Englishman an discriminate against West Indians:

'We have no chance. They don't even listen to the case in the Magistrates Courts. They fall asleep and then they wake up and sentence you. That's why they won't get a lot of coloureds joinin the force because it's not fair to them.' (West Indian male: factor sample)

'I would think that they treat them worse than they would the English because they don't like them. It's an Englishman's country and they have come over here and all the English are moving out. They've taken over the country. That's why they are not liked.' (English male: factory sample)

Of the West Indians who claimed that the courts discriminate against them, not all directly referred to racism as the explanation, although this may have been implicit in some of the references to their inability to explain themselves to the judiciary:

' A lot of black people get done for things they don't do. A lot of us can't explain themselves out of some situation. Up in the witness box you just turn into a fool and they either fine you or send you to jail.' (West Indian male: factory sample)

'Well, maybe they don't understand them properly and they don't give them a chance to explain themselves. Sometimes they may not answer the question, so they can't answer because they don't understand it, but the judge or magistrate would say they are rude.' (West Indian male: factory sample)

Other West Indians explained discrimination by the courts in terms of their ignorance of their rights:

'I think that they [i.e. West Indians] stand more chance of going to jail because some of them really don't know their rights: some of them are not really interested.' (West Indian male: factory sample)

Thus, our West Indian workers do not necessarily or directly explain their perceived disadvantage in terms of racism. Indeed, a small minority said that West Indians brought trouble on themselves as a consequence of their own behaviour:

'Well, I think they treat themselves as if they are being picked on and then they rake against the police who make a statement, pass it on to the solicitor and it comes back on them.' (West Indian male: factory sample)

Racism was clearly apparent, however, in the responses of that 20 per cent of the English sample who claimed that the courts discriminate in favour of West Indians and against the English:

'Well, I think the English people in this country are frightened of what they say to them because straight away they are in trouble with the courts. Even in the court you have to be careful. They have this Race Relations Act done and it's like an angel on the black man's back all the time so he can't ever do any wrong which is wrong.' (English male: factory sample)

'Well, the Sikhs have just had his helmet law reversed and they can now go about on bikes with their turbans. I think that's wrong. I don't think it could be called religious grounds. I think it's just a case of "Right, we'll let them off this and perhaps they will be a bit more cooperative in other respects." In some cases they probably get an easier deal in the courts simply because they don't want to cause a riot.' (English male: factory sample)

We have more to say about this response in chapter 7.

In sum, there is unambiguous evidence here that the majority of our factory sample holds the view that the upper class receives preferential treatment from the police and courts, with the consequence that they (the working class) are disadvantaged. Money again figures as an important element in their explanation for the picture that they present: this time, money is seen to buy 'justice'. But, in addition, we have evidence of another form of racist response from the English workers and of an awareness on the part of West Indians that they constitute an excluded racial category in addition to being disadvantaged as a result of being working class.

Perceptions of private property

Moorhouse and Chamberlain (1974) have drawn attention to the lack of interest shown by social scientists in working-class attitudes to private property. Such neglect by those interested in class consciousness is difficult to comprehend given both the subjective and objective importance attached to property in the establishment of class relations. For the purpose of comparability with their data, we adopted two questions used in their own study of such attitudes. They were asked only of the residential sample. The first concerned the utilisation of private property: 'Do you think that homeless families should be allowed to squat in empty houses?' This question was not identical to that asked by Moorhouse and Chamberlain because we introduced the term 'squat'. We did this because at the time of our interviewing, the media was portraying squatting (particularly in North London) in an unfavourable manner. We were interested to see how often our respondents articulated the media image of the rent-evading squatters who moved into the 'family' home while the occupants were on holiday.

In fact, the majority of our respondents not only rejected the 'updated' image of squatting but also the basic principle of the sanctity of private property:

'I would say yes. Just around this one area I could show you about six or seven houses that have been empty for at least one year or more. That's a waste of money and someone should be living in them. So why shouldn't they squat? I think they should take them over and use them.' (West Indian male: residential sample)

'If it's empty for so long, why not occupy it? Why is it empty for so long?' (English male: residential sample)

'Well, the houses down there are all pulled down now but before they were pulled down they were quite nice but standing empty. Well, I can understand them moving in. I mean, they want somewhere to live and it must make them feel desperate. I think I would do the same thing if I was homeless and there are places standing empty which were habitable.' (English female: residential sample)

'Yes, why not, if you can't get, you have to take. I don't blame them at all ... if I didn't have mine I would go and squat myself. The council buys these houses and lets them go derelict.' (West Indian female: residential sample)

About three-quarters of the West Indians in our sample approved of squatting, although nearly half made reservations such as exhausting all possible channels to find a home first and being prepared to pay rent. A slightly higher proportion of the English, nearly a third, were opposed to squatting in principle:

'I don't think anyone should be allowed to squat in empty houses. It is someone's property.' (English male: residential sample)

The level of support for squatting would appear to confirm the conclusion drawn by Moorhouse and Chamberlain (who identified similar levels of support in their study) that the majority of our respondents approve of action which defies the sanctity of property but which meets a basic need (1974, p. 394). Very few of our respondents had not, at some point, experienced real hardship in finding somewhere to live and the continuing housing shortage in Brent provides a very obvious material basis for the level of support for squatting.

However, when we asked our respondents about the ownership of private property, we found an overwhelming acceptance of the market principle. We put the following question: 'Some people say that until everyone has a home to live in, no one should be allowed to have more than one home. What do you think?' Moorhouse and Chamberlain found a majority supporting this statement and concluded that their responses indicated a belief that the ownership of property should be allocated according to need and not money and were therefore rejecting the market principle. We found a majority of both the English and West Indians disagreeing with the statement: over 50 per cent of West Indian men and 60 per cent of West Indian women and English men believed that 'people should be allowed to do whatever they want with their money'. The following quotes are illustrative:

> 'Now we're talking about communism, aren't we? At one time I would have said yes, but now no. When everybody starts to have everything equally then you get some lazy bastards.' (West Indian male: residential sample)

> 'That's hard to answer because the man who didn't have the house might have been on the dole for the last four or five years and didn't want to work while the man with more than one house started off in the same position and worked for all he's got. So who's to say that he doesn't deserve all he's got. It's how they get it, not the fact that they have got it. Some people who have three or four houses might seem ridiculous but if they worked hard for it then they deserve it. And unless you are going to go into the commune situation and share everything out then you can't really touch them at all.' (English male: residential sample)

> 'You could have as many as you want as long as you've got the money.' (West Indian female: residential sample)

Nearly half of those expressing this view went on to qualify it by saying that anyone owning more than one house would be renting out the 'extra' property and therefore providing accommodation for someone else:

> 'If a person can afford more than one home, he can only live in one so he must be doing something for the other people because he lets it to somebody else and he's helping the situation, isn't he? So, if he's helping the situation I don't see why he shouldn't have twenty houses.' (West Indian male: residential sample)

> 'Well, I think if someone wants to buy six homes and he can afford to do so, then he should. He can't occupy the whole six so therefore he will be helping someone to get a house.' (West Indian female: residential sample)

It is possible to suggest an explanation for the 'internal contradiction' in our respondents' replies, but less easy to explain the discrepancy between our findings and those of Moorhouse and Chamberlain. Concerning the latter, it could be argued that, because over half of our West Indian respondents and a proportion of our English respondents were owner-occupiers, they would be less likely to reject bourgeois values concerning the ownership of private property than would Moorhouse and Chamberlain's sample of council tenants. But this is not the case. First, there is no obvious difference in the answers of our owner-occupiers as compared to council tenants. Second, one cannot automatically assume that our West Indian owner-occupiers will demonstrate beliefs as a consequence of such ownership because, for the majority of them, they had little choice other than to buy rather than rent.

One way of explaining the contradiction between their attitudes towards ownership as opposed to the use of property follows from the view that they are materially based, i.e. they are ideological constructs based on their immediate (and therefore limited) experience. This is clearly important in connection with their attitudes to squatting: approval of squatting derived from their own experience of the difficulty of obtaining accommodation. As far as the ownership of property was concerned, what they perceived (either in themselves, or in others around them), was the 'hard-working man' who had earned enough to buy a house(s) and this legitimated ownership. Private property was not conceived of in terms of inheritance or speculation. But if the 'hard-working man' was willing to allow his property to 'stand idle' then homeless families were quite justified in squatting because they were homeless and the owner was not making available accommodation for others.

This data therefore illustrates the lack of consistency in our respondents' consciousness: the majority reject bourgeois values about the use of private property but support them on the matter of the ownership of private property. However, in so far as their support is based on the view that 'people should be allowed to do whatever they want with their money', that support is somewhat tenuous because of, in many cases, their limited earning capacity and job insecurity.

Perception of an alternative society

Mann has argued that there is no appraisal amongst the manual working class of an alternative society and that this absence is the most important factor in preventing the political consciousness of the working class attaining a fully revolutionary form (1973, p. 69). Moorhouse and Chamberlain have challenged this view by presenting evidence that sections of the working class do hold to an alternative principle for the organisation of society (1974, p. 399). The dispute would seem to be an empirical one, but we believe there to be underlying conceptual problems which are unresolved because they are unacknowledged. These follow in part from the fact that Mann says very little about this dimension of class consciousness and does not break it down into what can be identified as its constituent parts. As we shall show, Moorhouse and Chamberlain have produced evidence only with respect to one of these parts. We suggest that a conception of an alternative society involves the following beliefs:

(1) that capitalist society should be replaced by an alternative (socialist) society (i.e. a belief in an alternative principle for social organisation);

(2) that this alternative society is realisable;

(3) that the individual can participate in the realisation of this alternative.

We asked our samples a series of questions which have produced evidence relevant to all three of these parts.

At the end of the interview, the respondents in the factory sample were asked whether they were happy with the way things were in Britain or whether they would like to see changes made, while just over three-quarters of the residential sample were asked 'Would you like to see any big changes in the way things are run in this country?'. Over three-quarters of those asked these questions in both samples (86 per cent in the case of the factory sample) said that they would like to see changes. The sort of changes desired were usually mentioned spontaneously by the men in the factory, but where they were not, the respondent was specifically asked. Apart from the fact that a quarter of the residential sample said that they did not know what changes they would like to see, the pattern of response (shown in Table 6.12) was very similar for both samples and so the data is analysed together.

First, the vast majority of those desiring change do not describe or discuss this desired change in terms of an alternative society or revolution. With the exception of the two individuals who are members of revolutionary parties in the factory sample and one West Indian man in the residential sample, all of our respondents spoke about change in terms of altering specific disliked features of Britain, most being of a material kind (e.g. reducing the cost of

Table 6.12 Desired economic and social changes in Britain

	English		West Indian	
	Factory % (N=36)	Residential % (N=31)	Factory % (N=36)	Residential % (N=31)
Stop immigration/ repatriation	36 (13)	32 (10)	—	—
Reduce cost of living (prices, inflation)	17 (6)	6 (2)	36 (13)	23 (7)
More jobs/end unemployment	11 (4)	3 (1)	36 (13)	13 (4)
Build more houses/ improve housing	14 (5)	—	22 (8)	3 (1)
End racialism	3 (1)	—	11 (4)	—
Reduce taxation	6 (2)	—	9 (3)	16 (5)
Stop abuse of State benefits	3 (1)	3 (1)	9 (3)	10 (3)
Stronger government/or coalition	9 (3)	16 (5)	—	—
Revolutionary change or Socialism	6 (2)	—	—	3 (1)
Other	31 (11)	19 (6)	22 (8)	16 (5)
Don't know	—	23 (7)	—	26 (8)

Note Columns total more than 100 per cent because several respondents mentioned more than one aspect of desired change

living, providing more jobs). It is, of course, arguable that the sort of changes envisaged by our respondents are not in fact realisable without a revolutionary transition but our data suggests that this fact is not apparently lodged in the consciousness of the workers we interviewed. Our point is that, when invited to conceive of changes to contemporary capitalism, hardly any of our respondents replied in terms which suggested an explicit desire for an alternative form of social organisation. Indeed, many conceived of change without reference to either capitalism or socialism.

Second, the most common desired change mentioned by the

English respondents was an end to black immigration and/or repatriation of black people:

'I think I'd like to see some more equality and a better relationship within ourselves. I think it's about time this country started to look after itself and forgot the other countries. We can't keep paying for crimes committed in other countries. Like these coloured people: they come and they say "You made us slaves". What I say to that is "How the hell could I because I wasn't even alive". I think they should start to look after today and forget about yesterday. I mean, Amin throws them out and we take them in because they have a piece of paper which says they have a British passport. I think it's ridiculous.' (English male: factory sample)

'I think we let too many immigrants into the country to start off with. What we have here can stop but we shouldn't let any more in. That's the only sore problem I have about England at the moment. I've lived here all my life and I can't get anywhere to live, yet they fly half-way round the world and land at Heathrow and get somewhere.' (English male: factory sample)

'One thing that bugs me is the coloureds. I think they have to do something because there's going to be trouble as there has been recently. Enoch Powell knows the problem but he seems to be the only one. Close the door before any more comes in, that's one thing. Try and get them out of the country because I'm sure we can survive without them ... I think Britain's still great but they fall down on this colour thing.' (English male: factory sample)

'Kick the wogs out and there would be more room for the whites.' (English female: residential sample)

We shall have more to say about this form of response in the following chapter so we will only mention here that the most commonly stated change desired by the English workers was a racist one, although it was not without its material dimension, at least in so far as some of the workers themselves were concerned:

'I don't like all these immigrants coming over. There are just too many. I don't mind a few and I get on well with some of them but it's like the white man in Africa. The black man out there would say I like the white people but they are in my country. I'm not prejudiced at all. I like them but they are in my country taking something from me.' (English male: factory sample)

'Don't let any more in and send the trouble-makers away. I

mean, how many of them are in the nick, how much are we paying for them to stay there and then they'll come out and start all over again.' (English female: residential sample)

Third, whereas over a third of the English workers conceived of change in racist terms, most of the West Indian workers conceived of change in the material sense of a reduction in the cost of living, in the provision of more jobs and of reduced taxation:

'Well, there are quite a few changes I would like to see. Mainly like employment (more jobs), the rates, fares, petrol price, road tax and all these food prices. Everything.' (West Indian male: factory sample)

'I would like to see changes. Wages, prices and some houses for the people to live in. They need jobs too. Control the prices: the people are being robbed. I don't want to see Britain become a communist country.' (West Indian male: factory sample)

'Yes, there should be more money in the wage packet of the working population and they should be taxed less. More money in the wage packet is the main thing. At least give us a bit of freedom.' (West Indian female: residential sample)

'Get the inflation down, stop taking too much tax from people. You go to work because you have to nowadays and they take so much out of our wages that you don't have enough left to run a house and family. If inflation were down and they froze the prices, then I think things would be a little better.' (West Indian female: residential sample)

These changes were also desired by the English workers but the proportion mentioning them was much smaller. In sum, our West Indian workers' desired changes were predominantly and directly expressed as materialistic whereas the dominant single desire (although the desire of a minority) amongst the English workers was to stop all further immigration of black workers, many of them adding that they believed this to be a means of improving their own material circumstances.

Fourth, there was an expression of opposition to racist practice, mainly from the West Indian workers, although from only a small minority (all of whom were in the factory sample):

'I would like to see the economic situation in this country better. And I would like to see black and white get the same treatment. I think everyone should work together for the good of the country and if the government had stricter laws on the police and harassment of black people I think everyone would work together more.' (West Indian male: factory sample)

'I would like to see black people in this country get a better treatment because back home we treat the white people with respect and we try to help them but the treatment we get here makes me wonder. Also, these black youths can't get jobs. I know some of them don't want to work because they are rude but there are others who want to work and they can't work. Some take one black and judge the whole black race by that person. They say dirty or smelly but we aren't all the same. I know some white people who are the nastiest and filthiest thing you have. I've shared a multi-racial house so I know how some of them live. There's a lot of changes that I'd like to see.' (West Indian male: factory sample)

Given the extent of racial discrimination (Smith, 1977), it may come as a surprise that only a small proportion of West Indian workers refer to it in the context of their perception of a 'better society', even though references to racial discrimination were evident in responses to other questions as we shall show in chapter 7. But, as we have already pointed out, the level of awareness of discrimination would seem to be much lower than its extent. Moreover, as again we shall see in chapter 7, even if racial discrimination is recognised as an important element of the black experience in England, the fact that it is sometimes perceived not to affect the respondent but only other black workers may absolve some (our sample does not allow us to be more specific about how many) West Indians from expressing concern about it.

Fifth, our West Indians were more concerned than the English about the abuse of state benefits:

'One of the things is the services that we get. I think people should pay for them. People wouldn't mind paying money when they know where it's going but now what does all the tax that we pay go on? The national health services and the rates. People wouldn't mind paying if they can see what they pay for. Are the right people getting cared for by the social services? So many people don't bother to take care of themselves because they know they can just throw themselves at the mercy of the social security and they will take care of them.' (West Indian male: residential sample)

'Well, the only thing I feel that's wrong is so many people not working. I think they should have enough work to give them. Also, they should make the ones that don't want to work go out to work because the ones that are working pay for the ones that don't want to work. The government should build more factories and give them work to do, then the tax would be less.' (West Indian male: factory sample)

Set against this difference is the proportion of English respondents in both samples who want stronger government, a coalition government or some form of constitutional change:

'Yes, when you have the Conservatives in power they stand for wealth and privilege in the House and the socialists try to soak the rich which you can't do because rich people put money into the country and they give employment. So, I would like to see some sort of coalition government at the moment.' (English female: residential sample)

'I would like to see the abolition of all political parties. I would like people just to stop thinking about their particular party for a while and just think about Britain so that we can straighten the whole thing out. I don't think there is room for all this nonsense about Labour, Conservative, Liberals and all the rest of it. I don't think we need a coalition either. I just think we need the best brains of everyone in the country to do the job. It's as simple as that. Why do we have to have parties?' (English male: residential sample)

'I don't think the government are decisive enough and I think this is what's wrong at the moment. I don't think the industry is progressive enough either. I wouldn't mind working harder for a better standard of living. Look at West Germany: they've progressed since the war. We haven't.' (English male: factory sample)

Put together, a belief in strong government, reduced taxes and the prevention of the abuse of state benefits might be said to constitute part of specific Conservative ideology. There was little evidence of this being the case in either sample: these particular beliefs were always articulated with a number of others, with rarely any logical relationship between them.

Finally, following on from this last comment, there was no clear majority opinion in favour of any single (reformist) change. The question seemed to produce a vague miscellany of desired changes, evident also in Table 6.12, in the 'other' category which included reference to a stronger incentive to work, an end to nationalisation and an improvement in the conditions of old age pensioners. There was certainly no clear and passionate vision of a future radically different from that of today. This inchoateness increases the significance of the unanimity about a desired future that did exist in our samples, notably the racist desires of the English workers and the materialist desires of the West Indians.

But is it possible to explain this vagueness and inchoateness by reference to a belief that there is no expectation of change in Britain: why work out a vision of the future if change is not seen as a practical possibility? When asked whether they thought that things would change or that they would stay as they are, 54 per cent of the factory sample said that they expected things to change, while 34.5 per cent had no expectation of change. However, there was much greater optimism about the possibility of change amongst the West Indian workers: 67 per cent said they expected things to change compared to 39 per cent of the English workers. Thus, although it was scarcely a majority view, changes were foreseen (albeit reformist in nature), but the West Indian workers were far more optimistic than the English.

This limited optimism has to be viewed in the context of how these changes are foreseen to occur, and particularly whether the individual himself expects to be able to participate in bringing them about. A majority of the West Indian workers believed that government action was the crucial factor in bringing about the changes that they desired:

'Governmental again. I think they have to do something about it.' (West Indian male: factory sample)

'The main problem that we have is inflation. That is what I think the government have to work on. It's their responsibility.' (West Indian male: factory sample)

'I think if the government puts some pressure on all these things they will get by. It will take some time, maybe years, but they will get by.' (West Indian male: factory sample)

While the residential sample were not asked whether they thought changes would occur or how they would come about, it was evident from the responses to the previous question that many West Indians believed that government was the initiator of change.

This view is consistent with the earlier finding that the West Indian workers are more likely to believe that government has the power to determine events, compared with big business and the trade unions. Most of the remainder of the West Indian workers expressed uncertainty about how the changes would come about. For them 'something' would or must happen:

'I've got no idea but it's got to be done somehow.' (West Indian male: factory sample)

'It is changing. It's changing all the time.' (West Indian male: factory sample)

'We can't stay at this level. Things will be better in times to come.' (West Indian male: factory sample)

A somewhat similar pattern of response was found amongst the English workers who believed in the possibility of change, although the proportion referring to the government as the initiator of change was much smaller. Other sources of change were mentioned:

'I think if all the parties were thrown out and there was some new thinking put into the country, there might be a hell of a lot of difference. If they could get all the economists and the rest of the experts together. It's very unlikely because it would have to be done under a coalition government. It always takes a war to sort things out.' (English male: factory sample)

'Certainly being honest and treating my neighbours right. If everyone did that the whole world would change.' (English male: factory sample)

'It's just going to carry on until something forces us I think. When a man can't afford to buy a pint of beer or have his smokes then something might happen. The trouble is the ordinary man couldn't cope with it.' (English male: factory sample)

The same type of response was articulated spontaneously in the residential sample.

What was clearly implicit in most of these responses was that the respondents did not see themselves as the initiators of change. For the majority, change was the responsibility of 'them' (usually the government, especially in the case of the West Indians) or 'something'. This was confirmed as a result of asking the factory sample whether they believed that they could help to change things. Only 15 per cent said that they believed that they could, including the two Englishmen who were politically active as members of revolutionary organisations. The vast majority (79 per cent) said that they could do nothing to help change things:

'No, I don't think that what I have to say would make any

difference. People would probably say I was a bloody idiot. I don't think there is anything I could do. I'm not a big enough person anyway. You have to be big and have some influence to get something done.' (English male: factory sample)

'What can I do. I'm only a little cog in the machine.' (English male: factory sample)

'At the present time and the position I am in, I can't do anything. If I tried now I would be called a rebel.' (West Indian male: factory sample)

'I doubt it but if we have some good leaders to push for things that we need, we might achieve something.' (West Indian male: factory sample)

As these responses suggest, many of the answers to this question revealed again a sense of powerlessness and belief that the power to influence events lay with the 'big men'. There was little difference between our English and West Indian workers in their response to this question. Of those who said that they did believe that they could do something to bring about change, only a few of the West Indians had any specific proposals or ideas for action, all of which were very specific and localised:

'Start with your local community. In Harlesden here we could form some sort of community organisation to deal with taxes and also do something to the kids in the area, find somewhere for them to go at night. That means white as well as black.' (West Indian male: factory sample)

'The only thing that I could do is to try and tell my friends to live better with the people around them. That's all.' (West Indian male: factory sample)

In sum, as we expected, there is very little evidence that our sample possessed a vision of an alternative society, a major dimension of revolutionary class consciousness. This is not to say that there was general satisfaction with the existing economic and social arrangements in England. Rather, the opposite was the case, but the desired changes referred to were not discussed in terms of a revolutionary transformation of capitalism. For both English and West Indian respondents there was no majority opinion in favour of any single change, although a third of the former wanted an end to the immigration of black workers to England, or their repatriation, while a third of the latter wanted material changes in the form of an end to inflation and unemployment. Just about half of the factory sample did believe that changes were possible (this view being most common amongst the West Indian workers), although most saw them as being the responsibility of the existing government or as arising from processes of which they had no real conception. In other words, despite a perception of class inequality, what was viewed as realisable was a reformed capitalism, although this was not expressed in these terms. Finally, despite there being a greater proportion of West Indians who believed that change was possible, an almost equal and very large proportion of both English and West Indian workers believed that they could do nothing themselves to bring about change.

Discussion

We believe that the data presented in this chapter demonstrates, first, that the political consciousness of between 60 and 75 per cent of our working class sample contains ideas which are central to the constitution of class consciousness and, second, that with certain exceptions this is true for both our English and West Indian respondents.

Concerning the first, and returning to our definition of class consciousness, the factory sample data showed a majority believing in the existence of a class society and identifying itself as working class. These beliefs were defined as parameters of restricted class consciousness. Additionally, data from both of the samples demonstrated a majority belief that the power to determine decisions and events certainly did not lie with the working class, although there was no single consensus on where power did lie. 'Big business' and the trade unions were commonly mentioned as the loci of decision-making (the former more often than the latter) but so was the government by one group in the sample (to be discussed below). Implicit here was a notion of collective disadvantage: 'they' have the power to make 'the important decisions' while 'we' have little or no influence. In so far as government was not seen to take such decisions, there was a rejection of the grounds upon which bourgeois democracy defends itself. A feeling of collective disadvantage was also clearly evident in the responses to the questions on police and court practice: a majority of the factory sample believed that the 'rich' receive favourable treatment from both the police and the courts. Finally, there was no consistent endorsement of the rights that supposedly accrue to those who own private property: a majority of the residential sample believed that squatters had a right to live in someone else's property if it was empty.

Much of the perceived advantage of the ruling/rich/big business class (and hence the corresponding disadvantage of the working class) was seen to be related to money. Class itself was generally seen to be measured by money (often being given concrete expression in the rich/poor dichotomy), and those that had money were seen to have the greatest power. Money was also perceived to buy 'justice'. This leads us to suggest that the cash nexus is important not only in the context of selling labour for a wage (Westergaard, 1970) but also in structuring the nature of the political consciousness of the working class. Not only does the cash nexus bind the worker to his or her employer but it also serves to structure his or her perception of the class structure and the advantages and disadvantages that accrue to the 'rich' and to the working class respectively. That this is so should not be surprising given that it is the sale of labour power that ensures a livelihood through receipt of a money wage, and given that a livelihood is actually obtained by exchanging that money for the commodities that both actually are (e.g. food, shelter) and are perceived to be (e.g. washing machine, wallpaper) essential to the maintenance and reproduction of life. In other words, given that capitalism distinctly expresses itself as a mode of production through the commodity form and given that commodities are exchanged by means of money, a conception of social structure which is expressed in terms of money can be seen not as an alternative to class consciousness but as its supreme (although simplistic) expression. Thus, in so far as a direct experience is but a source of workers' class consciousness, money is an important medium for the expression of class relations. This is the most important reason why a majority of our working-class sample (*both English and West Indian*) express almost all the elements that define the existence of restricted class consciousness.

We say 'almost all' because we have not shown that the collective interests that derive from the perceived material and social disadvantages of being working class are acknowledged to give rise to a need for collective organisation and action. Such a need is recognised in the context of work, as chapter 5 has shown, but we could find little evidence of such recognition outside of this context. This is probably to be explained by the sense of powerlessness that was revealed by our questions on the exercise of power and, indeed, is consistent with our finding that, although a majority of our respondents desired economic and social change, an even larger majority believed that they could do nothing themselves to bring change about. (Taken together with the fact that the majority of our respondents had no conception of an alternative society, it is clear that it is the absence of a recognition of the need for collective action that is an ideological barrier both to the expression through action of restricted class consciousness and to the development of a radical class consciousness.) But it must be added that this does not completely preclude the development of a radical class consciousness expressed through action. The economic and political context (as well as political consciousness) are crucial factors in the determination of political action and, as Westergaard (1970) has noted in connection with working-class beliefs about work and trade unions, the cash nexus constitutes a brittle binding force.

We must add in this connection that this is not the only source of political consciousness because not all of our respondents exhibited class consciousness, while those that did often also held contradictory beliefs too (this point is taken up in a specific way in the next chapter). Indeed, our questions on private property revealed a majority supporting one aspect of the sanctity of the ownership of private property: the individualism that is evident in the view that people, especially hard-working people, 'should be allowed to do whatever they want with their money' is just one instance of dominant beliefs being reproduced within the working class.

Finally, there was not complete unanimity between our English and West Indian respondents. Certainly amongst the West Indian men we interviewed (this is less true for West Indian women) there was greater faith in the ability of the government to actually take 'the important decisions' and to be the initiator of economic and social change. Moreover, they were more likely to be optimistic about the possibility of change. In addition, and it is to this that we now turn in some detail in the next chapter, some of our data suggests that racism is an important element in the political consciousness of our English respondents and that at least some of our West Indian respondents were aware of their being racially categorised.

CHAPTER 7

Class consciousness, racism and racial consciousness

So far we have established the existence of important continuities as well as discontinuities in the political consciousness of our white and black respondents and we have suggested that these continuities are explicable in terms of their common class position. However the fact that the working class is objectively internally stratified gives rise to the possibility that political consciousness will contain references to 'race': in the case of English workers this is likely to take the form of racism, while in the case of West Indian workers, as we have already suggested, these elements are likely to reflect their position as a racially excluded class fraction.

In presenting our data relevant to these aspects of political consciousness, it is important to recognise that we did not locate the research in a 'race relations' problematic, and so did not ask 'race relations' questions (although the factory sample were asked whether they believed that the police and courts discriminate against black people). Our interviews were specifically designed to allow, *inter alia*, the respondent to define his or her view as to what were his or her own experienced problems or perceived problems at both a local and national level. We anticipated that such questions would elicit references to racism and racial discrimination from at least some of our black respondents. What we did not anticipate was the extent of deeply held racist beliefs expressed by our white respondents in answer to such questions.

Our task, in this chapter, is therefore not an easy one because we are forced to consider the dialectical relationship between class consciousness and racism on the one hand and racial consciousness on the other. This is not an easy task and our analysis is offered extremely tentatively, because we know of no British study which has touched on the topic (for the US see Leggett, 1968) and because our data largely comprises spontaneous responses to questions designed to elicit information on other topics.

In order to give some structure to our analysis, we will therefore examine first the responses to questions which elicited the highest level of racist responses from our white respondents and the responses of our black respondents to the same questions. We will go on to discuss why we believe racist beliefs can co-exist with elements of class consciousness. Second, we will examine the nature and extent of racial consciousness among our black workers and the degree to which such consciousness can co-exist with or preclude the development of class consciousness. Finally we will attempt to draw some conclusions on the relationship between these two areas.

Perceptions of socio-economic decline among the English and West Indian working class

In relation to our first aim we will consider the answers of all our respondents to four questions which relate to their perceptions of socio-economic decline.

The first of these questions asked the respondents what they saw as the local problems facing ordinary people in the area. Over a third of our English men and women articulated the belief that the 'coloureds' or 'Asians' were *the* local problem:

'It's just the wogs isn't it?' (English female: residential sample)

'Immigration, they are putting too many into this area. I'd like to see some of them moved to the new towns. They put them all in the industrial areas like Park Royal and that causes discrimination. Look in the playground and you can count the white kids on your hands and that's what causes the bad feeling.' (English male: residential sample)

'Too many coloureds.' (English male: residential sample)

A further third of the residential sample believed 'mugging' to be a local problem, some explicitly identifying 'muggers' as black people.

A further quarter of the English men and women referred to the scarcity or inadequacy of housing and 17 per cent to the lack of work. Other problems which were identified were inadequate social services, public transport and entertainment. Education and environmental problems were also identified as problems. These responses indicated an intense feeling of social and material disadvantage and decline, interlinked with hostility towards the presence of the 'coloureds'.

This raises the question as to whether our West Indian respondents perceived this hostility as a local problem. The short answer is no. Taking the two samples together, it is work, housing and inflation which are the most commonly perceived local problems among our West Indians. Having said this, 15 per cent of the residential sample did identify racism and racial discrimination as problems as the following extracts show:

'I went for a job some time ago at an agency and the girl told me I would definitely get the job because I was just the sort of person they were looking for. When I went for the interview they took one look at me and said it was a mistake, the job should have been advertised for internal personnel only, and the position had been filled. Things like this happen to the black youths in the area all the time. They ring up for an appointment and as soon as they get to the place they are told the job has been taken. Yet if they ring up again through an agency for the same position it's still available. That's why so many black youths are out of work. I know they don't all want to work, but the ones that do find it almost impossible to do so.' (West Indian female: residential sample)

'All my worries presently in Harlesden is for my children. I mean if my son was walking down the road or at a bus stop and there was a mugging nearby, how could he explain to the police that he wanted to go because he wasn't one of them with the relationship we have here between the police and the black youth. The police will say "they all look alike", they always say that. I would like people to tell my children apart from others because of their conduct. The hardest thing for these people is to prove their innocence.' (West Indian female: residential sample)

This is not to say that only 15 per cent of our West Indians perceived racism and racial discrimination as problems affecting black people. On the contrary, we will show in the next section that nearly half of our sample are aware of at least some aspect of the disadvantaged position of black migrants in Britain (though they may not express this view in a way which directly implicates themselves). What we are emphasising here is that in relation to local problems, the majority of West Indian respondents perceive housing, inflation and work as the most critical problems facing ordinary people in the area. The following extracts are illustrative:

'Jobs, at the moment it's very bad. I think I would find it difficult to find another job if I lost this one.' (West Indian female: residential sample)

'Getting work and housing.' (West Indian female: residential sam

'The high cost of living I think. I would like to see everyone get a reasonable wage. Prices keep rising, home expenditure and the cost of living keeps rising and your wage stays the same.' (West Indian male: residential sample).

'Well this area isn't much different from any other because the problem is widespread, but this area has definitely had it because of the decline of the industries. People are moving out all the time.' (West Indian male: residential sample).

What is perhaps most striking when reading the English, as compared to the West Indians', responses to this question, is the former's sense of loss, of being left behind in a decaying area which has been taken over by the 'coloureds'. This is obviously most strong in the residential sample because the majority of English respondents had been born in the Harlesden area and *had* witnessed the socio-economic decline of that area. They are in a sense too young to resign themselves to changes whose causes, in the main, they do not understand. What they do perceive is the change of colour of the faces that have replaced people they knew and grew up with. If, as we will show in the next chapter, you also feel powerless to manipulate in any meaningful way your present circumstances, through individual advancenent or collective political action, then a scapegoat is truly manna from heaven. When all else fails, blame the 'coloureds'.

In contrast our West Indians are migrants. While not all admit that this migration sprang from material reasons, it is clear from our data that material concerns are pre-eminent in understanding their continued residence in Britain. An improved standard of living and good prospects for their children are their major concerns. They are therefore very concerned when they see their standard of living increasingly eroded by rising prices, and threatened by job loss, and when their children's prospects are perceived to be undermined by racism and racial discrimination.

In addition to asking our respondents about local problems, we asked them specifically if they saw housing as a problem locally and what they saw as its reason. In the residential sample a third of the English identified the 'coloureds' or 'coloured immigrants' as the cause of the local housing problem, while only 17 per cent of the factory sample responded in this way. Thus taking the two samples together it is the failure to deal with the problem of scarcity in housing that emerges as the most commonly attributed explanation amongst the English. These explanations relate to shortage in itself, the shortage of decent housing and the failure to take action over empty houses in the area. The latter explanations characterised the majority of responses from the West Indians in the residential sample, but only 19 per cent in the factory. In fact nearly half the West Indians in the factory said that they did not think there was a housing problem or that they simply did not know of any. The marked differences between the two samples on this question emphasises the importance of housing, or more precisely, the lack of it, for the residents of the Harlesden area. Black and white residents face the same problem, they see themselves or others in the area denied the right to decent housing. But for a third of the English the denial of the right was not due to the failure of the council or private enterprise to build or rehabilitate houses, but to the 'coloured immigrants' who lived in houses that they believed 'the English' should be occupying.

This apparent injustice was, we believe, most widely articulated by English respondents in the residential sample because the majority were or had been involved in the bewildering struggle to gain decent housing from the council. That struggle centres around the waiting-list: thus all the respondents in the residential sample were asked if they thought the allocatory system for council housing was fair. Forty-two per cent of the English respondents articulated the belief that the 'coloureds' or 'Asians' got preference.

A report by the Working Party of Housing Directors (1976) indicates that the movement of 'ethnic minorities', particularly West Indians, into the public sector of housing is now much faster than in the past, and this is due mainly to the fact that they live in areas of 'housing stress' (p. 29). Nevertheless there is considerable evidence to show that black migrants remain relatively disadvantaged in the public housing sector when compared to the indigenous working class (Smith, 1978, p. 20; Parker and Dugmore, 1978, pp. 27–40). These may be the 'facts' of the situation, but to 42 per cent of the residential sample it is a 'fact' that these perceived competitors in the struggle for housing are deemed illegitimate, non-local, queue-jumping *and* black, as the following quotes illustrate:

'We would love to know how the Asians and West Indians get their housing because there is a definite bias in this community ... this Borough bends over backwards to help the blacks.' (English female: residential sample)

'My children have waited 15 years to see a bathroom and some hot water, but the coloureds, they're all right.' (English female: residential sample)

The majority of West Indians who expressed an opinion on the fairness of the allocatory system felt that it *was* fair, although three expressed similar objections to those made by their white counterparts:

'Well one thing I don't like is to see all the "Pakis" getting all the houses at the front of the queue when you've had all the English and the West Indian people waiting for a place for years, they say they are homeless but I think they have more money put away than I have. They are very crafty. The council says not more than 3 people in these flats but you go into an Asian flat and see how many of them are in there and everyone of them will be working. We suffer for them to have more.' (West Indian female: residential sample)

Two West Indian men expressed similar views:

'Well the white people get first preference, then mostly the Indians and we are almost in the last place.' (West Indian male: residential sample)

Unmarried mothers were also seen as being given unfair preference by two of our West Indian respondents.

Thus, in response to the questions on local problems and housing there is a basic similarity in the perceptions of our English and West Indian respondents, a perception of social and material disadvantage. But amongst at least a third of the English this perception is obscured by racist beliefs; specifically that the presence of black people in the area constitutes a problem and that black people take 'our' housing.

These discontinuities in perception which result from the intrusion of racist beliefs are markedly absent from the responses to the third question we wish to consider. We asked our respondents what they thought were the reasons for local unemployment and redundancies. The most frequent responses to this question amongst the English as a whole and the West Indian men in the factory was to admit complete ignorance of the reasons for local unemployment. This is possibly related to the fact that all were either engaged in wage labour or were not actively seeking work.

But the most common explanation amongst the English was the high cost of rates and rents locally (well publicised in the local paper), and amongst the West Indians it was a case of profitability and rising costs, with the government often taking the blame:

'I don't actually know but it could be that the government is pressuring the employers. Some of them have to pay too much overheads and they can't cope so the best thing for them to do is to close the place down. Some of these closures are definitely to do with the government. Then again you have the higher management with all their perks which helps to put the overheads up. They get company cars, they don't pay for petrol so they get everything free. But the ordinary worker has to pay for everything.' (West Indian male: residential sample)

What is apparently lacking for a large proportion of our respondents, particularly the English, is a source of local knowledge other than direct experience on this issue. The fact that the West Indians in the residential sample were more 'knowledgeable' may be partly explained by a number referring to such direct experience:

'My husband is redundant right now from GKN, they were losing money and the rates were too high.' (West Indian female: residential sample)

Finally we will consider the responses to a question on national unemployment. We asked our respondents to tell us whether they thought this was a problem and, if so, what they perceived to be the main reasons for it. The most popular response was to blame 'people who don't want to work' preferring to live off what they perceived to be generous state benefits. This constituted the response of a third of the English and West Indians in the factory and a quarter in the residential sample. The following quotes are illustrative:

'A lot of people don't want to go out to work because they feel it's not worth their while going to work when they can get the same or more money from the social security for staying home. They have no incentive to go out to work.' (West Indian male: residential sample)

'I think they've got to get out and get themselves jobs, because there are plenty going. The majority of them just don't want to work. If I was getting £30 a week off the dole I wouldn't go out to work.' (English female: residential sample)

A further 17 per cent of the English blamed unemployment on coloured immigration, 13 per cent of the English and West Indians mentioned profitability, and 9 per cent inflation.

If we compare the responses to the question on national unemployment with those on local unemployment, we find that the two frames of reference are reasonably distinct. When the question was posed at the local level our respondents seemed somewhat unwilling to hazard a guess at the reasons for unemployment unless they had some experience of the situation, or had possibly been reading the local paper. Neither source was likely to convey the message that the problems involved stemmed from the attitude of the workers, but to forces over which the latter had little control. In contrast, when the question was pitched at the national level it appeared to tap responses whose origin can possibly be traced to 'information' received from the national media rather than from local sources. This is further illustrated by the way 'coloured immigration' is mentioned as a reason for national, but not local, unemployment.

Working-class racism in declining centres of capitalist production

We believe that the responses to these four questions illustrate a basic continuity in belief between our English and West Indian respondents, but that this basic continuity is overlaid by racist beliefs among the English. We will first consider what we believe to be the source of this discontinuity. Taking the interviews with our English respondents as a whole (not just their responses to these four questions) we find that 75 per cent articulate some form of racist belief, although not one of our questions produced a majority of responses which can be labelled racist. What is in fact the case is that these racist beliefs and explanations are articulated alongside other types of explanations which are often as vague and inconsistent as the former, or, as we have seen, with self-professed ignorance. They reflect our respondents' individual and collective experience as well as messages mediated by the television and newspapers. It might be argued that if this is the case then all that is necessary to eliminate the articulation of racist beliefs is a systematic anti-racist campaign which both challenges the racist perspective and offers a competing interpretation of reality. We would like to agree, but cannot do so for the following reasons.

Firstly, to reiterate a previous argument (Phizacklea and Miles, 1979, pp. 97–8), we believe that the racist ideas expressed by our respondents are not simply an ideological 'hangover' from Britain's imperial past. The racial stereotypes which are a part of this inheritance (that black people are inferior, uncivilised etc.; the use of the word black to denote unclean and dirty) may serve as a foundation for racial categorisation and may, if necessary, be used as ultimate justifications for the expression of racist beliefs. We emphasise that they 'may' because such stereotypes were rarely articulated by our respondents. But the racist beliefs articulated by the English in our samples are more than this because they are grounded in the daily experience and the material realities of working-class life in an area experiencing both social and economic decline. The presence of black people provides an easy and immediate explanation for that decline and its attendant problems. If those racist beliefs are an attempt to understand and explain immediate daily experience, those who do not share this 'experience' cannot be expected to understand, as the following quote illustrates:

> 'They could have taken a few thousand of these coloured people that we've got into areas like Hampstead, the nice elite areas and let them see how we have to live among them. Politicians who bring them or allow them in never have to really mix with them; they don't see them in the way the working people do. And they don't have to work with them.' (English male: residential sample)

It is this sentiment that Enoch Powell, MP, recognised and used when he claimed to speak for the ordinary English man and woman whom, he argued, had the 'experience'. Thus if working-class racism is grounded in a material reality for our respondents, alternative explanations of socio-economic decline and material disadvantage will appear quite abstract and unreal.

Secondly, the 'racialisation' of British politics since 1945 (but particularly since the late 1960s) is of critical importance in those urban areas undergoing a process of socio-economic decline and containing black residents, because the speeches of Enoch Powell, MP, on immigration and the activities of the National Front can so easily be interpreted as legitimating those racist ideas which are an ideological product of material decline. Nor can the ambivalent postures of successive Labour and Conservative governments be ignored. Both parties are pledged to fighting racism but British immigration policy is (and becomes more so through each successive proposal) racist in both intent and effect. If governments proclaim 'coloured immigration' to be a problem, it is hardly surprising that racism remains a reality nationally.

These factors will work to severely undermine any ideological challenge to the racist perspective, and this leads us to a pessimistic conclusion about the persistence of racism as a feature of British culture, particularly in those areas undergoing socio-economic decline and which contain black residents. Thus if we maintain that racist beliefs are possibly an enduring feature of the political consciousness of our English respondents, we are also forced to consider the possibility that they provide the basis of support for right-wing (including nationalist) movements. The short answer to this is that they do for a small number of people for a short space of time as is evidenced by the high turnover in membership and fluctuating fortunes of the National Front party (see Walker, 1977; Taylor, 1979).

Nairn is probably right in arguing that there is a limit to the exploitability of racist sentiment focused on Britain's black population because 'England's Indians and West Indians can scarcely be identified with "the system" by which the majority feels obscurely oppressed' (1977, p. 276). This is implicitly evident in the political practice of the National Front: it uses racism as the means to obtain popular support, but then urges its members to deflect that hatred to the politicians who, in the words of our English male respondent, 'bring them in or allow them in'. It is also implicitly evident in the consciousness of the majority of our respondents whose racism we can describe as piecemeal. They see themselves as continually duped by politicians and, as Westergaard argues, 'see blacks singled out for a liberal concern from which they themselves have been long excluded' (1975, p. 406). As one young woman explained:

> 'People might say I'm prejudiced but I think that someone who has lived in this Borough for twenty-six years should be more entitled to get a house or flat than someone who has just come from Malawi or Uganda. Why should they get preference? Is it that the people who've lived here all their lives aren't good enough to have these places, I don't understand it. I don't feel that people like us have any control over anything. Not our children in schools, where we live, who we live with, where you want to work.' (English female: residential sample)

Her acute sense of social and material disadvantage and feelings of powerlessness to do anything about this situation are given a focus by what she perceives to be the privileged treatment of black people.

Class consciousness and racism

Only a radical class consciousness can provide a competing explanation of reality or an 'alternative' to a racist perspective. But the majority of our respondents exhibit 'only' the elements of what we have termed a restricted class consciousness, a consciousness which may be ridden with contradictions and which, like racism, is a product of both personal and collective experience and cultural transmission (Beynon, 1973). If we see both processes in this context then we can understand why racism can co-exist with a restricted class consciousness.

Firstly, viewed within the parameters of a restricted class consciousness, racist beliefs are not so much an aberration as a likely response to the current circumstances in which our respondents find themselves: they reflect the perception of disadvantage amongst 'us' who have to take the brunt of inflation, unemployment and the shortage of housing. In this way the 'coloureds' come to be seen as just another problem that has been hoisted upon a beleaguered working class by politicians who 'don't have to mix with them'.

Secondly, there is very little in the history of the British labour movement (bar a brief anti-racist campaign in 1976) to indicate that such beliefs are contradictory. The role of trade unionism in Britain is ultimately defensive: trade unions may extol the principles of the international brotherhood of the working class but as we have shown elsewhere (Miles and Phizacklea, 1977b) there is a long history of such principles being sacrificed in the defence of the *British* working class and British *capitalism* at particular conjunctures. Thirdly, such sacrifices are more easily justified if socialisation in a racist culture has taught you that these supposed potential competitors in the fight for scarce resources are innately inferior (see Lawrence, 1974, pp. 55–6).

Racist beliefs therefore provide a major source of discontinuity in the belief of our English, as compared to West Indian, respondents. But as we have emphasised, the racism of the majority of our respondents is piecemeal: the racist explanation for material disadvantage/decline is only one of a number of explanations which are often as vague and inconsistent as the former. Racist beliefs are one element, albeit an important one, of a wider and equally inchoate political consciousness. Our West Indians demonstrate equally disparate explanations drawing upon their own individual experiences as well as ideological messages mediated by the television and newspapers. But what is clear from their responses to the question on local problems is that only a small proportion of our West Indians perceive racism to be a 'problem' in the area. This raises the question as to how far a perception of racism and racial discrimination structures the overall political consciousness of our West Indian respondents.

Racial consciousness and the black working class

In chapters 1 and 2 we have argued a case for conceiving of black migrant labour as a racialised fraction of the working class because of its subordinate role in economic, political and ideological relations. We have also argued that in so far as this subordinate role is a function of racial categorisation and a supporting ideology of racism and of racial discrimination, it follows that those black workers who become conscious of their structural position are likely to assess this position in racial terms, although simultaneously rejecting or even reversing the negative evaluation implicit in racism and racial discrimination.

Identifying the nature and extent of racial consciousness is not an easy task and our own analysis is offered tentatively, rather than with certainty, because there is little extant British research on this topic. In part the problem is methodological because, as we have already emphasised, we did not ask any of our respondents 'race relations' questions. Neither did we place any great emphasis in our interviews with West Indian workers upon their experience of and attitudes towards racial discrimination in general, although, as we have already seen, the factory sample was asked whether they believed that the police and the courts discriminate against black workers. Rather, our interviews were specifically designed to allow the respondent to define his or her view as to what were his or her own experienced problems or perceived problems at both a local and national level. This procedure proved useful in the identification of racism amongst the English workers as we have already shown, and we have attempted to use the same procedure to identify the nature and extent of racial consciousness, although for the factory sample this is complicated by the fact that the respondents were asked about discrimination by the police and the courts. Accordingly, all of the interview transcripts for our West Indian workers were read specifically to locate references to racism and racial discrimination.

This form of analysis produces three main categories. First, those respondents in both the residential and factory samples who spontaneously referred to racism and/or racial discrimination in the course of the interview. This constituted 34 per cent of the residential sample and 33 per cent of the factory sample. The second category relates to the 30 per cent of the factory sample workers who mentioned racism and/or racial discrimination as evident only in relation to the practice of the police and the courts. The third category relates to those men in the factory sample who denied that the police and the courts treated West Indians differently from the English and who nowhere else in the interview said that they or other West Indians were the subjects of racism and/or discrimination. This group constituted 31 per cent of the sample and a further

6 per cent of the West Indians in the factory denied that they or other West Indians experienced racism and/or discrimination.

Taking the spontaneous references to racism and/or discrimination first, the most frequent reference amongst the West Indian factory workers was to discrimination in employment (either in terms of actually getting a job or whilst carrying out a job) or in public places (pubs were specifically mentioned). The following quotes illustrate the extent to which this experience of discrimination was unanticipated upon migration and therefore came as a great shock:

'I can remember when I first tried to get work. Myself and a cousin went for a job and were the first two outside the factory in the morning and afterwards fifteen other white blokes came along and they all got work and they told us that they didn't have any jobs. But I just got used to it and said that if you can't do anything about it you have to ignore it ... I think they (white people) are scared and a lot of them aren't fair-minded. In Jamaica we treat them completely different. I feel the ones in this country are scared that if a black man gets a good education and then a good job he will step on them.'

'Well, the truth is now, Britain is in a hole. The first choice for the bread and butter jobs are the white folks, not the aliens. It's done diplomatically. A white man out of a job now would be in one quicker than a black man with the same experience and qualifications.'

'Well, I think there are a few [i.e. who are prejudiced], mostly the working class, the ones that don't have a good home and a good job. They see some black people with good homes and good jobs and they cause trouble.'

'London Transport: it was horrible. I hated it. Well, it opened my eyes to people. I didn't know they could react in that way. I'd heard about it but it's to prove it. In my country I didn't know what prejudice meant. It was class-divided between the rich and the poor but not black and white ... Sometimes I would go for the money and they would put it on the seat because they didn't want to touch my hand. There was an incident about ten years ago on the buses when it used to be old pence. And an old fellow came on and said 4p please. I gave him the 4p ticket and about six stops later he said to me "Where is my change?" I said "You didn't give me anything to get change. You gave me 4p." He then said he gave me half-a-crown and started calling me a black so-and-so, asking me why I came to this country.'

In the residential sample personal references to discrimination in work and public places were far less common: only three made reference to such incidents. What was more common were personal or generalised references to their position in British society as an excluded racial fraction. The following quotes are illustrative:

'Every time I look out onto the street and I see all the muck and dust out there I wonder why I pay the rates. I think they are ignoring the area as they always do whenever there is a concentration of blacks, trying to say look what they done to the area and it was so nice one time. I mean, you get all these people coming in to the area, eating their Kentucky fried chicken and just throwing the paper on the floor and back they go to their so called Gin and Tonic belt and leave the place in a mess for us to live in.' (West Indian female)

How much influence do you think that people like you can have over the way things are run in this area?

'If you go back years, even before 1958, black people had no influence at all, right? But they've got a long way since and there will probably be a lot of years before they get any further. If you take, for instance, the race riot, before then people used to say, "Well look he's only a black man, he's a wog, he's nothing". But now they don't say that right, things have changed. Men have changed with the times, but it will probably be a lot of years before they get any more influence.' (West Indian male)

Have you ever had to make a fuss yourself to get some complaint aired or to get some official to take notice of you?

'Well the most that a coloured man could do around this area to try and get some assistance is to make trouble. As a black man you aren't accepted regardless of what you say, it would take a black man with more influence than me to get them to listen to him. Once a man threw two bricks through my front window and damaged my furniture so I contacted the police. Two police officers came along, saw the bricks and the broken furniture and then they drove off. You get no help from the police.' (West Indian male)

In contrast to such references there were those men in the factory who said that they believed that both the police and the courts treated West Indians in the same way as English people and who nowhere else in the interview said that they or other West Indians were the subject of racism and/or discrimination. A further 6 per cent of the West Indians in the factory specifically denied that they or other West Indians experienced racism and/or discrimination:

> 'Personally speaking, I don't believe in colour prejudice because the English people and myself get on very well. I don't think the police treat anyone different at all. But in every nation or every race, there is the odd ones out who are awkward. I just ignore them. If you are speaking to someone and you are rude to them, then you must expect them to be rude to you and I think that's what the trouble is. All these people running around saying the English do this and the police do that. I think they have to take some of the blame as well. If you are not civil to a man, then you can't expect him to be civil to you.' (West Indian male: factory sample)

> 'It's all right in Wembley and everyone seems to live good together. You never get much trouble there. People go in the pubs, whether black or white and they will buy each other drinks and they get on so there isn't anything bad to say about the place. It's more on the quiet side really.' (West Indian male: factory sample)

Taking the two samples together, it is possible to argue that roughly a third of our West Indian respondents felt strongly enough about some aspect of their disadvantaged position as an excluded racial category to spontaneously refer to it, although the fact that a further 30 per cent of the factory sample referred to racism and discrimination when prompted by the question on the police and courts suggests that this consciousness of themselves as an excluded racial category may be more widespread.

However, this awareness needs to be evaluated in the context of other beliefs and only a small minority of the group who spontaneously referred to racism or discrimination made regular and consistent reference to either. The majority made only occasional or passing reference and indicated concern about other problems and issues more often. To return to our findings of the last section, it is clear that only a small proportion of our West Indians saw racism and/or discrimination as the most significant problem that they faced locally. They were far more concerned about the level of inflation and taxation and the scarcity of housing and work. Additionally, a proportion made other qualifying comments which indicate either that, although they were aware of their disadvantaged position, it was not something that they could or needed to do anything about, or that they themselves advanced similar sorts of ideas with respect to other groups. Thus 13 per cent of this group in the factory acknowledged the experience of racism and discrimination but added that they took no notice of it:

> 'Well, a couple of "black bastards" thrown my way don't really trouble me. But there are blokes who will floor you if you call them that. It don't worry me as long as no one hits me.' (West Indian male: factory sample)

> 'I have no complaints about this country because since I've been in the country and they had all this colour bar and things, I didn't get affected because I try to keep out of things.' (West Indian male: factory sample)

Some West Indian workers in the factory qualified their reference to racism and/or discrimination by adding that blacks were equally as 'prejudiced' as whites. Thus, 22 per cent made the following sort of statement:

> '[Some West Indians] say they are black and that's that. They say that they don't want to be involved into white people's business and I think that's wrong. I think they have a chip on their shoulders and they are prejudiced. They must be prejudiced to say such a thing. If they are living in the country, they must be part of the country. Everybody do discriminate, that's one thing that you can't help. It's all over the world. It could be anything. It could be someone who don't like Pakistanis, or West Indians or whites. Anything.' (West Indian male: factory sample)

> 'It's just like some of the coloured people here don't like the white man. You will find this wherever you go.' (West Indian male: factory sample)

And as if to illustrate the latter point, 22 per cent of those in the factory sample who referred to racism expressed by, or discrimination practised by, the English expressed negative attitudes about Indians and/or Pakistanis (attitudes that were rarely different from those expressed by some of the English about these same groups). This is illustrated by this quotation from a West Indian worker:

> 'Prejudice will always exist, not only in the white man but in the black man also. The black man will always be ready to shout that the white man is prejudiced but he forgets that he is prejudiced too. Indian people are people I can't stand. They get on your nerves. They are the worst drivers on the road and then there's the saris and all that. I know it's their national dress but there's

something about them I just can't stand. But Britain itself is putting its own neck in the noose. Take all these Asians that have come here, especially the ones from Uganda and Kenya. Now they couldn't turn them away because they gave them all British passports and told them that Britain was their Mother Country. So the Asians come here and they work and save. And believe me that they do save. If they work £10 per week, they will save £9 because when they buy a house together, as they usually do, they live in every part of it. Also, this is why the balance of payments is the way it is because they will find some way to invest their money somewhere else other than Britain. They come here and they've found out that it's not the Mother Country they expected with people calling them names so they earn their money because if you put them on the moon they would earn money, and then they get it out of the country. You notice that the Indians are always the people with wealth. They are always in the richest part of the country and if they have to take this piece of paper and survive with it, they will do it. So they draw out their money and they buy Southall and they really do own it because the police there are about the only white people still living there and now they are thinking of buying Wembley. Now a man in the corner shop starts thinking "I've got a Paki next to me" and so he starts sizing up his shop for about £8,000 and then an Indian comes along and says "I'll buy it for £16,000" and he sells it on the dot. You now decide to go down to the corner shop to buy something and sees this Indian. You'll swallow your spit and turn round to go home.'

It was also argued that Asian immigration disadvantaged West Indians in Britain:

'Well, they say they [i.e. Indians] have British passports. They are not like us because we have our own countries to go back to but they are coming from Kenya, Uganda and now Malawi. They can't go back to India because Mrs Gandhi won't have them. The biggest trouble in this country now is them. There's too much of them in the country. I got nothing against them but the population's too big and they are making it harder for us.'

Both types of sentiment were also expressed by a few West Indians in the residential sample:

'They [Asians] have no expenses, no overheads. The children come from school and they help out, the wife stays in the shop when the husband is out and so there is no bills at the end of the week except for the normal run of the house. An Indian family of man and wife and about three children I can guarantee that they can feed themselves on about £8 a week. They don't eat meat and they'll get by on anything. They can borrow money at any interest rates whatsoever and they can pay it back because they have no overheads and they eat every little thing so their diet isn't expensive. Things can't be too hard for the Asians to survive so they will get their little shops and they will do well. The man in the high street who's been left a little business by his father is going to go out of business to one of them. There is an Indian shop round the corner, he opens every night until about 8 p.m. and he opens every Sunday morning so how can a man run a business similar to his and compete? They will grab all the money and keep it amongst themselves and there is where the crunch is going to come. You will find that any jobs that they have got going will only go to another Indian and that was the trouble in Uganda and Kenya, they kept all the jobs and the money to themselves. That's what caused the trouble. I've no time for them at all for the simple reason they don't mix with anyone else, they would even kill a girl for marrying someone who wasn't one of them. The Ugandan Indians in this country didn't even want to be known as Ugandans because they didn't want to be ruled by a black man.'

Additionally, in both samples there were those who argued that while there might be 'problems' between black and white neighbours, or those who referred specifically to racial discrimination, they themselves nevertheless maintained good relations with the English.

We believe it is possible to argue that racial consciousness is, like class consciousness and racism, in most individual cases inchoate. Amongst a majority of the West Indians in the factory sample and a third of the residential sample, there is an awareness of black people being the object of racism and discrimination though the individual may distance himself or herself from the process. This inchoateness and ambivalence is particularly evident in their views about black youth.

Firstly there are those, particularly West Indian women, who are deeply concerned about the education of their children, as one woman explained:

'I don't think the teachers or even the labour exchange is helping the kids at all and I think the reason for this is the majority of kids around here are coloureds. I hear that they say why worry about the coloureds. That's very bad.'

A West Indian father told us that he believed the police were making sure that black youths had some sort of criminal record to prevent their gaining reasonable work. Similarly, a proportion of the factory sample who expressed an awareness of racism and discrimination made specific reference to black youth, half of whom saw black youth as unwarranted victims of discrimination and so refused to condemn outright the youths' reaction to their circumstances:

> 'I think the thing the government have to look about now is this race prejudice thing. I think it's getting worse now and one day it's going to be out of control so if the government can't do something now before it gets bad, I don't know what will happen. I'm not worrying for myself but for the kids who were born in this country because they are British and they are the ones you have to worry about. I was watching Panorama the other night and there was this coloured bloke and he had about 15 "O" levels and he was saying that there were other blokes around his standard and they go for jobs and people tell them "Wait there a minute" and then they come back and say the vacancy is filled and they don't get the job because they are coloured. They are getting bitter as a result of this. That's why you see flare-ups like the Notting Hill thing the other day. All these kids can't get a job. I know some of them don't want jobs, but a lot of them try but they just can't get work.'

Amongst the young West Indian men in the residential sample there was a very real ambivalence towards black youth, as the following quotes illustrate:

> 'I think some of my own black youngsters want to stretch themselves out more within this society. Forget about the cliquism. Jamaicans have their own heritage, they have their own music, but I don't appreciate this cliquism. And so often the light does not really hit them until they're about twenty-five, not everybody can be a teacher or this or that but at twenty-five it's slightly too late, then you are breaking your back to see what you can gather in. So if we are not careful and if the government is not careful, Harlesden will be another Harlem. It might be coming slowly but to me it has symptoms of deterioration.'

Another said:

> 'Even Willesden is better than Harlesden because there is so much trouble going on here with all these youths. Some of these

youths are black and it comes back onto you because if people see
this and they will say all black people are the same and that's the
reason why I don't like this area. 'I notice with the police they put
everyone on a level. If they have trouble with some of one race
they will say they are all the same, so if they get an innocent West
Indian he will be treated as guilty even before they find out
because of what some of the youths are doing. The police have a
job to do but the way they go about it sometimes is wrong. For a
start, if they stop a black youth on the road the first thing they
will ask him is, where is your knife. Some of them do carry knives
but the innocent ones get lumbered as well.'

But a small proportion of both factory and residential sample
respondents held a more extreme view, indicating a belief that black
youth got the treatment they deserved:

'The young coloured youths these days give a lot of trouble. They
also think that the police shouldn't speak to them when they do
anything wrong. They think they should be left alone which is all
wrong.'

'There are a lot of youngsters who could pick up some sort of job.
It's probably not the one they really want but it would keep them
off the streets and out of trouble for a while. But they don't seem
to want to get involved in work. In Brent as a whole there are a
lot of them who are pretty light-fingered and rude. I don't really
feel too good about it knowing that a lot of them is my colour. It's
not very nice. I think that something should be done to get them
settled. They aren't settled. They seem to be from one place to
another and they don't know what they are going to do
tomorrow and what they are going to. A lot of them are more or
less living on the streets because they have been too rude at home
so they got thrown out. So a lot of things build it all up.'

These views about discrimination and black youth are of interest
not only because they suggest that opinion is divided as to the
legitimacy of the behaviour of black youth but also because, for at
least some of the respondents, they imply that racism and discrimination is not a problem for themselves but for other blacks,
specifically British-born blacks. As with some of the 'qualifications'
previously discussed, this belief can absolve the respondent from
himself or herself responding to racism and discrimination because
it is viewed as inevitable or because it does not affect them directly.
In the factory and residential samples there was only one respondent

in each (both male) who articulated elements of a racial conscious
ness which were not subject to these sorts of qualifications. Both c
them, throughout the interview, drew attention to racism an
discrimination and to the fact that, because of this, there wer
specific black interests that had to be taken account of. We wi
consider the views of one of these men in some detail. He, like man
other West Indians, did not expect the hostile reaction upon arriva
in Britain and has now come to believe that:

'Once you are a black man here you always have to look over
your shoulder and know that someone is after you. You may go
to a pub and ask for a drink. The barman may turn his back at
you. All these kind of things could happen.'

For him, racism and discrimination are everyday occurrences an
constitute the major problem in Harlesden:

'The problem is anywhere you get a lot of black people together,
you always find a lot of hostility between the whites. They alway
think the black people are there to take over and it causes a lot o
trouble. I don't know why the white people are frightened
because the majority of the black people who live here do the jol
that the white people wouldn't do and they have the worst
housing that the white people wouldn't have so I don't see what
they should be frightened about ... I don't think the race
relations is very good in Harlesden and I think in the next five to
ten years this will be a very bad place to live in because of the
hostility between black and white people.'

He argued that both Enoch Powell and the National Front ha
legitimated and encouraged racism and that the trade unior
(whose role he defined as being 'to protect the workers') 'could hav
a one- or two-day strike and force the government to smash th
National Front'. That strike action was necessary because h
believed that no government 'helps black people at all'. For th
reason he also strongly supported West Indian participation i
British politics, seeing as the aim the election of black MPs. Ther
was no doubt in his mind that the police discriminated against blac
people:

'They will treat the rich man differently according to what he ha
done because the rich man may have the money to fight him. Bu
the ordinary black man in the street if he picks you up and plant
some hash in your pocket and you have no money to fight, you
may go to prison innocently. The ordinary white man gets

treated differently as well. So, if you are rich you are all right, if you are poor, you've had it and if you are black and poor, you are at the bottom of the gutter.'

Not surprisingly, then, his view of the class structure (in which there were just two classes, the rich and the poor) was mediated by what he saw as the effect of racism.

Class and racial consciousness

The political consciousness of this West Indian may be seen as containing elements of both a class and a racial consciousness, but this is to suggest a relative inchoateness which would be inaccurate. We believe that this man demonstrates a class-racial consciousness which on the one hand enables him to correctly analyse the material basis of working-class racism and on the other perceive the fight against fascism as the responsibility of traditional working-class organisations. This class-racial consciousness transcends the compartmentalised view articulated by the vast majority of our West Indians who refer to the existence of racism but whose attitude is best illustrated by the belief that it 'does not affect me personally'. This is not to say that the latter are living in a 'fools' paradise'. Such a conclusion would also be incorrect. What we are saying (and we will discuss this point more fully in the next chapter) is that racism clearly does not structure *all* situations for the majority of our West Indians.

They, like their white working-class counterparts, are wage labourers, but there are also migrants whose presence in Britain is largely materially inspired, so making them particularly concerned about wages, prices and inflation. Some deny the existence of racism and racial discrimination, while others will live with the routinised expression of racism and the knowledge that there is racial discrimination as long as neither are perceived as directly interfering with their own and their children's well-being. When they do, black migrants will assess their position in racial, rather than class, terms. This co-existence of beliefs is possible because a racial consciousness is, like racism, partly derived from direct experience. This is not to say that those West Indian respondents who did not refer to racism or racial discrimination had no experience of either: this is highly unlikely. But as migrant labourers there are many other experiences which will be as, if not more, important in the structuring of their political consciousness.

In chapter 6 we argued that direct experience was an important source of working-class consciousness. What we hope to have shown in this chapter is that racism and racial consciousness are also partly derived from direct experience. In the chapter which follows we consider which of these orientations, if any, become translated into political action among our English and West Indian working-class respondents.

CHAPTER 8

Political action: class consciousness in action?

Since the Second World War we have witnessed in Britain a decline in support for the major political parties and an increase in the use of tactics within the sphere of informal politics by certain sections of the population (Crewe, Sarlvik and Alt, 1976; Chamberlain and Moorhouse, 1974; Chamberlain, 1977; Crouch, 1977). This has raised the issue as to whether such developments mark a basic questioning of the legitimacy attributed to present political arrangements, particularly by those least likely to benefit from such arrangements. Thus for the working class it is arguable that a questioning of the legitimacy of existing political arrangements can lead to the development of class consciousness. In this chapter we wish to examine this possibility as evidenced in the political practice of our respondents. We therefore consider the political action of our respondents in three different areas.

First, in the formal sphere of politics, we will concentrate on the voting behaviour of our working-class sample because we believe that such behaviour can be viewed as a basic source of legitimation for present political arrangements. In addition we will consider our samples' formal membership of political parties. Second, we will consider our respondents' involvement in industrial action and the legitimacy which they attribute to such action. Third, we will consider our respondents' involvement in local collective action focusing attention on whether such action reflects particular elements in the political consciousness of our respondents.

We shall draw together the conclusions we reach from these three forms of political action in a discussion of the relationship between the strategies of class unity and ethnic organisation.

Involvement in the formal sphere of politics

Voting
In 1951, 81 per cent of the British electorate voted either for the

Labour or the Conservative party, while in 1974 only 56 per cent of the electorate voted for one or other of these parties (Crewe, Sarlvik and Alt, 1976, p. 142). This decline in partisanship has more recently been paralleled by a tendency for Labour Party supporters to criticise the party's major ideological platform. Crewe *et al.* argue that

> there occurred in the 1960s a major haemorrhaging of support for the party's main tenets ... Between 1964 and 1970 the gap grew wider still ... a near 60 per cent rejection of the idea that trade unions were too powerful in 1964 turned into a 60 per cent agreement six years later; and declarations of general sympathy towards strikers were more than halved, from 37 per cent down to a minuscule 16 per cent. Only the belief that big business was too powerful was steadily and heavily upheld (p. 152).

This ideological decline was most pronounced among the 'core' group of Labour partisans, the one in three who were working-class trade unionists with a very or fairly strong Labour identification (p. 153). It is against these national patterns that we will consider the

Table 8.1 Reported voting behaviour of English and West Indian respondents in October 1974 (%)

	English men (N = 55)	West Indian men (N = 57)	English women (N = 17)	West Indian women (N = 20)
Conservative	13 (7)	9 (5)	6 (1)	5 (1)
Labour	53 (29)	58 (33)	47 (8)	30 (6)
Liberal	5 (3)	—	18 (3)	—
National Front	2 (1)	—	—	—
Communist	2 (1)	—	—	—
Did not vote	20 (11)	23 (13)	29 (5)	35 (7)
Voted, but would not say whom for	5 (3)	10 (6)	—	30 (6)
Per cent who voted	80	77	71	65

electoral behaviour of our working-class samples. In Table 8.1 we show their reported voting behaviour in the October 1974 General Election.

One note of caution in the interpretation of these figures: there was a noticeable tendency amongst our West Indians, particularly the women, to refuse to tell us who they had voted for even though it became clear in their responses to later questions that at least four of the women had voted Labour. Moreover, well over a quarter of our respondents did not vote in the General Election of October 1974. Non-registration explains only a small percentage of this non-voting. The majority did not vote for reasons we will look at shortly.

The most important point arising from Table 8.1 is that while variations exist between the various groupings, overall our West Indian and English respondents have broadly similar voting patterns. The main exception is the minority of English who are attracted to minor parties, a tendency which we would expect to find in a period of declining identification with the major parties, but an option which obviously does not appeal to any of our West Indians. The differences between men and women are more pronounced than the differences between the English and West Indians taken as a whole.

We asked our respondents why they had voted in the way they did. Most of the English Conservative voters explained their practice in terms of support for, or perceived benefits of, Conservative policies:

'I will vote for the one who is going to do the best for the housing in the area. I feel very strongly about the housing.' (English male: factory sample)

'I just think that they could do a better job than the Labour Party.' (English male: factory sample)

'I like the Conservatives. There are lot of things I don't agree with the Labour Party for. I think they make mistakes.' (English male: factory sample)

Only one explained his vote for the Conservative Party in a way that could be described as in part deferential:

'Well, my mother voted Conservative and her father. Well, they all come from up there where they all vote Conservative. I vote for them because most of them know about industry. They have more property than the Labour Party and they have more money to speculate to get things to work.' (English male: factory sample)

The very small number of Conservative voters amongst the West Indians makes generalisation about motive impossible.

The explanations provided by our Labour voters show that a substantial proportion of our respondents (46 per cent of the English and 31 per cent of the West Indians) vote for the Labour Party because they see it as in their 'class' interest to do so:

'I believe in voting for the working-class people.' (English male: residential sample)

'Well I reckon that Labour is more for the working people and I'm one of them.' (West Indian male: residential sample)

'Well I thought they were for ordinary working-class people and we are ordinary working-class people. I just thought they were going to do better because the Conservatives give me the impression they are just for the rich people' (English female: residential sample)

'Well I think Labour is more for the working-class people. The Tories is for the big man: if you have money you will be all right with them.' (West Indian male: factory sample)

'I never go against Labour. I think a working-class man should always vote Labour. I take the word "labour" to mean hard work and that's what the party stands for. So I feel that if a man knows what hard work means, then he will try to make it a bit easier for you.' (West Indian male: factory sample)

'Well I believe the Tories represent the capitalists, the industrialists. That's proven by who pays for the Tory party isn't it? The Labour Party's supported by the unions which comes from the working man. For me, to see a working man voting Tory, he's a complete hypocrite. If I was a millionaire I would go out and vote Tory but I'm not arguing their point of view. I'm arguing my point of view.' (English male: factory sample).

Not a single West Indian woman gave what we might call a 'class' interest reason for her voting.

Our West Indian respondents as a whole were just as likely to suggest that they voted Labour because they approved of the party's policies as they were to mention 'class' interest. A similar proportion of the English gave this also as their reason for voting Labour:

'They are the only ones that seem to do us any good, to get us out of the red.' (English male: factory worker)

'Well, in the general election last time I was seriously thinking of changing my vote but listening to them I thought Labour's policies sounded better. They seemed to be more beneficial to me so I voted Labour.' (English female: residential sample)

'All I know is that if Labour wasn't in the House people like me who are single wouldn't get any family income supplement. When the Tories were in no single woman with her first child could get any money. But since Labour has been in every one-parent family gets £1.50 for their first child. I think this is a great big help for a lot of women today. Also look at the way people are getting more in their wages every week, all you used to get from the Conservatives was rate increases.' (West Indian female: residential sample)

A few West Indian men in the factory believed that the Labour Party had a more acceptable policy on the 'race issue':

'I think they are more down to earth and for the poorer people. I think the Conservatives may be a bit snobbish, they only think about the rich. I think Labour will be more concerned about the poorer people and also when it comes to black people, they might be more on our side than the Conservatives would be.' (West Indian male: factory sample)

'I think they are much more cool on the racial issue and that determines how I feel about a lot of people. Then again, the Labour Party is usually on the side of the trade unions which is on the same side as me. I think the Tories have got it all anyway: they are all for themselves so why should I vote for them?' (West Indian male: factory sample)

In addition, both quotations again alert us to the fact that there are some West Indians who are consciously aware of their position as a racialised fraction of the working class.

So far, Labour voting has been explained in terms of a positive orientation to the Labour Party; that is to say, Labour voting is explained as expressing class interests or an approval of Labour policy. But Labour voting was also explained to us by roughly 20 per cent of our sample as a matter of habit or family socialisation. This explanation seems primarily relevant to our English respondents because the parents of our West Indian respondents could not have been Labour voters in England. Nevertheless, some West Indians transferred their allegiance from a Caribbean 'Labour' Party to the Labour Party in England, even though the political aims and objectives of the Caribbean party may not be the same as those of the Labour Party in England.

Taking Jamaica as an example, it is understandable, given the overall lack of ideological difference between the two major parties, that a Jamaican Labour Party supporter who came to England fifteen years ago might transfer his or her allegiance to either the Labour or Conservative Party. One man explained:

> 'Why did I vote Conservative, or why have I been a Conservative all my life? I was a JLP supporter in Jamaica.'

But his response is unique. The more common transference is to the Labour Party in Britain:

> We always stay with the Labour Party because from when we were small we hear our parents say that they had to work so hard for everything and that the Labour Party was for the working people. The Tories are like the PNP back home, they are well off, but the Labour people have to work to gain what they have.'
> (West Indian female: residential sample)

Carl Stone argues that collective political action in Jamaica 'has grown more out of the attachment to strong leaders than out of a tradition of radical class organisation and class awareness among the peasantry and working class' (1974, p. 56). When the working class is divided along partisan lines and the governing parties' supporters receive a few pay-offs for that support, then class conflict can be avoided by channelling discontent into partisan antagonism.

Without an understanding of this intense partisanship, of the material pay-offs for support and the importance attributed to strong leadership, we fail to understand much of the reasoning behind Jamaican migrants' current political choices in Britain fifteen or twenty years after their emigration. These are points to which we will return later, but we believe they provide a valuable insight into one final reason for voting Labour in Britain, voiced only by our West Indian respondents:

> 'Well it's very funny because that same year my general rates were very high and when Labour got into power in the February of that year, the rates came down about £20 so I said, "All right, I'll vote for Labour in the October election." ' (West Indian male; factory sample)

> 'At the time there was a housing problem in the Borough where I lived and many people were struggling. Mr Wilson made it easier for people to get a mortgage so I worked hard to get a maisonette

for myself and I'm only sorry a lot of people didn't do the same thing. But I couldn't have done anything about it if Mr Wilson hadn't made it easy for me.' (West Indian male: factory sample)

'I vote Labour because I know what Labour does for me.' (West Indian male: factory sample)

These responses were distinct from those which we have labelled 'Labour Party policy'. The latter were general in origin, having no reference to the benefits of Labour Party policy for the respondent, while these specifically emphasise the perceived benefits for self. We believe that the increased tendency among the West Indians, as compared to the English, to exhibit material instrumentalism as a basis for their vote is due not only to the fact that they are migrant target workers but also because of the nature of their previous political socialisation. The former reinforces rather than erodes the influence of the latter.

Finally, we must consider why a third of our sample did not vote. A few of our non-voters gave non-registration as their reason for not voting, but the most common explanation was that voting was perceived as ineffective or as being an issue of little interest:

'I don't believe in voting myself. I don't believe that any of them are doing any good, Labour or Conservative, not at the moment anyway. So I don't bother voting at all.' (English male: factory sample)

'I don't think my one vote would make any difference, I'm sure thousands of people vote twice anyway.' (West Indian female: residential sample)

'I've never voted. I just didn't bother, most people go to the polls in the evenings but working nights I find that when that time comes round I just say I can't be bothered, it's time to go to work.' (West Indian male: residential sample)

'I'm not registered to vote, I don't want to vote because either way it's going to be run by the same thing, I'm not saying the same person, only the same influence.' (West Indian male: residential sample)

'Why put them there? They don't do anything at all.' (West Indian male: factory sample)

Just one West Indian drew attention to his migrant status in explaining his non-voting:

'I don't vote. I don't think that immigrants should vote to that extent because we are just there to make up the numbers for one party or the other. There are very few, if any, immigrants working in local or government councils.' (West Indian male: factory sample)

This was the only West Indian respondent in the factory who hinted that immigrant (black?) interests needed to be represented by immigrants (blacks?) and in their absence there was no point in participating in the electoral process. The significance of this has to be assessed in the context of the fact that over 70 per cent of the West Indian respondents in the factory were prepared to participate, even if, as we shall see, they did also doubt the efficacy of voting.

Future voting intentions

The factory sample was also asked about future voting intentions. Their responses indicate clearly the fragility of the Labour vote amongst both English and West Indian workers: only about half of the 1974 Labour voters said they would definitely vote Labour in the future. A variety of reasons was given by our respondents in explaining why they would or would not necessarily vote Labour in the future. The most common explanation given by the English men was that the Labour Party had lost its radicalism and could not be expected to advance working-class interests:

'I might not vote. They seem to be letting us down just a little bit at the moment. They seem to be squeezing us a little bit.' (English male: factory sample)

'Well really I shouldn't vote at all because at the present time Callaghan's milk and water: he might as well be a Liberal. I think Wedgwood Benn is the ideal politician for a working man. At least he gives you alternatives. If things go on the same way we will get the situation that they have in America where the Democrats and Republicans are really the same except for the name.' (English male: factory sample)

But there were also a minority of references to 'left-wing bias':

'They seem to be getting left-wing in the main. For example, this nationalisation. I don't agree with it.' (English male: factory sample)

Most of the West Indian Labour voters, on the other hand, explained their uncertainty (the level of which was much higher than amongst the English workers as indicated by the proportion of

'Don't know' responses) in terms of wishing to wait and evaluate the benefits of a Labour Government:

> 'My boy will soon be going to school and so I'll have to start swotting up on the education issue and see how it goes, how they intend the schooling to go, what they intend to do for the younger generation, because I've got much to do with it.' (West Indian male: factory sample)

> 'Well, they [the Labour Government] have another two years to go yet and I think I'll wait a while and see how things go. I won't flip a coin this time, I'll make up my own mind.' (West Indian male: factory sample)

> 'I think I may still vote for the Labour Party. But you don't know how these things go with inflation and the rising prices. You have to wait and see how things go before you decide whether they can make a go of things.' (West Indian male: factory sample)

A small number doubted not only the efficacy of voting for the Labour Party but of voting at all:

> 'Well generally I always look at it and think that whoever I vote for or whoever comes out the winner, it won't make any difference to me.' (West Indian male: factory sample)

The predominance of 'wait and see' responses amongst the West Indian workers is a partial reflection of the fact that a larger proportion of West Indian workers explain their electoral support for the Labour Party in terms of 'Labour Party policy' and 'self-interest' whereas 'family tradition/habit' is a more common explanation for Labour voting amongst the English workers.

Of course, not all of the sample voted Labour, and for those who did not, there is little evidence of a changed orientation for the future. Most of those who voted Conservative in October 1974 said that they would vote Conservative in the future, while the majority of those who said that they did not vote in that election or that they never vote indicated that they would not be changing their practice. The only doubt expressed amongst the Conservative voters concerned the fact that the Conservative Party was led by a woman.

In sum, considering the responses to the question on future voting intentions in themselves, it would seem that it is the Labour vote that is the most unstable. This instability can be explained for English and West Indian workers in terms of a combination of doubts about the efficacy of voting and about the ability of the Labour Party to 'deliver the goods'.

Efficacy of voting

Doubts about the political efficacy of voting were much more widespread than this data suggests. The residential sample was asked two questions, one on the efficacy of voting, the other on the efficacy of alternative forms of political action. The factory sample was asked two significantly different questions, one focusing on whether it was believed that voting did or did not lead to economic and social change in England, and another on whether it made any difference to the respondent which party formed the government. We will look first at the factory sample.

The questions asked were significantly different because it is possible that voters may believe that the act of voting does lead to socio-economic change, but also that the change has no (positive) impact on their own circumstances. The first question produced an interesting difference of opinion between English and West Indian workers, 56 per cent of the former saying that voting did not lead to changes while 64 per cent of the latter said that voting did. Despite this difference, the reasoning behind the two different opinions was very similar. Thus, those (both English and West Indian) who believed that voting did not change things said that this was because all politicians make promises that they do not keep, or because all parties have the same views/policies or because all the issues are 'fixed' in advance of elections, or, finally, because each new government has to implement policy in the context of the situation inherited from the previous one:

> 'Well at the moment, from what I can see, it doesn't make any difference. You are promised this and that but when they are voted in, you don't get anything done.' (English male: factory sample)

> 'They all say they will do this and that when they want you to vote but when they get into the House, they don't do it. So it doesn't make any difference to the ones that were in before.' (West Indian male: factory sample)

> 'It's a waste of time. It's just a con because they all have the same views and they all work together!' (English male: factory sample)

> 'I don't think the voting makes a lot of difference because it seems to me that the both of them are the same thing. It doesn't make much difference who gets elected.' (West Indian male: factory sample)

What all these explanations have in common is the underlying view that the electoral system does not offer a 'real choice': for the workers who subscribe to this view, 'they' are able to determine political issues and hence socio-economic circumstances, without reference to and without taking into account 'our' interests and problems.

But not all of our factory workers subscribe to this view. Indeed, as we have already indicated, a majority of our West Indian workers said they thought that voting did change things (along with 33 per cent of the English workers), almost all of them claiming that there was a 'real' electoral choice:

'Voting is good because you'll find good people and you'll find bad people in politics so it's up to you to vote for the one who is trying to help everyone, not just himself. It does make a difference because when the Conservatives were there, if we didn't push them out, things would become more difficult. By changing them, things became different.' (West Indian male: factory sample)

'Well obviously if you have bad government then things are going to get worse so the thing to do is to have a vote and get them changed. Other than that, the place would go to ruins altogether. So, I think that voting is a good thing: everyone gets their say. It's only the people who have the authority to change the government.' (English male: factory sample)

'I think it makes a lot of difference, especially these days because the parties have different ideas about things.' (West Indian male: factory sample)

'I think it does make a difference who gets elected. I mean the Labour Government have negotiated with the unions for this 4 per cent pay restraint. I think if the Conservatives had been in power they wouldn't have got it, if they wanted to do it, that is.' (English male: factory sample)

These explanations indicate not only a perception of electoral choice but also imply a belief that the elected government is both capable and able to effect socio-economic change, if only in a limited way. This view is not implied by those who believe that voting does not change things. In other words, what is implicit in the original question is a perception of the exercise of power and the fact that 64 per cent of the West Indians believe that voting can change things is consistent with our earlier reported finding that our West Indian workers were more likely than the English workers to believe that it is the government that runs the country.

However, despite the fact that they are more likely to believe that the government does have the power to determine socio-economic change, our West Indian workers were at least as likely as our English workers to believe that a change of government has very little effect on their own circumstances: 67 per cent of the English workers and 75 per cent of the West Indian workers agreed with the proposition that 'it makes no difference to me which party forms the government'. The English workers explained this in very similar terms to the way in which they explained why voting does not change things (i.e. there is no 'real' electoral choice) but other views were also expressed:

'No, not to me. I still have to come to work tomorrow, whoever is in.' (English male: factory sample)

A small proportion of the West Indian workers interpreted the question in a slightly different way, believing it to focus on their personal feelings about which party held government office rather than the impact on their own financial and other affairs. Those who interpreted it in this way expressed a classless, almost nationalistic, sentiment:

'I wouldn't say it makes any difference. Once they are doing something good for the country, then it doesn't make any difference which government is in.' (West Indian male: factory sample)

'It doesn't make any difference to me as long as the one that forms the government is a good one.' (West Indian male: factory sample)

But the vast majority of those who believed that it made no difference to them which party formed the government explained their view in very similar terms to the English workers:

'Because there was a Conservative government in before and they didn't do me much good. Before them, there was a Labour government and they didn't do me any good either.' (West Indian male: factory sample)

'You've got to want to have the government that you support in power but I don't think it makes any difference financially.' (West Indian male: factory sample)

'No I don't think it makes any difference because regardless what they say that Labour forms the government it's the Conservatives who still rule. You name any of them Lords who aren't Conservatives.' (West Indian male: factory sample)

'To me personally? No. I come here to work and take care of myself and my family and that's it.' (West Indian male: factory sample)

So, with the exception noted above, the majority of our factory sample believe that the political complexion of the government has no effect on their own affairs and circumstances, despite the fact that 64 per cent of the West Indian workers (but only 33 per cent of the English workers) said that they thought that voting did ensure that change could be brought about. It might be argued that the questions tap different dimensions of belief, the question on change relating to abstract, universal action and the other tapping orientations which can be squared with individual experience. If this explanation is valid then we are suggesting that our West Indians are more likely than the English to draw on dominant values in response to questions of a general ideological nature.

The first question asked of the residential sample could be interpreted as allowing the respondent to draw on either system of belief. In response to the question 'Do you feel that by voting people like yourself have some say about the way things are run in this country?', a quarter of the sample indicate an awareness of both systems of belief by responding that they should have had some say in theory, but did not in practice. Overall, 58 per cent of the sample did not feel that they had any say over the way things were run in the country through voting. The following quotes are illustrative:

'Well, it should be that way but it isn't, whichever party is in power leaves everything the same as before.' (West Indian female: residential sample)

'No, MPs are too detached from the grass roots.' (English male: residential sample)

'Whether you vote in the Conservative or the Labour party they don't do anything for the country or for the working-class people.' (West Indian female: residential sample)

'No, I don't think voting and elections do anything.' (West Indian female: residential sample)

But roughly 45 per cent of the men who responded, English and West Indian, expressed the view that voting was a necessity:

'Well yes, the actual vote, although you're only one in millions, it's necessary.' (English male: residential sample)

'Yes, because when the average working man doesn't go and vote you will have a Conservative government because the Conservatives do go and vote. That's why the Labour majority fell so much in the last by-election because the average working man thinks it's nothing really important.' (West Indian male: residential sample)

Thus, amongst the men, in both the factory and residential samples, we find a relatively high level of voting (around 75 per cent), paralleled by a relatively high level of cynicism about the efficacy of voting itself. Amongst the women, we find the same level of cynicism, but a higher level of non-voting.

The residential sample was also asked: 'Can people like ourselves do anything else to make our influence felt over the way things are run in this country?' This was not a 'core' question: only three-quarters of our respondents answered the question and 18 per cent said they did not know. The remainder were divided between a third who answered 'No', a third who believed that some form of direct action was an alternative means of exerting influence, and a further 15 per cent of the respondents, mainly English men, who suggested other 'conventional' forms of political action, such as writing to an MP, the papers or lobbying. The following dialogue between husband and wife is illustrative of those who believed that direct action was the only alternative method of exerting influence:

Husband: 'The only alternative for people like us is to withdraw our labour, strike, let those people know we are dissatisfied with things.'

Wife: 'You could write to your MP.'

Husband: 'What MP? They don't take any notice.'

Wife: 'He would answer you, he should take some notice of what you have to say.'

Husband: 'Yes, the secretary answers you. He don't even see it, does he? That's what the secretary's for. If I write to the Queen that don't mean she gonna see the letter. She's got a secretary to look after that.' (Male and female West Indian: residential sample)

Overall (but with the exception noted above), the responses to these four questions support the conclusions drawn by Chamberlain and Moorhouse (1974) in that they do not indicate a widespread commitment to existing political procedures and institutions. Furthermore, a third of the residential sample believe that some form of direct action is necessary if the working class is to make its influence felt, which would seem to indicate the presence of radical, as opposed to merely accommodative, beliefs in the political consciousness of at least a proportion of our working-class sample.

Voting and the efficacy of voting: a summary

Thus, what can we conclude overall from our data on voting behaviour and attitudes relating to the efficacy of voting? First, the majority of our sample voted Labour in October 1974, and while the proportion of West Indian workers in this total is slightly higher than the English, it disguises the fact that fewer West Indian women than men voted Labour. If they did not vote Labour, they, like the rest of the sample, were more likely not to have voted than to have voted for another political party, though there appeared to be growing support for the Liberal Party amongst English women.

Second, of those voting Labour, only amongst the English men did the largest proportion explain their vote as an expression of class interest, while the West Indian Labour supporters were more likely to refer to their support of Labour Party policies or to self-interest. We believe this difference can be partly explained by differing socialisation processes of support for so called 'working-class' parties in the country of origin and their status as migrant workers. However, these differences should not blind us to the fact that they are attributable to only small numbers of respondents and so should be interpreted with some caution.

Third, and this applies only to the factory sample, despite 40 per cent of the Labour voters explaining their vote as an expression of class interests, only about 30 per cent of the sample said that they would definitely vote Labour in the future. In other words, the electoral support for the Labour Party was not universal and unconditional. Amongst the English workers there was concern as to whether the Labour Party did represent their class interests and as to whether any political party can effect change. The West Indian workers expressed a more calculating and hesitant attitude. They were more likely to explain their uncertainty by saying that they wanted to evaluate the practice of the Labour Government before deciding to vote Labour in the future. Again, these conclusions are based on relatively small numbers and so are offered with some hesitation.

Fourth, the fact that only 38 per cent of the Labour voters expressed their support as a reflection of their class interests indicates that only a minority of the sample see electoral politics as an expression of class conflict. However, it does not follow from this that the majority of the sample believes that the electoral process is a 'fair' and effective means by which they can influence political decisions and have their personal interests taken into account.

Fifth, roughly a quarter of our sample and over a third of the women did not vote at all, the majority making it very clear that voting was of no real importance to them as a political act. In addition, even though 73 per cent of the sample did vote in October 1974, there was little indication of a widespread belief in the efficacy of voting or of other conventional channels of influencing governmental decisions. There is, of course, the qualifying case of the West Indian men in the factory, a majority of whom believed in the efficacy of voting to bring about change which might be interpreted to mean that West Indian men are more committed to the norms of bourgeois democracy. But, to reiterate an earlier point, the conceptual leap from 'ought' to 'does' in the context of individual perceptions is a large one. The fact that only a minority actually believed that changing the government had any direct effect upon themselves demonstrates that care should be taken when considering responses to a single question. There is, in fact, little evidence to support the notion that West Indian men are any more committed than English men to existing political procedures on the basis of the data collected from the residential sample. In addition, as far as support for the Labour Party is concerned, there would appear to be a more conditional commitment amongst our West Indians than our English.

Sixth, while our numbers are small, we must tentatively comment on what appear to be differences in belief and action between the men and women in our sample. The most striking difference is the higher level of non-voting amongst the women. Nearly all the non-voting women had voted in the past and many were disillusioned Labour voters. Others who did vote for the Labour Party said it was from habit. What is missing amongst this potential reservoir of Labour Party support is any sense of loyalty to a party which represents their working-class interests. For many women, cut off from the Labour movement, appeals to the 'workers' can be viewed as quite irrelevant when those appeals are directed to workers in factories and not in the home. Unless political parties seriously consider issues of concern to women and consciously encourage their participation, then women's support for any of the bourgeois parties is likely to decline.

Involvement in political parties

It is commonly observed in the academic literature that the working class, particularly the semi- and unskilled fractions of that class, are only rarely involved in any form of political action other than voting (Dowse and Hughes, 1977). Our data relating to actual involvement in political parties is quite consistent with this observation. Only 7 per cent of the factory sample, all of whom were English, reported that they had joined or were still members of a political party. In the residential sample, 4 per cent reported that they were or had been members of political parties. Of those who had joined or were still members of a political party in the factory at the time of interview, two were members of Trotskyist revolutionary groups and three had been members of the Labour Party. This should not be interpreted to mean that revolutionary groups had a large membership at Food Co. Only what is now known as the Socialist Workers' Party (SWP) was active in an organised sense at Food Co. during the period of participant observation. It appeared to be undergoing dissolution. The number of active members had declined and the total was in single figures. One of the workers interviewed was a member of SWP: the other, although claiming to be a member of another revolutionary group, was not politically active in the factory itself. In the residential sample one West Indian was an ex-member of the Labour Party and one Englishman was an active member. There was also an ex-member of the National Front.

We also asked our respondents if they attended political meetings or rallies: 14 per cent of the factory sample and 18 per cent of the residential sample said that they had. The two young West Indian women in the residential sample reported going to meetings relating to black politics in Britain.

Thus only a tiny proportion of our English and West Indian respondents had any experience of political action in the formal sphere of politics other than voting. In addition, the only women who had attended political meetings were West Indian, and neither of these meetings had been organised by political parties but by black pressure groups which operated in both the formal and informal spheres of politics.

But the other side of the involvement coin is the belief that elected representatives are amenable to influence. We asked our respondents whether they had ever written to, or gone to see, their MP, or a local councillor, on a particular matter. In the factory only 3 per cent had done so, but in the residential sample 42 per cent of the English men and women had at some time contacted a local councillor on a particular problem, the most frequent being housing. None of the West Indians interviewed had made such a contact. A further 11 per cent of the English respondents had contacted their MP, and 14 per cent had written a letter to the local newspaper. Some of this difference between our English and West Indian respondents relates to the differing tenure patterns between the two groups in the residential sample, the majority of our English respondents living in council accommodation. During the time that one of the researchers worked and observed in a local advice centre it was common to find that a client with housing 'problems' had a council waiting-list problem and would be well aware of the different ploys and interests that might be mobilised to help shorten the wait. Local councillors were a particular favourite.

Political activity of West Indians before migration

It is conceivable that our West Indian workers had a higher level of political activity in the Caribbean, perhaps expressing a higher level of class consciousness, than they have now that they are resident in England. If this is so, it could be explained in terms of their awareness of migrant status, accompanied by the belief that, as migrants, they have no political rights in a country that is not 'their own'. Alternatively, they may feel that there is a high level of hostility towards them and that withdrawal from the political process is the safest response (cf. Lawrence 1974). Assessing whether this is the case is not easy because many of the migrants left the Caribbean before they were old enough to vote and most of them were not resident in the Caribbean long enough to develop a political 'career'. Moreover, in many of the islands, trade union organisation was very limited or even non-existent in the period before they migrated so that they had little opportunity for involvement in labour politics (as we have already explained in chapter 5).

Concerning the factory sample, 42 per cent said that they had had an opportunity to vote before they migrated and, of these, 67 per cent said that they had voted. However, only 6 per cent claimed to have been a member of a political party before migration and only 14 per cent had helped a political party at an election. These levels of activity certainly do not indicate widespread involvement in the formal political process before migration. However, 44 per cent did say that they had attended a political meeting, a far higher proportion than had been to a political meeting since migration (and higher than for our English workers). A very similar level of political involvement was reported by the West Indian men in the residential sample, but not the women. Only two women reported having had any interest in politics when they were in the West Indies.

All of these differences need to be evaluated in the context of the nature of Caribbean politics. Many of our respondents pointed out that the political style of Caribbean politicians and the small scale of rural (and also urban) communities ensure that political campaigning is a major local event in which people and politicians have face-to-face contact:

'There would be public meetings and everyone be outside somewhere like Hyde Park and the candidate would tell you what he thinks a long time before you would have to vote, so you could go along and make up your mind. You know where the meetings would be, but in this country you don't know anything. We just hear who is who and then the next minute, who has won, that's all.' (West Indian female: residential sample)

In a sense, then, going to a political meeting in the Caribbean is not the same sort of activity as going to a political meeting in England. In the latter case, an arrangement has to be made to attend an organised meeting in the context of competing 'attractions' whereas in the Caribbean the 'meeting' is a 'community event'. What is interesting is that a number of West Indian men told us that they went to Hyde Park on Sundays and really enjoyed the informal atmosphere and heckling. Others complained that while politics were freely and heatedly discussed in the bars at home, this was not the case in England:

'The communication between people is really bad because if I go into the pub they don't want to discuss politics there, you transgress the laws of the pub, so now our political life is based here in the home with your own little clique. My friends come here on a Saturday night and I'm in pocket, I buy a bottle, or we'll go to a friend's house and we discuss politics from one hour to the next ... nobody in this country ever invite me to a meeting, nobody seems to bother about that.' (West Indian male: residential sample)

But for many women, politics in the West Indies simply meant trouble and violence and they dissociated themselves from party politics altogether. It is quite possible that this type of association has some bearing on their political behaviour in England. When asked if they had attended political meetings or rallies in England, a number responded that this might involve 'violence'. It could be argued that with the appearance of the National Front on the scene they were quite correct, but apart from a few scuffles at election time there was, in 1976, none of the street warfare that ensued the following year.

Thus it is very difficult to say that West Indians are less active politically in England than in the West Indies, because we are not comparing like with like. But if cross-national comparisons of political activity are unreliable, we were at least able to measure the level of interest in politics in the home country. The factory sample was asked whether they were still interested in what happens in the Caribbean. Seventy-eight per cent said that they were, and identified two main sources of political information: correspondence with relatives, and newspapers. Most seemed to read *West Indian World* (a paper published in England) and half also mentioned occasionally reading a newspaper from their island of origin.

This interest in the political process in the island of origin, derived from the black worker's migrant status, could logically have as a corollary an opposition to involvement in the political process in England. Accordingly, the factory sample was asked 'How do you feel about West Indians getting involved in British politics?' In reply 72 per cent said that they favoured such involvement:

> 'Yes. They live here for so long and they become part of the nation. I don't see any difference between them and the people who were born here and grow up.'

> 'I suppose yes. If he's going to make this place his home for some time like I suppose I will. I suppose you should try and keep up with the everyday things that go on. You've got to support the country that you live.'

> 'Yes, they should get involved. There are a lot of West Indians living here now. They are getting coloured policemen now. They have plenty doctors and nurses. Mr Wilson said on television once that if they took the coloured people out of Britain, the hospitals would be paralysed. He said without the coloured immigrants the buses, railways and hospitals would be paralysed.'

> 'Yes. I'm British right now. If anything goes wrong I still have to be in it and join in it. I have my home here, all my family is here. I've been here for sixteen years and that's a long time so I have to take part.'

A minority of this 72 per cent specifically stated that involvement in

British politics was a necessity in order to ensure the representation of black interests:

> 'Well, in the past no. But now yes, because if you are here for ten years you automatically become a citizen so I think they should become more involved now, especially in the local councils. They need someone to talk for them.'

> 'Yes, I think they should because the black population in this country is quite big and there should be someone to represent them.'

Just one worker was not certain that black people in England would benefit from such representation:

> 'I don't know. There is man for every job and it's up to the individual to say what he wants to do. If it means should you have a black MP, well maybe he's going in there and become the same as the white ones. Quite frankly, I think if they put a black man in there now as an MP he would become an Uncle Tom so I think it should stay as it is. He wouldn't become the head of the party, that you would never see.'

So, far from being opposed to involvement in the British political process, the majority of West Indians in the factory sample believed that they should participate. They argued that they had been living in Britain for many years and were now 'part of the country', doing indispensable jobs, with the consequence that they were entitled to the same rights as anyone born in Britain. A minority volunteered the additional view that such involvement was essential to ensure representation of black interests. Clearly, then, objective migrant status was not considered to be relevant by these black workers to their views about involvement in the British political process but, rather, they defined themselves as 'belonging' (to the extent that some explicitly defined themselves as 'British') and so entitled to participate. At the level of 'principle', there is little sign of a desire to withdraw from the political process, although it should be remembered that our respondents were not asked whether such involvement was feasible and would bring rewards. It is the case, as we have seen, that their actual involvement, apart from voting, is very low, although this characteristic is also shared by the English workers we interviewed. This suggests that the West Indian worker has divided political loyalties. Perhaps the final word should then be left to a Jamaican who, as a Labour Party activist, spent most of his leisure time drumming up support among fellow West Indians:

'West Indians exercise their constitutional rights by voting but they don't want to get involved in any party. They are in a foreign country, they are regarded as foreigners and they regard themselves as foreign so they don't get involved. In their own country they feel as if they belong and they know that no one will kick them out, if they want to fight for something they will fight.'

Involvement in industrial action

It is commonly argued that involvement in industrial action is a crucial trigger to the development of class consciousness (Mann, 1973). We asked our respondents both whether or not they had ever been involved in industrial action and also questions which we believed would elicit some generalised ideological orientation to industrial action. In relation to the responses of the factory workers it is important to note that there had not been a major strike at the factory within the memory of both senior management and senior shop stewards.

In answer to the first question 31 per cent of the factory sample and 32 per cent of the residential sample said that they had been involved in industrial action, the majority saying that they had been on strike. However, there were large differences between our English and West Indian respondents and between men and women. Approximately half of the English men in the factory and in the residential sample said that they had been involved in industrial action, compared to only 18 per cent of the West Indian men. Amongst the women, 33 per cent of the West Indians, compared to only 12 per cent of the English, reported involvement in industrial action. We would expect to find an overall lower level of industrial action amongst the women for two reasons, first because large areas of 'woman's work' have a low level of trade union organisation and, second, because fewer English women than men were currently engaged in wage labour. But why the difference between English and West Indian men?

Here we are forced to turn to our attitudinal data to seek a possible explanation: is it the case that our West Indian male workers are more likely to be ideologically opposed to strike action? Data from the factory sample suggests that this is not so. In the factory, the men were asked what they thought about strike action. Only 17 per cent of the English and 6 per cent of the West Indians indicated a general and unqualified approval of strike action. The majority of the sample was nearly equally divided between those who indicated general disapproval of strike action and those who were equivocal, saying that strike action was appropriate only in certain circumstances. The following quotations illustrate the responses of those who expressed general disapproval:

'I think they are diabolical. I don't know how half of them live. I certainly couldn't. What you get off the union on strike pay isn't worth looking at and you would have to go to the Social Security and fill out forms and things. I wouldn't like to be involved in one at all.' (English male: factory sample)

'I don't like it at all. I don't believe in it. I've seen quite a few firms close down that were doing very well before the strikes crippled them. I think strikes should be abolished entirely. I don't think people should be allowed to go on any strikes.' (West Indian male: factory sample)

'I don't like them at all. Well, we are poor people and we can't afford to go on strikes and things. That could be one of the reasons why we are suffering, I suppose. I mean, there are times when we should go on strike but we can't afford to so we just have to suffer some more.' (West Indian male: factory sample)

Three main themes run through these explanations for being opposed to strike action: the individual claims either that such action contradicts his own financial self-interest, or that it benefits management rather than the workers, or that strikes 'ruin the country/firm'.

The following quotations illustrate the views of those who believe that strike action is appropriate only in certain circumstances:

'Well, I don't like strikes myself but it's all according to what you are striking for. Sometimes I read about things people strike for and I don't think it is worth it. It only brings down the government and worsens the situation of the country.' (West Indian male: factory sample)

'Well, there are strikes and there are strikes. If it's for money that you need, then yes, but you get people like Fords who are never satisfied. They get one pay rise and they walk out again. It's especially so in the car industry and they have a lot of strikes that are unnecessary. I would strike for money but anything else I would think twice about it.' (English male: factory sample)

These workers often articulate views similar to those referred to in the previous paragraph but also acknowledge that there are situations where personal interests dictate that strike action is appropriate and necessary. For these workers, strike action is a matter for rational calculation. To consider strike action at all is to imply recognition of the conflicting interests of worker and employer, but recognition of this does not mean that the worker is not liable to pick up and reproduce the ideological messages about strikes that abound in the media (e.g. Glasgow University Media Group, 1976; Beharell and Philo, 1977). Indeed, given the nature of media coverage and the fact that the worker is often completely dependent upon it for knowledge and information about other industrial disputes, one would be surprised if arguments about the 'national interest' were not articulated and made the context of equivocation over the desirability of strike action. But it does not follow from the fact that such arguments are reproduced that they cancel out the view that strike action is necessary in certain circumstances because, as we have previously stressed, the criterion of logic is not necessarily the best criterion with which to 'measure' class consciousness. The residential sample were not asked a direct question about strike action, but the majority of respondents were asked what they thought about the proposal that men and women who strike should not be allowed social security payments. It was only amongst the West Indian women that we found a majority who disagreed with this proposal.

What conclusions can we therefore draw about class consciousness from our data on industrial action? First, as strike action is nearly always taken against an employer, usually to advance the immediate interests of those taking the action, it expresses a conflict of class interests. The fact that roughly half the English men in our combined samples had been involved in some form of industrial action, and that over half of the men in the factory said that they would support strike action if they found the circumstances acceptable, is an indication of at least an implicit recognition of this conflict of interests.

Second, only 18 per cent of the West Indian men (compared with about half of the English men) had been involved in some form of industrial action. However, the attitudinal data from the factory sample does not reveal any major differences between our English and West Indian workers. Moreover, extant evidence indicates that black workers are as willing as white workers, if not more so, to take industrial action (Brooks, 1975a; Smith, 1977). We can find no obvious explanation for the resulting discrepancy.

Third, we must consider the belief and action of West Indian women. We know of no statistics relating to the percentage of women wage labourers who have been involved in industrial action, but we do know that West Indian women in Britain have formed the backbone of some forms of industrial action (see *Race Today*, May 1975, pp. 108–13). We also know from our data that nearly twice as many West Indian women as men had been involved in industrial action and that their attitudes to such action cannot be described as conservative. How do we explain this? We believe that West Indian women's attitude to the wage labour relation is qualitatively different from that of their male counterparts for two reasons. First, there was the necessity for self-reliance in the West Indies but the denial for most of earning a regular wage. Second, while migration to Britain affords the opportunity of earning a regular wage it is quite evident that many express resentment towards the control of their labour which the wage relation imposes. Their refusal 'to be pushed around' is one element of their resistance to this control which we have already mentioned.

Involvement in local collective action

But industrial action is not the only available channel for the expression of class interests. In asking the residential sample, 'Have you ever got together with others in this area to do something about a local problem?', we were interested in the basis of any form of collective action that our respondents had been involved in as well as 'who' were the activists. When we refer to the basis for action we had in mind the strategies of class unity or ethnic organisation. But a third possibility became obvious to us: collective action that was racist in nature.

In answer to the question only 17 per cent of our West Indian respondents as compared to 36 per cent of the English replied in the affirmative. But for the vast majority this action extended to signing a petition. One of these petitions was against 'muggings'. It was organised by local white residents and signed by some of our English respondents. Another petition organised by an English respondent asked for the abolition of a play area on the grounds of noise, the vast majority of children who used the play area being black. A third petition was borough based and opposed a rate increase. In this case the organisers were obviously willing to lose the potential support of black owner-occupiers by having a public relations officer who seemed to spend most of his time publicising the 'misuse' of public funds for Hindu community centres.

Only one petition, expressing opposition to the size of electricity bills, had been signed by both English and West Indian respondents. This issue did become the basis for collective action among the tenants on one council estate. With the help of the local advice centre and Law Centre they had a professional survey of the heating installations carried out and they used this information, along with various forms of direct action (e.g. demonstrating at the Town Hall), to press their point. While the tenants' association had a black chairman, English women provided the 'hard core' of activists.

Amongst the West Indians, several women mentioned attending parent-teachers' associations and it is relevant to note that a few months after our leaving the area West Indian women were instrumental in organising a black parents movement because of growing concern over the education of black youth. Another woman was an active member of the Campaign Against Racial Discrimination, which still exists in Brent. In all three cases, therefore, the West Indians' activity stemmed from concerns relevant to their position as members of a racialised fraction of the working class.

Apart from one instance, we are therefore presented with a picture of limited political action structured by racism and black reaction to racism. The strength of the former should not be underestimated and while we cannot draw clear-cut conclusions on the basis of two cases it is pertinent to note that the two individuals who articulated the most systematic racist beliefs were also the most politically active. In both cases the activities were not exclusively racist in nature, as the following extracts from an interview with one of these individuals, an Englishwoman, illustrates. She was unemployed at the time of interview, she left school at fourteen and she no longer voted because 'one is as bad as the other when they get in. The only party I can see now is the National Front.' She claims to have no interest in politics whatsoever which makes her answers to three consecutive questions very interesting:

Have you ever been to see or contacted your MP about anything?

'Yes, I had to go to the consumer people about my gas bill and they sent someone round from the gas board. They told me that the boiler had been badly used. So I went to see Mr Freeson (MP and then Minister for Housing) and then they couldn't come down quick enough to collect the thing and replace it with a new one.'

Have you ever written to a newspaper?

'Yes, I got in touch with the Brent Chronicle, I sent a letter to their public section about all the trouble on this estate, but it didn't get published. They didn't even answer.'

Have you ever had to take any other type of action to try and get the people who matter to take notice of a problem?

'Yes, we went on a march to the House of Commons a couple of weeks ago about people's electricity bills, especially the old people. To keep the boiler going for the gas central heating you have to keep the electric on, so if they come and cut your electric off for not paying, the heating goes off as well.'

Later in the interview she was asked whether she had ever been involved in any type of industrial action:

'Oh yes, when I lived in Wiltshire the women up there were so asleep, if there were four of them short they would do about the same amount of work. I'd only been there a couple of days and I said "Oh, no, why should I work four women's shifts, do I get four women's pay?" The management says "no" and they were all right after that. They thanked me for it in the end.'

There were, in fact, very few types of political action that she had not been involved in but she saw black people as the cause of all local and national problems, although her black neighbour was seen as an exception:

'She has to bring up children on her own, it would be all right if they were all like her but you don't get them like that.'

She was in favour of repatriating all other black people. In sum, her political activism had little to do with fighting class issues in solidarity with other working-class people. Her fights were, in the main, solitary struggles for the material well-being of herself and her two children and she was prepared to use any channel, conventional or not, to secure that end.

The other individual was a man, an ex-member of the National Front. He gave as his reason for leaving the National Front:

'It sounds very rosy when you first get into it but after a while it doesn't sound so good. England for the English which is a good thing but the methods that they wish to attain that by are not so nice. We gain these things by fighting for them which I took as meaning fighting in the political sense, but their idea was more physical.'

He was a firm believer in the 'democratic' process. While chairman of the tenants' association he had organised a rent strike, and as a shop steward he had helped organise several successful strikes. He was also an active member of his local parent–teachers' association.

It might be argued that the articulation of racist beliefs by such individuals is unimportant because such beliefs are not being manifested in political activity in an overtly racist manner. We believe this is a dangerous conclusion. The open expression of racist beliefs, particularly by the articulate and more active section of the white population, is rarely seriously challenged and they serve to demarcate a boundary between 'us' and 'them'. This can be illustrated by two examples: involvement in tenants' associations on one council estate and relationships between black and white workers at Food Co.

Black participation in the tenants' associations of one council estate (60 per cent of whose residents were black) was minimal. When asked why black people did not participate in the tenants' association one English committee member replied:

> 'Racial discrimination is always pointed against the whites but nobody talks about racial discrimination by the blacks. But they discriminate against us. They will not join whites in any social events. They will not join the tenants' association.'

Similar views were articulated by other English tenants, the caretakers and the local police constable. The Housing Department was aware of these views and the implications they had for plans for the introduction of tenant management schemes on such estates. The then Director of Housing argued that black people knew of the boundary of exclusion which operated within a number of the tenants' associations and this effectively blocked their participation.

No one would want to belittle the problems experienced by all tenants on this particular estate. Physically, it is unattractive, it is constantly vandalised, and robberies take place. But they are the problems which beset similar estates all over Britain. However, for the white tenants, the 'cause' was the 'coloureds'. During the period we were interviewing on the estate much of this anger was directed towards certain 'anti-social' tenants who held noisy parties. On one occasion a dispute arose between a caretaker and several party-goers, culminating in a caretaker's door being 'kicked in'. The caretakers took strike action following the incident, seeking stronger support from the council in handling 'anti-social' tenants. While it was officially recognised that elements of 'racialism' were operating, the council took a number of steps to take the immediate heat out of what had become an explosive situation. The caretakers returned to work but remained dissatisfied with the council's reaction on the matter of assault. The caretakers had a legitimate grievance, but for the English tenants we spoke to at the time the dispute was about the inequity of the council's 'soft line' towards the handling of black tenants. As one put it, 'The Labour Party rely on the coloured vote.'

The expression of racist beliefs within all-white groups on the estate is routinised, but they are only rarely openly expressed outside of all-white groups or acted upon. Why? A very basic reason was articulated, mainly by women, on the estate:

> 'Well, as I said, we are so outnumbered that people like myself are afraid to do anything for fear of repercussions. We get a lot of muggings, people are afraid to go out and they lock themselves in their flats in the evenings.'

> 'The problem is it's too coloured. They've been kept down so long they must want to get their own back, it's true. I'm afraid of what they could do to me.'

It is within the context of these beliefs that the stand taken by the caretakers was seen as so crucial by some white tenants.

The distinction between routinised and dramatic expressions of racism is further illustrated by the patterns of interaction between black and white workers at Food Co. 'Social segregation' was not absolute at Food Co.: some groups regularly formed during breaks in which both English and West Indian workers were members and English workers would temporarily join West Indian groups (and vice-versa) for specific purposes (to pass on messages, to sell various items, to organise a return to work, etc.). The pattern and process of social interaction was therefore not a simple one but racism was an element in this complex equation of processes.

Our interview data has shown that racist ideas and sentiment were commonly expressed in social interaction in the factory (as well as on the toilet wall). They were usually expressed in all-white groups, although West Indians might also be present (but racist ideas would only then be mentioned if the West Indians were well-known by the white workers). The stimulus for discussion about 'the coloureds' varied: it might be a particular incident in the factory or a newspaper report on 'race'. On occasion the stimulus was of such a nature that it entered into the vast majority of conversations, as in the case of the media coverage of the Notting Hill Carnival and the events following the murder of a young Sikh boy in Southall in the summer of 1976. On such occasions, a high level of collective hostility was generated amongst the white workers which was expressed much more openly, and so structured interaction with black workers much more precisely than the more routinised discussions. The same process occurred if physical violence arose out of a dispute between a white and a black worker in the factory or if there was a public allegation of racial discrimination by a black worker. Such events were rare but when they did occur a high level of collective hostility developed amongst both English and West Indian workers, with the consequence that interaction between them diminished to the lowest possible level and the incident and its repercussions later became elements of shop-floor mythology.

Implicit here is the analytical distinction between routinised and dramatic expressions of racism, although there is an important dialectic between the two in practice. As far as the English workers were concerned, both served to create and continually reaffirm a sense of 'us' (i.e. the whites), although it was usually only in the latter instances that the sense of 'us' was expressed in an outward show of hostility towards black workers.

The routinised expression of racist beliefs by white workers at Food Co. and on the neighbouring estates was not usually meant for the ears of black workers and tenants, but it is impossible for the latter to be completely unaware of them. Nevertheless the extent to which this awareness fosters withdrawal from social interaction (other than that which is necessary for work and work-related tasks) on the part of West Indian workers and tenants is not easy to determine. In chapter 7 we reported that a small minority of West Indian workers at Food Co. denied the existence of racism, while a larger minority emphasised that they took little notice of it or accepted it as a 'fact of life'. Indeed, only a minority of West Indians seem to have a well developed racial consciousness in which the awareness and experience of racism played a prominent role and could serve to justify a conscious strategy of avoiding contact with white workers and neighbours. Nevertheless, such individuals play the role of opinion leaders within West Indian work and social groups and discourage interaction.

But one should not ignore the effect of other factors which encourage the 'social segregation' observed at Food Co. For example, particularly amongst Jamaicans, the playing of dominoes is a practice derived from the culture of the 'homeland' and the manner in which the game is played specifically excludes English workers. Hence, in so far as West Indian workers simply wish to maintain social patterns of interaction relating to their migrant status, 'social segregation' is encouraged. Migrant status can also act as a deterrent to 'involvement' in, for instance, tenants' associations. When asked why he had not thought of joining or starting a residents' association in his neighbourhood, one West Indian replied, 'My idea was not to stop here for long you see. I would like to go home to the West Indies and settle down.' The extent to which an awareness of racism in turn reinforces the desire to return is very much an open question.

Thus, we are making several points which bear repeating. First, by no means all the English men and women who work at Food Co. or live in Willesden are party to or agree with what we call the 'routinised' expression of racist beliefs, but very few are prepared to take a public stand against the consensus. Second, this routinised expression of racism is a practice limited mainly to all-white groups and serves to define and maintain a (racialised) group identity. This is not to deny that racism is not openly expressed but such expression is not as common as the actual prevalence of the ideas might lead one to expect. This is to be explained by a number of reasons. For instance, at Food Co. those individuals whose racist beliefs we have described as piecemeal were usually concerned that such ideas be not openly expressed in the presence of black workers for fear of being labelled as racists.

Finally, there is a heterogeneous reaction to the articulation of racism amongst the West Indians at Food Co. and on the estates. For many, racism is not seen as being directed at them personally but at black youth, for instance. Consequently there is no immediate cue for reaction. But the fact that racism is routinely expressed within the white working class means that there exists an important precondition for conflict to develop.

What conclusions can we draw from this with regard to the political strategies which are open to black migrant workers as a consequence of their fractionalised class position?

Class unity or ethnic organisation?

We have argued in chapter 2 that it is necessary at all stages of analysis to compare the political action of black workers with that of indigenous workers in order to identify continuities in belief and behaviour which might then be explained in terms of their shared position in class relations.

We believe that we have shown very clearly that continuity in belief and action between our English and West Indian respondents is more common than discontinuity if our level of analysis is a very general one. For example, amongst our respondents there is an overall low level of participation in the political process, participation being restricted to voting and trade union membership, though a quarter of the sample do not vote and the majority demonstrate a low level of voting efficacy.

But if we move from the general to the more specific level of analysis we find important discontinuities which are relatively consistent and which can only be explained by reference to a fractionalised class position. English men can form a baseline for comparison, not because they are the 'core' of the working class, but because they usually dominate studies of working-class consciousness and action.

We have found little evidence of a radical class consciousness amongst our English men. What we find instead is a consciousness ridden with contradictions but which is consistent in one fundamental respect, that money is power and power is money. This structures their perceptions of the class structure in Britain, particularly the disadvantages of the working class. But it is in only one sphere of life, work, that this perception of disadvantage leads to a recognition of the need for collective organisation and action through trade union membership, but even this allegiance is highly pragmatic and conditional. Outside of work most battles are personal battles and as a result the enemy is the council, or the Housing Department, and the blacks whom they are perceived as favouring. 'Us' are disadvantaged workers in the factory, and the disadvantaged English outside the factory gates; life is compartmentalised and an overall perception of the source of disadvantage is submerged.

Our English women are occupationally the most diverse group: just over half were engaged in wage labour, some of whom were part-time workers and only two currently working were members of trade unions. There is, therefore, very little direct contact with the Labour movement as such. The media frequently portrays the image of working-class wives organising in opposition to the strike action of their husbands and we have presented evidence to show that the majority of English women articulated the view that the unions 'were too powerful', but this presents only half the picture. Our data leads us to agree very strongly with Porter who suggests that working-class women may appear to be hostile to the Labour movement but in practice are not so, she argues:

> This is partly because of a traditional loyalty to these organisations, but also because there is little point of contact. They are seen as belonging in the 'other' world and in having little

relevance for women. They are, at worst, fairly detached (1978, p. 188).

But we also believe that this detachment more easily erodes traditional loyalities. Three women who had previously voted Labour all their adult lives had voted for the Liberal Party in October 1974, five others had not voted at all, three of whom professed support for the National Front. Half of the English women were turning away from what they saw as class politics: as one woman put it,

'I thought Labour was for the working people, but with prices the way they are, I don't know any more.'

In many respects West Indian men demonstrate very similar beliefs to those articulated by English women, even though they may have arrived there from different starting-points. What they have in common is a fractionalised class position which results in a fragile and conditional allegiance to working-class organisations. The fact that West Indian men are more likely to vote Labour and be members of trade unions is not in itself a significant difference between these two groups because we regard such actions as merely expedient or necessary in the circumstances. While both groups appear to be drawing more heavily on dominant beliefs, it is not possible to provide a blanket explanation for this apparent similarity. West Indian men left their homelands at a point when class organisation was still, as it were, in its infancy, but they all had experience of wage labour. As economic migrants their willingness to join and support the traditional organisations of the working class is entirely consistent with realising their original goal. But if racial discrimination and racism are seen to operate in the workplace and the union, any sense of loyalty bred from a sense of belonging or inclusion will be weak. But whereas we have shown that English women do sometimes organise around issues of concern to them without the aid of established class organisations, we have found no evidence of this amongst our West Indian men.

Finally, we must consider the belief and practice of West Indian women who, in many instances, articulate the most radical beliefs of all our respondents. We have already mentioned several factors which we believe go some way towards explaining this. These factors relate to the position of women in the West Indies and their subsequent resistance to the control of their labour which the wage relation imposes. But we believe that these factors take on a particular significance within the British social formation because

West Indian women occupy a distinct position in economic, political and ideological relations: they experience both racial and sexual categorisation. What this means in practice is best described by one West Indian woman's experiences.

Mary came from Jamaica twenty years ago on her own with two small children (two were left behind with her mother). She found a room, a job, a baby minder, and any spare money at the end of the week was sent home. Her first job was in a hospital where she met racism on a daily basis, particularly from patients. The pay was bad so she searched for another job. She heard of work at an iron foundry where the workforce was 90 per cent black and they took her on as a fettler. She was appalled by the dangerous conditions in the factory, the workers did not even get a tea-break, but she was so grateful to be in a job at all she kept her mouth shut for the first three months. By this time she felt confident enough to take a stand on the question of tea-breaks. The foreman resented her speaking out and on the Monday she found her name on the top of the redundancy list. Fortunately the union had just started at the factory and the women were asking why Mary could not be made their shop steward. The convenor pointed out to management that on the principle of last come, first out, there were forty-eight workers on the list before Mary. They took her name off the list and she started to organise, as a shop steward, tea-breaks, safety regulations, equal pay for women.

When asked about her role as shop steward she stated that she enjoyed the work but wanted to achieve a situation where women would attend union meetings, speak out and get elected to positions within the union but she was pessimistic about what this would achieve:

> 'as shop steward I've never been higher than going to the office and paying the dues, black people are going nowhere in the trade unions, we're just "dues" collectors.'

But her awareness of racial and sexual categorisation also led her to the conclusion that

> 'I would take any action to keep jobs, we don't want to be out on the street, being black, being a woman, that's two things you can't hide.'

On racism she had this to say:

> 'The working class are the worst, they are plain ignorant.'

After years of work and organisation in the factory Mary left and started an organisation for West Indian women in the community. She was not turning her back on factory organisation (her group were quick to offer support to the Asian women at a local factory who took strike action to protest about their pay, working conditions and union recognition and she remains a member of the Trades Council), but she does believe that she and the other West Indian women will achieve more through their own organisation. They know the problems that West Indians, particularly women, encounter in this country and work hard to achieve unity between young and old by emphasising what the generations have in common culturally. They run play schemes, drama groups and supplementary education classes and have in a short time made a significant impact in numerous areas.

What we hope this example illustrates is that certain fractions of the working-class perceive a need to organise in their own way. Within the industrial sphere, black workers and women have so far not chosen to do so, but we believe that Mary's experience shows that this does not mean that all is well. What we feel to be equally serious is that amongst our small samples we have found that those English who might be termed the most politically active articulated the most systematic racist beliefs. We know from our observational work that most individuals in positions of leadership in the area condemn such views (particularly the Labour movement which has campaigned to combat racism) but their positions in themselves would, in our respondents' eyes, distance them from grass-roots experience, and it is this 'daily' experience overlaid by various dominant beliefs, particularly messages picked up from the media, which constitute the basis of our respondents' beliefs about the world they inhabit.

Thus we have found little evidence of what we term class unity in action amongst our black and white respondents, but this cannot be attributed only to the existence of racist beliefs and practice among the white working class. There are a number of other important reasons why this is the case. Firstly, because our West Indian respondents are migrants and are continually reminded of this, many react accordingly to involvement in what they perceive to be 'other people's' struggles. Secondly, and most importantly, those struggles are very rarely waged outside of the workplace. If class unity in action is not a reality for the white working class outside of very specific (and rare) contexts, how can it be anything else for black migrants?

CHAPTER 9

Conclusion: labour and racism

We began this book by rejecting the 'race relations' approach as an adequate analytical framework within which to interpret our data. In drawing together our conclusions, we begin by returning to those early points in order to emphasise their relevance to the general arguments of the book. In this connection, we wish to make three points,

Concerning the importance of class determination

First, the 'race relations' problematic, by attributing explanatory primacy to the supposed factor of 'race', tends to explain the structural position, belief and action of black migrant labour almost solely in terms of racism and racial discrimination. We must emphasise that in posing an alternative analytical framework we are not wishing to deny or ignore the extent of racist belief and racial discrimination in Britain. Indeed, here and elsewhere we have been concerned to stress that racist ideas are widely expressed within the working class. Rather, we are arguing that racism and racial discrimination do not occur in a vacuum, and that it is only by considering the context that one can more accurately consider their impact, both on the black and the white working class, and the resulting political dialectic between these two (and other) fractions of the working class. Hence, we have argued that it is essential to commence with concepts which acknowledge the nature of the dominant mode of production within the British social formation (i.e. capitalism) and the major class divisions to which that mode of production gives rise. From such an analysis we are able to conclude that black migrant labour shares with the rest of the British working class the same relationship to the means of production, that is, the same position in class relations.

Only at this point in the analysis do we introduce the concept of class fraction as a means of taking account of the economic, political and ideological bases of stratification within the working class. Both racism and sexism are instrumental in creating ideological fractions, although these ideologies cannot be understood in isolation from the economic divisions to which they give rise and/or sanction. Consequently, to speak of black migrant labour as a fraction of the working class is to simultaneously acknowledge both a class position *vis-à-vis* capital and a distinct position within the working class. By adopting such an analytical framework, we are forced to search for basic continuities in the political belief and action of our respondents (be they male or female, black or white) which are a consequence of a common class position. However, given the existence of class fractions, such continuities may coexist with certain discontinuities which express different interests within the class.

When we speak of continuities in belief and action we are not referring to some logically consistent, holistic view of the world which dictates certain types of political action. Political consciousness is usually inchoate and contradictory, and consequently class consciousness is not consistently evident, either in belief or in political action. What is most consistent and common to all class fractions is our respondents' feelings of material and social disadvantage, accompanied by a feeling that they are powerless to alter their circumstances, either individually or collectively. We have shown that this perceived disadvantage is usually conceptualised in terms of money, or more precisely for our respondents, their lack of money. As they see it, *with* money one has power: one can buy oneself out of prison, out of an area being 'taken over by the coloureds', or back to the West Indies to enjoy a more comfortable and prosperous life. But for the majority there was only a hypothetical vision of changing this situation (apart, perhaps, from winning the pools). Change was not perceived as emanating from the ballot box and given the low level of political activity other than voting amongst our respondents, there was little evidence of active support for alternative methods of bringing about change. With the partial exception of the West Indian men we interviewed, our data points to a generalised feeling of disapproval of existing socioeconomic organisation juxtaposed with a sense of powerlessness to change this situation, let alone conceive of an alternative form of socio-economic organisation. These continuities in belief and (non-)action are only explicable if one acknowledges the common class position of our respondents. But in addition to these continuities, we have also identified important discontinuities which coincide with and can be explained in terms of the fractions of the working class that we identified at the outset. Consequently, we are claiming that the political belief and practice of our black workers is explicable in terms of both their class position and as a racialised and/or sexually categorised fraction of that class. Hence, we reject those theories which dichotomise the position of black and white workers (see, for instance, Leggett, 1968; Rex and Tomlinson, 1979).

The emphasis on rebellion

Second, an analysis which focuses upon racism and discrimination will tend to place a great deal of emphasis upon reactions to both processes. In the absence of an objective class analysis this can lead to a misplaced and undue emphasis upon the political importance and impact of, for instance, wageless black youth – the hustlers (cf. Pryce, 1979) and the Rastas (cf. Rex and Tomlinson, 1979). Again, we must emphasise that the ideology and political practice of these groups (particularly the Rastas) are not without considerable political importance because, by their manipulation of the idea of an historically oppressed 'race', they could potentially provide a justification and leadership for black workers as a racialised fraction. However, such developments cannot be examined in isolation from the political belief and practice of the black working class as a whole. In so far as it is possible to generalise from our research experience and findings, we are not convinced that there is widespread passive, let alone active, support for the militancy of what to date is only a minority amongst the young and often British-born black population. We agree with Pryce when he emphasises that the vast majority of the West Indian working class are law-abiding and pursue stable employment as wage labourers (1979, p. 184–97) and it is these workers who constitute the population within which the wageless, the hustlers and the Rastas must live. That one cannot expect such support for the 'politics of race' to be automatically given follows from the fact that, as we have shown, the political consciousness of the West Indian working class combines elements of what we have defined as class and racial consciousness, as well as elements of the ideology of the ruling class. Indeed, amongst a substantial minority of the West Indian workers we interviewed there was considerable hostility expressed towards young West Indians who were seen as unwilling to work and who behave in such a way as to warrant the attention of the police. Such views may well be grounded in the economic motivation for migration to Britain from the Caribbean: in the light of their own experience of wage labour, these West Indian migrants may regard with some suspicion the perceived motives of those who are seen to be wageless. The lifestyle of the wageless, the hustler and the Rasta may appear 'exotic' to the 'sociological outsider' and thereby warrant attention but the rebellion that it signifies must be interpreted within a theoretical context which admits more than the realities of racism and discrimination.

The relevance of migrant status

We believe that any study of the political consciousness and action of the black working class as a whole cannot afford to neglect the fact that a large proportion of the men and women in question are migrants. The theoretical significance of this lies in the fact that the concept of migrant labour permits an analytical starting-point within political economy rather than within the 'sociology of race relations' (Worsley, 1976). But recognition of black workers as migrants is necessary at the micro-level of explanation too. For example, our data has shown that, as economic migrants, black workers have certain goals which will enhance an instrumental approach to life and work in the country to which they have migrated (cf. Lawrence, 1974, p. 35). Moreover, as migrants, black workers experienced their primary political socialisation in a colonial social formation and so could not have inherited any of the traditional British working-class beliefs and loyalties. We have shown this to be relevant not only to an understanding of the political ideology and practice of black workers when compared to that of white workers but also to an understanding of the different political ideology and practice of West Indian men compared to West Indian women.

This is one reason why we cannot accept those arguments that suggest that the problems and experiences of black workers are 'really' only class problems and experiences (e.g. Westergaard and Resler, 1976). Not only does racism and discrimination bring about specific problems and experiences for black workers over and above those which arise from their position in class relations, but also the fact that they are migrants should alert us both to potential differences in political socialisation and to a desire, whether or not it is 'unrealistic', to return to the country of origin to join the petit-bourgeoisie.

Labour and racism: a diagnosis

In conclusion, how do these arguments and findings fit into the more general debate about working-class consciousness and action? On this, we state our case with caution, not so much because our samples were relatively small (for we believe that our lengthy period of participant observation provided us with considerable contextual information and a substantially larger 'informal' sample on which to support the conclusions drawn from our formal interviewing) but because, first, we have only limited evidence relating to the skilled fraction of the manual working class. The class struggles of the 1970s, concerning wage control and legal restrictions on the defensive institutions of the working class, clearly demonstrate the political significance of the relatively highly paid and skilled fraction of the working class. At the same time, given the position of black migrant labour in economic relations (outlined in chapter 1), the West Indian workers we interviewed (most of whom were semi-skilled) are likely to have been more representative of the class fraction. Second, because of the tenuous relationship between political consciousness and political action, and the importance of the 'situational context' (in the current conjuncture, this means the economic crisis of profitability and its corresponding political crisis) to the development of radical political action, we find it difficult to make very specific claims because they will inevitably take on a static character while our interest in political action is in fact an interest in a dynamic process.

We have found little evidence of a radical class consciousness amongst our working-class sample, although this is not surprising. Rather, our evidence points in the direction of the existence of an inchoate restricted class consciousness amongst a majority of our sample, combined with a pragmatic acceptance of capitalism. These conclusions hold generally for both our English and West Indian workers, both male and female. An awareness of class structure and inequality does, however, provide an ideological foundation for the development of a more radical consciousness, but in so far as it is possible to show that working-class political consciousness develops out of the direct experience of the impact of capitalism upon daily life, we cannot agree with those who expect the development of such a consciousness to result solely from the appearance of a 'new' radical leadership.

In so far as black migrant labour constitutes a fraction of the *working class* it of necessity shares similar problems with the rest of the working class: in this connection, it is important to note our findings on the problems identified by our West Indian workers at both the local and national level, most of which were material ones relating to prices, wages, inflation etc. We have presented some evidence to show that class unity can be expressed in political action which transcends fractional boundaries. At the national level, one can also point to involvement of black workers in trade union struggles arising out of state-imposed wage controls, particularly in the public sector. It is, of course, correct to point out the limit-ations of these struggles (for they are certainly not evidence of the existence of a radical class consciousness), but that is not the point. We believe that the significance lies in the fact that such struggles bring together fractions of the working class in common political action, an important precondition for the development of a consciousness of a common class position which transcends awareness of the different interests which arise out of and express fractionalisation. Moreover, evidence of such action on the part of black workers must lead us to at least qualify the view that black workers have 'withdrawn' from the political process (cf. Lawrence, 1974).

The fact that black workers do constitute a *fraction* of the working class reflects not only the position they occupy in economic relations but also their position in political and ideological relations. In the latter connection, racism and discrimination are not the prerogative of the state and employers but are clearly evident within the institutions of the working class. We have stressed that working-class racism must be viewed as something more than 'ideological baggage' which is fed to an unquestioning working class or which is simply an inheritance from the colonial past (cf. Lawrence, 1974; Rex and Tomlinson, 1979). We have suggested that these ideas are materially grounded and are reproduced because of the *appearance* of certain economic and social processes in the urban context (the underlying movement being hidden). This carries with it the im-plication that it is only through the eradication of (and therefore through the struggle for the eradication of) those material inequali-ties that one major basis for racist belief can be eliminated. We say one, because we do not deny that certain cultural values in Western culture give rise to racist belief. On the other hand, we have been at pains to stress, using our data, that it does not follow from the fact that racist ideas are widespread amongst the working class that they are constantly given expression and determine political action. Only by conceding this point is it possible to explain both those instances where black and white workers are in conflict with each other and those where they are not.

Having said that, we would argue that racism has been given increasing and more extreme political expression in the 1970s, although this cannot be divorced from the state's sanctioning of racism, in the form of legislation on immigration control which characterised the 1960s (see Miles and Phizacklea, 1979). The most significant events of the 1970s have been the increase in racist-inspired political violence, the identification of young blacks as a 'law and order' problem (Hall, *et al.* 1978), and the emergence of the National Front. All of these events have taken place against the background of an increasing support for conservative and reactionary political arguments, which received expression in the election of a Conservative government in 1979. We are unwilling to assume that these developments have had an immediate 'radicalising' effect on the black working class: certainly our evidence obtained during the mid 1970s suggests not. Moreover, as we have said before, there is more than one potential response: a return to the West Indies or emigration to North America for instance is as logically possible as a development of racial consciousness when one considers that the black working class is predominantly composed of migrants. Nevertheless, these developments have produced a defensive reaction amongst some sections of the black working class, manifested in local self-organisation as we witnessed in Willesden. Only a small minority of the black working class seem to have been actively involved, and often the initiative has been taken by young blacks, many of whom are not wage labourers. Our evidence regarding the limited nature and extent of racial consciousness suggests that there is an ideological basis for further support to be given to such political action, but, as we stressed above, it also suggests that such initiatives will not meet with universal support from the black working class as a whole.

An equally serious threat to the black working class emanates from the renewed ideological campaign to define women as principally responsible for the care and socialisation of their children (see speech made by Social Services Secretary reported in the *Guardian*, 22.9.79, also the *Observer*, 7.10.79 and Editorial, *Spare Rib*, No. 88, November 1979).

In a period of economic and political crisis the effect of such campaigns on the public at large, including women themselves, is to define certain sections of the labour force as illegitimate competitors: women do after all (we are led to believe) have 'a sphere of their own' to which they can return (West, 1979, p. 14). While the threat is particularly obvious in the case of West Indian women (the majority of whom are wage labourers who also have children), such campaigns pose an ideological threat to the unity of the working class as a whole. It remains to be seen how easily women can be pushed back into the home, but one thing is sure: any campaign which is mounted to combat such pressure is likely to be supported by black female labour, from the West Indies and the Indian sub-continent alike.

In such instances it is sexual rather than racial categorisation which is at issue and consequently ethnic boundaries within the black working class are unlikely to produce a fragmented response. But we are less sure of such unity in the response to racism and discrimination.

Our data and analysis has concentrated on West Indians as a racialised fraction of the working class yet our category of black migrant labour must also include workers who originate from the Indian sub-continent. There are good reasons for arguing that the political consciousness and action of these workers may not be the same as that of West Indian workers (e.g. Dahya, 1973; Lawrence, 1974; Khan, 1976; Rex and Tomlinson, 1979), and for arguing that they will not inevitably come to organise in common with West Indian workers against racism and discrimination (see Miles and Phizacklea, 1977a). We are therefore referring not to a potential but to a real source of fragmentation within black migrant labour as a working-class fraction, and this too must be recognised in any detailed analysis of political consciousness and action.

Nevertheless, the facts of black political organisation (albeit defensive in character) and a limited racial consciousness amongst at least a minority of the black working class pose a challenge both to black workers as a fraction of the working class and to the working class as a whole. That challenge will become ever more serious as the economic and political crisis deepens. In the same way that we would respond to those who argue that infant fascist parties are best ignored by pointing out to them that what is important is not so much the party as the conditions for its existence and its political impact irrespective of its size, so we would question those who might argue that the aforementioned facts are of little relevance. Unless the political expression of racism within the working class is decisively curbed, the fragmentation of the class will be even further advanced if it does result in a heightening of racial consciousness, while to curb it is one phase in the development of a radical class consciousness. We believe the evidence in this book suggests that both developments are possible, but the initiative is now with the white working class: if it is not taken, and as the crisis does deepen, the initiative may pass both to the remainder of the black working class whose racial consciousness is at present limited or non-existent, and to the racists, both inside and outside the institutions of bourgeois democracy.

METHODOLOGICAL APPENDIX

Having agreed the aims of our research we chose to focus attention on the English and West Indian working class in one geographical area. Our decision to focus on only one group of migrant labourers was governed by the fact that it is not possible for two researchers, given a limited time period, to gain a sufficient understanding of the values and motivations of more than one distinct group of migrant labourers.

In order to minimise the number of independent variables which were anticipated as having an attenuating influence upon political consciousness and action, we controlled for age (25–45 years) and class.

As far as age was concerned, we were keen to ensure a relatively long period of work experience amongst our respondents. In addition, for the English respondents we felt it important that none had previous direct experience of long-term economic recession. For the West Indian respondents this would ensure, in most cases, consideration of the influence of prior socialisation in the West Indies.

We used the following definition of 'working class' to select our sample: all those without control over investment or the physical means of production, who did not control the labour power of others and who either sold their labour power for a wage or, if not directly involved in the wage-labour relation, were dependent upon that sale.

We chose as our method of data collection a combination of participant observation and in-depth interviewing. We also decided that our joint energies would best be deployed by selecting our samples from different locations but within the same geographical area. One of us decided on a factory and the other on a residential location, both within South Brent.

In 1975 one of the researchers moved to the area and spent three months 'lending a hand' in a local advice centre. The purpose of this exercise was to test the feasibility of carrying out the planned

233

research. It proved an invaluable exercise in enabling the researcher to begin understanding the community context which shaped the socio-political beliefs of the relevant populations and the issues which determined the nature of conflict and political action in the area. On the basis of this experience we decided that the project was feasible and that South Brent was an excellent location for carrying out the research. Hereafter we will refer to the *factory sample* and the *residential sample.*

Factory sample: Having obtained sufficient specific information about the then current industrial structure of Willesden, six firms were contacted. Permission to carry out pilot interviews was given by the personnel manager at a food processing factory producing canned and bottled foods and sauces, known as Food Co.

Of the total number of employees, 2,000 were hourly paid and engaged in some form of manual job, either connected directly with production or with storage and distribution. The workforce was divided into a permanent day shift and a permanent night shift.

A small pilot sample from two production departments was interviewed in the autumn of 1975 for the dual purpose of developing and testing an interview schedule, and of establishing a presence in the factory which would permit observational techniques. The main sample was drawn using a listing supplied by the company of all hourly paid employees which identified each individual by sex, shift, date of birth, date of joining and department. As the skilled craftsmen were identified as belonging to separate departments, it was possible to exclude them from the sample. It was also possible to obtain information on self-reported 'nationality'. Using this information a sample of eighty individuals was drawn randomly from the population of English and West Indian males, aged twenty-five to forty years. The sample of eighty was equally divided into English and West Indian respondents, and by shift. A reserve sample was also randomly selected, from which an individual was drawn if any person from the main sample refused to participate, had left the company's employ, or had been promoted.

All interviews were conducted by one of the authors and were carried out in conjunction with continuous observational work in the factory. Interviewing began in June 1976 and was completed in September 1976. In sum, seventy-two individuals were interviewed, equally divided between English and West Indians, all of whom were semi-skilled workers.

Residential sample: A presence at the Advice Centre continued during a pilot phase of in-depth interviewing in late 1975. The major problem identified during this phase was non-response, and it was decided that initial access had to be handled very carefully in the main study. Thus letters of introduction outlining the aims of the study, age controls etc., were prepared and identity cards printed to this end.

Sampling in the residential sample was governed by two main factors. Firstly, the sample was to be broken down into four groups, West Indian men and women (40), English men and women (40). Secondly, although the response rate was much better in the public sector of housing we were keen to sample from both the private and public sectors since West Indian manual workers are over-represented in owner-occupation and under-represented in council housing when compared with manual workers in general (Smith, 1977, pp. 210–16).

We decided, therefore, to conduct half the interviews in the private sector and half in the public sector of housing. The areas to be sampled were not chosen randomly but were sought out on the basis of having fairly equal numbers of English and West Indian residents. Choosing these areas was simplified in the private sector by the availability of a relatively reliable if somewhat dated sampling frame in the form of the 1971 Census.

Using the small area statistics as a base, two virtually identical enumeration districts were selected. Sampling in both the private and public sector was conducted in the same way. Our first task was to carry out a full listing process of all eligibles in all households. Work began first in the private sector and our listing process indicated that since 1971 the English-born population had sharply decreased. Furthermore, half of those persons of English parentage who remained were old age pensioners. Nevertheless we decided to go ahead with the interviews in the first of the two enumeration districts but with a lower cut-off point (34 instead of 40 interviews) due to the shortfall of eligible English respondents. While we had decided to interview only one eligible person in each household, in two cases husbands and wives insisted on their being interviewed together. Every effort was made to overcome the problems of non-response, which meant in some cases up to ten return visits to obtain an interview, and as a result very few eligibles slipped through the net.

Locating eligible interviewees of English parentage was much easier in the council sector. Even though no sampling frames existed for any of the new redevelopment estates, it was clear that more of the English were located in the houses and maisonettes and more of the West Indians in the flats (some of which are high rise). We were therefore able to concentrate our efforts on two sections of housing on two different estates. Due to time constraints we interviewed only seventeen English women and two of our English male respondents were excluded from the total sample on occupational criteria (one was a quantity surveyor and the other a student). Nearly all the interviews with English men were conducted by Martin Bailey.

We make no claims that the sample is representative in a rigorous sense, but we made every effort to screen out undue biases (for example, conducting interviews only in the evenings and at the week-ends). If an eligible interviewee was particularly resistant to giving up an hour of his or her time we agreed to ask only 'core' questions: this meant that they were not asked some of the attitudinal questions and fortunately this compromise was necessary in only a few cases.

Observational work continued in Harlesden and on one large council estate throughout the main period of interviewing and any invitations to return to the house of interviewees for further discussion were readily taken up. This allowed a much wider network of informants to be built up during our presence in the area.

While our samples are small our lengthy period of participant observation provided us with evidence which confirmed and extended our interview findings. Having said this there were times when our being accepted as part of the local scenery presented us with problems in our role as researchers: suffice it to say that we left the field with some good friends and we hope not too many enemies.

BIBLIOGRAPHY

Anderson, P. (1967), 'The limits and possibilities of trade union action', in R. Blackburn and A. Cockburn (eds), *The Incompatibles*, Harmondsworth, Penguin.

Ballard, R., and Ballard, C. (1977), 'The Sikhs: the development of South Asian communities in Britain', in G.L. Watson (ed.), *Between Two Cultures*, Oxford, Blackwell.

Ballard, R., and Holden, B. (1975), 'The employment of coloured graduates in Britain', *New Community*, vol. IV, 3, pp. 325–36.

Banton, M. (1970), 'The concept of racism', in S. Zubaida (ed.), *Race and Racialism*, London, Tavistock.

Banton, M. (1977), *The Idea of Race*, London, Tavistock.

Banton, M., and Harwood, G. (1975), *The Race Concept*, Newton Abbot, David & Charles.

Beharell, P., and Philo, G. (eds) (1977), *Trade Unions and the Media*, London, Macmillan.

Benewick, R. (1972), *The Fascist Movement in Britain*, London, Allen Lane.

Beynon, H. (1973), *Working for Ford*, Harmondsworth, Penguin.

Blackburn, R. (1967), 'The unequal society' in R. Blackburn and A. Cockburn (eds), *The Incompatibles*, Harmondsworth, Penguin.

Bohning, W.R. (1972), *The Migration of Workers in the United Kingdom and the European Community*, London, Oxford University Press.

Borough of Brent (1977), *Brent: A Statement of Forward Planning Policies*, Planning Department, London Borough of Brent.

Brooks, D. (1975a), *Race and Labour in London Transport*, London, Oxford University Press.

Brooks, D. (1975b), *Black Employment in the Black Country: A Study of Walsall*, London, Runnymede Trust.

Bulmer, M. (ed.) (1975), *Working-Class Images of Society*, London, Routledge & Kegan Paul.

Cameron, G., and Evans, A. (1973), 'The British conurbation centres', *Regional Studies*, 7, pp. 47–55.

Castells, M. (1975), 'Immigrant workers and class struggles in advanced capitalism: the Western European experience', *Politics and Society*, vol. 5, no. 1, pp. 33–66.

Castles, S., and Kosack, G, (1973), *Immigrant Workers and the Class Structure*, London, Oxford University Press and the Institute of Race Relations.

238 · Bibliography

Chamberlain, C.W. (1977), 'Attitudes towards direct political action in Britain', in C. Crouch (ed.), *Participation in Politics, British Political Sociology Yearbook*, vol. 3, London, Croom Helm. pp. 164–201.

Chamberlain, C.W., and Moorhouse, H.F. (1974), 'Lower-class attitudes towards the British political system', *The Sociological Review*, vol. 22, no. 4.

Cohen, B.G., and Jenner, P.J. (1968), 'The employment of immigrants: a case study within the wool industry', *Race*, vol. 10, pp. 41–56.

Commission on Industrial Relations (1974), *Mansfield Hosiery Mills Ltd*, Report no. 76, London, HMSO.

Community Development Project (1977), *The Cost of Industrial Change*, London, CDP Inter-Project Editorial Team.

Community Relations Commission (1975), *Participation of Ethnic Minorities in the General Election, October 1974*, London, CRC.

Conference of Socialist Economists (1975), *On the Political Economy of Women*, Pamphlet no. 2, London, CSE.

Coulson, M., Magas, B., and Wainwright, H. (1975), ' "The housewife and her labour under capitalism" – a critique', *New Left Review*, 89, pp. 59–71.

Counter Information Services (1976), *Crisis: Women Under Attack*, London, CIS.

Counter Information Services (n.d.), *The General Electric Company Ltd*, London, CIS.

Cox, O.C. (1970), *Caste, Class and Race: a Study in Racial Dynamics*, Monthly Review Press.

Crewe, I., Sarlvik, B., and Alt, G. (1976), 'Partisan dealignment in Britain 1964–1974', *British Journal of Political Science*, 7, pp. 129–90.

Cross, C. (1978), *Ethnic Minorities in the Inner City*, London, Commission for Racial Equality.

Crouch, C. (ed.) (1977), *Participation in Politics, British Political Sociology Yearbook*, vol. 3, London, Croom Helm.

Curtis, L.P. (1968), *Anglo-Saxons and Celts*, Connecticut, University of Bridgeport.

Dahya, B. (1973), 'Pakistanis in Britain: transients or settlers', *Race*, vol. 14, pp. 246–77.

Dahya, B. (1974), 'The Nature of Pakistani ethnicity in industrial cities in Britain', in A. Cohen, *Urban Ethnicity*, London, Tavistock.

Daly, M. (1971), *Characteristics of 12 clusters of wards in Greater London*, London, GLC, Department of Planning and Transportation Research Report no. 13.

Daniel, W. (1968), *Racial Discrimination in England*, Harmondsworth, Penguin.

Davis, H. (1979), *Beyond Class Images*, London, Croom Helm.

Davison, R.B. (1962), *West Indian Migrants*, London, Oxford University Press and Institute of Race Relations.

Davison, R.B. (1966), *Black British: Immigrants to England*, London University Press.

Deakin, N. (1970), *Colour, Citizenship and British Society*, London, Panther Books.

Deakin, N., and Ungerson, C. (1977), *Leaving London*, London, Heinemann.

Demuth, C. (1978), *'Sus': A report on section 4 of the Vagrancy Act 1824*, London, Runnymede Trust.

Dennis R.D. (1978), 'The decline of manufacturing employment in Greater London', *Urban Studies*, 15, pp. 63–73.

Department of the Environment (1977), *Policy for the Inner Cities*, London, HMSO.

De Witt, J. (1969), *Indian Workers'.Associations in Britain*, London, Oxford University Press.

Dowse, R., and Hughes, G. (1977), 'Pre-adult origins of adult political activity: a sour note', in C. Crouch (ed.), *Participation in Politics, British Political Sociology Yearbook*, vol. 3, London, Croom Helm.

Drewett, R., Goddard, J.G., and Spence, N. (1976), 'What's happening in British cities?', *Town and Country Planning*, 44, pp. 14–24.

Dummett, A. (1976), *Citizenship and Nationality*, London, Runnymede Trust.

Engels, F. (1969 edn), *The Condition of the Working-Class in England*, London, Panther.

Evans, P. (1976), *Publish and Be Damned*, London, Runnymede Trust.

Foner, N. (1979), *Jamaica Farewell*, London, Routledge & Kegan Paul.

Foreman-Peck, G.S., and Gripaios, P. (1977), 'Inner-city problems and inner-city policies', *Regional Studies*, 11.

Form, W.H. (1973), 'The internal stratification of the working class: system involvements of the auto workers in four counties', *American Sociological Review*, 38.

Foster, C.D., and Richardson, R. (1973), 'Employment trends in London in the 1960s and their relevance for the future', in D. Donnison and D. Eversley (eds), *London: Urban Patterns, Problems and Policies*, London, Heinemann.

Gabriel, G., and Ben-Tovim, G. (1978), 'Marxism and the concept of racism', *Economy and Society*, 7 (2), pp. 118–54.

Gardiner, G. (1975), 'Women's domestic labour', *New Left Review*, 89, pp. 47–58.

Gardiner, G. (1977), 'Women in the labour process and class structure', in A. Hunt (ed.), *Class and Class Structure*, London, Lawrence & Wishart.

Gilley, S. (1978), 'English attitudes to the Irish in England, 1789–1900', in C. Holmes (ed.), *Immigrants and Minorities in British Society*, London, George Allen & Unwin.

Glasgow University Media Group (1976), *Bad News*, London, Routledge & Kegan Paul.

Glass, R. (1961), *London's Newcomers: The West Indian Migrants*, Cambridge, Mass., Harvard University Press.

Goldthorpe, J.H., Lockwood, D., Bechhofer, F., and Platt, G. (1968), *The Affluent Worker: Industrial Attitudes and Behaviour*, Cambridge University Press.

Goldthorpe, H.J., Lockwood, D., Bechhofer, F., and Platt, J. (1969), *The Affluent Worker in the Class Structure*, Cambridge University Press.

Gramsci, A. (1971), *Selections from the Prison Notebooks*, London, Lawrence & Wishart.

Greater London Council (1969), *Greater London Development Plan: Report of Studies*, London, GLC.

Greve, J., Page, P., and Greve, S. (1971), *Homelessness in London*, Edinburgh, Scottish Academic Press.

Gripaios, P. (1977), 'The closure of firms in the inner city: the South-East London case', *Regional Studies*, 11, pp. 1–6.

Haddon, R. (1970), 'A minority in a welfare state society: the location of West Indians in the London housing market', *The New Atlantis*, 2.

Hall, P.G. (1962), *The Industries of London since 1861*, London, Hutchinson.

Hall, S., *et.al.* (1978), *Policing the Crisis*, London, Macmillan.

Handley, J.E. (1943), *The Irish in Scotland*, Glasgow, John S. Burns.

Hartmann, P., and Husbands, C. (1974), *Racism and the Mass Media*, London, Davis-Poynter.

Hill, S. (1976), *The Dockers: Class and Tradition in London*, London, Heinemann.

Hiro, D. (1971), *Black British, White British*, Eyre & Spottiswoode.

Humphrey, D. (1972), *Police Power and Black People*, London, Granada Publishing.

Hunt, A. (1977), 'Theory and politics in the identification of the working class', in A. Hunt (ed.) *Class and Class Structure*, London, Lawrence & Wishart.

Husbands, C. (1979), 'The "threat" hypothesis and racist voting in England and the United States', in R. Miles and A. Phizacklea (eds), *Racism and Political Action in Britain*, London, Routledge & Kegan Paul.

Hyman, R. (1971), *Marxism and the Sociology of Trade Unionism*, London, Pluto Press.

Institute of Race Relations (1979), *Police Against Black People*, Race and Class Pamphlet no. 6, London, IRR.

Jackson, J.A. (1963), *The Irish in Britain*, London, Routledge & Kegan Paul.

Karn, V. (1979), 'Low income owner-occupation in the inner-city', in C. Jones (ed.), *Urban Deprivation and the Inner City*, London, Croom Helm.

Katznelson, I. (1973), *Black Men, White Cities*, London, Oxford University Press.

Keeble, D.E. (1968), 'Industrial decentralisation and the metropolis: the north-west London case', *Transactions of the Institute of British Geographers*, 44, pp. 1–54.

Khan, V.S. (1976), 'Pakistanis in Britain: perceptions of a population' *New Community*, vol. 5, pp. 222–9.

Khan, V.S. (1977), 'The Pakistanis: Mirpuri villagers at home and in Bradford', in J.L. Watson (ed.), *Between Two Cultures*, Oxford, Blackwell.

Lambert, J., Blackaby, B., and Paris, C. (1975), 'Neighbourhood politics and housing opportunities', *Community Development Journal*, April 1975, pp. 95–112.

Lawrence, D. (1974), *Black Migrants, White Natives*, Cambridge University Press.

Lee, T.R. (1977), *Race and Residence: The Concentration and Dispersal of*

Immigrants in London, Oxford, Clarendon Press.

Leff, V., and Blunden, G.H. (n.d.), *The Willesden Study*, London, Research Writers.

Leggett, J.C. (1968), *Class, Race and Labour*, New York, Oxford University Press.

Le Lohé, M. (1979), 'The effects of the presence of immigrants upon the local political system in Bradford, 1945–1977', in R. Miles and A. Phizacklea (eds), *Racism and Political Action in Britain*, London, Routledge & Kegan Paul.

Lenin, V.I. (1963), 'Imperialism, the highest stage of capitalism', *Selected Works, vol. 1*, pp. 679–768.

Lipman, V.D. (1954), *Social History of the Jews in England, 1850–1950*, London, Watts.

Lockwood, D. (1966), 'Sources of variation in working-class images of society', *Sociological Review*, 14, pp. 249–67.

Lockwood, D. (1975), 'Sources of variation in working-class images of society', in M. Bulmer (ed.), *Working-Class Images of Society*, London, Routledge & Kegan Paul.

Lomas, G. (1973), *The Coloured Population of Great Britain*, London, Runny-mede Trust.

Lomas, G. (1975), *The Inner City*, London, London Council of Social Service.

McCarthy, I. (1977), 'Women in trade unions', in L. Middleton (ed.), *Women in the Labour Movement*, London, Croom Helm.

McCarthy, W.E.J., and Parker, S.R. (1968), *Workshop Relations in Britain: Research Paper for Royal Commission on Trade Unions and Employers Associations*, London, HMSO.

MacDonald, J.S., and MacDonald, L.B. (1964), 'Chain migration, ethnic neighbourhood formation and social networks,' *Milbank Memorial Fund Quarterly*, 42, pp. 82–92.

Mackie, L., and Pattullo, P. (1977), *Women at Work*, London, Tavistock.

Mann, M. (1973), *Consciousness and Action Among the Western Working Class*, London, Macmillan.

Martin, J.E. (1966), *Greater London: An Industrial Geography*, London, Bell.

Meszaros, I. (ed.) (1971), *Aspects of History and Class Consciousness*, London, Routledge & Kegan Paul.

Midgett, D. (1975), 'West Indian ethnicity in Great Britain', in H. Safa and B. du Toit (eds), *Migration and Development*, The Hague, Mouton.

Miles, R. (1979), *Between Two Cultures, the Case of Rastafarianism*, Research Unit on Ethnic Relations Working Papers, no. 10, University of Aston in Birmingham.

Miles, R. (1980), 'Class, race and ethnicity: a critique of Cox's theory', *Ethnic and Racial Studies*, vol. 3, no. 2, pp. 169–87.

Miles, R., and Phizacklea, A. (1977a), 'Class, race, ethnicity and political action', *Political Studies*, vol. XXV, no. 4, pp. 491–507.

Miles, R., and Phizacklea, A. (1977b), *The T.U.C., Black Workers and New Commonwealth Immigration, 1954–1973*, Research Unit on Ethnic Relations Working Papers, no. 6, University of Aston in Birmingham.

Miles, R., and Phizacklea, A. (1978), 'The TUC and black workers,

1974–1976', *British Journal of Industrial Relations*, vol. XVI, no. 2, pp. 195–207.

Miles, R., and Phizacklea, A. (1979), 'Some introductory observations on race and politics in Britain', in R. Miles and A. Phizacklea (eds), *Racism and Political Action in Britain*, London, Routledge & Kegan Paul.

Moore, R. (1975), *Racism and Black Resistance in Britain*, London, Pluto Press.

Moore, R., and Wallace, T. (1975), *Slamming the Door*, London, Martin Robertson.

Moorhouse, H. F. (1976), 'Attitudes to class and class relationships in Britain', *Sociology*, vol. 10, pp. 469–96.

Moorhouse, H.F., and Chamberlain, C.W. (1974), 'Lower-class attitudes to property: aspects of the counter-ideology', *Sociology*, 8 (3), pp. 387–405.

Morris, J.C. (1950), *The Willesden Survey, 1949*, London, Corporation of Willesden.

Morrison, L. (1976), *As They See It*, London, Community Relations Commission.

Nairn, T. (1977), *The Break-Up of Britain*, London, New Left Books.

Newman, A. (1977), *The United Synagogue 1870–1970*, London, Routledge & Kegan Paul.

Newton, K. (1976), *Second City Politics*, Oxford, Clarendon Press.

Nichols, T., and Armstrong, P. (1976), *Workers Divided*, London, Fontana.

Nikolinakos, N. (1975), 'Draft of a general theory of migration in late capitalism', *Proceedings of International Conference on Migrant Workers*, International Institute for Comparative Social Studies of the Science Centre, Berlin.

Nugent, N., and King, R. (1979), 'Ethnic minorities, scape-goating and the extreme right', in R. Miles and A. Phizacklea (eds), *Racism and Political Action in Britain*, London, Routledge & Kegan Paul.

Olsen, D.J. (1976), *The Growth of Victorian London*, London, Batsford.

Paine, S. (1974), *Exporting Workers: The Turkish Case*, Cambridge University Press.

Paris, C. (1978), ' "The parallels are striking" … Crisis in the inner city? GB 1977', *International Journal of Urban and Regional Research*, 2 (i), pp. 160–70.

Parker, J., and Dugmore, K. (1978), 'Race and the allocation of public housing – a GLC survey', *New Community*, vol. VI, nos. 1 and 2, pp. 27–40.

Parkin, F. (1971), *Class Inequality and Political Order*, London, Paladin.

Patterson, S. (1969), *Immigration and Race Relations in Britain, 1960–67*. London, Oxford University Press and Institute of Race Relations.

Peach, C. (1968), *West Indian Migration to Britain*, London, Oxford University Press.

Peach, G.C.K. (1975), 'Immigrants in the inner city', *The Geographical Journal*, 141, pp. 372–9.

Pearson, D.G. (1977), 'West Indian communal associations in Britain: some observations', *New Community*, vol. 5, pp. 371–80.

Philpott. S. (1973), *West Indian Migration: The Montserrat Case*, London, Athlone Press.

Phizacklea, A. and Miles, R. (1978), 'The strike at Grunwick', *New Community*, vol. IV, no. 3, pp. 268–78.

Phizacklea, A., and Miles, R. (1979), 'Working-class racist beliefs', in R. Miles and A. Phizacklea (eds), *Racism and Political Action in Britain*, London, Routledge & Kegan Paul.

Porter, Marilyn (1978), 'Worlds apart: the class consciousness of working-class women', *Women's Studies International Quarterly*, vol. 1, pp. 175–88.

Poulantzas, N. (1973), *Political Power and Social Classes*, London, New Left Books and Sheed & Ward.

Poulantzas, N. (1975, paperback edn 1978), *Classes in Contemporary Capitalism*, London, New Left Books.

Prais, S.J. (1972), 'Synagogue statistics and the Jewish population of Great Britain', *Jewish Journal of Sociology*, vol. XIV, pp. 215–28.

Price, C. (1968), 'The study of assimilation', in J.A. Jackson (ed.) *Migration*, Cambridge University Press.

Prince, H.C. (1964), 'North-west London, 1864–1964', in J. Coppock and H.C. Prince (eds), *Greater London*, London, Faber.

Pryce, K. (1979), *Endless Pressure*, Harmondsworth, Penguin.

Pulle, S. (1973), *Police–Immigrant Relations in Ealing*, London, Runnymede Trust.

Redford, A. (1976), *Labour Migration in England, 1800–1850*, Manchester University Press (3rd edn).

Reich, W. (1971), *What is Class Consciousness?*, London, Socialist Reproduction.

Rex, J. (1970), *Race Relations in Sociological Theory*, London, Weidenfeld & Nicolson.

Rex, J. (1973), *Race, Colonialism and the City*, London, Routledge & Kegan Paul.

Rex, J. (1979), 'Black militancy and class conflict', in R. Miles and A. Phizacklea (eds), *Racism and Political Action in Britain*, London, Routledge & Kegan Paul.

Rex, J., and Moore, R. (1967), *Race, Community and Conflict*, London, Oxford University Press and Institute of Race Relations.

Rex, J., and Tomlinson, S. (1979), *Colonial Immigrants in a British City*, London, Routledge & Kegan Paul.

Schoen, D.S. (1977), *Enoch Powell and the Powellites*, London, Macmillan.

Seccombe, W. (1974), 'The housewife and her labour under capitalism', *New Left Review*, 93, pp.3–24.

Select Committee on Race Relations and Immigration (1977), *The West Indian Community*, London, HMSO.

Sivanandan, A. (1976), 'Race, class and the state: the black experience in Britain', *Race and Class*, vol. XVII, spring, no. 4, pp. 347–68.

Smith, D.J. (1976), *The Facts of Racial Disadvantage*, London, Political and Economic Planning.

Smith, D.J. (1977), *Racial Disadvantage in Britain, The PEP Report*, Harmondsworth, Penguin

Smith, D.J. (1978), 'The housing of racial minorities: its unusual nature', *New Community*, vol. VI, nos. 1 and 2, pp. 18–26.

Smith, D.M. (1933), *The Industries of Greater London*, London, P.S. King.

Smith, P. (1979), 'Domestic labour and Marx's theory of value', in A. Kuhn and A. Wolpe (eds), *Feminism and Materialism*, London, Routledge & Kegan Paul, pp. 198–219.

Smith, R.T. (1956), *The Negro Family in Guiana*, London, Routledge & Kegan Paul.

Stone, C. (1974), *Class, Race and Political Behaviour in Urban Jamaica*, Kingston, Jamaica, University of West Indies, Institute of Social and Economic Research.

Sutton, C.R., and Makiesky, S. (1975), 'Migration and West Indian racial and ethnic consciousness', in H. Safa and B. du Toit (eds), *Migration and Development*, The Hague, Mouton.

Taylor, S. (1979), 'The National Front: anatomy of a political movement', in R. Miles and A. Phizacklea (eds), *Racism and Political Action in Britain*, London, Routledge & Kegan Paul.

Unit for Manpower Services (1977), *The Role of Immigrants in the Labour Market*, Department of Employment.

Walker, M. (1977), *The National Front*, London, Fontana.

Wallman, S. (1975/6), 'A street in Waterloo', *New Community*, vol. IV, 4, pp. 517–23.

Ward, R. (1979), 'Where race didn't divide: some reflections on slum clearance in Moss Side', in R. Miles and A. Phizacklea (eds), *Racism and Political Action in Britain*, London, Routledge & Kegan Paul.

Weintraub, A.L. (1972), *Race and Local Politics in England: A Case Study of Willesden*, Ph.D. Thesis, Faculty of Political Science, Columbia University, New York.

West, J. (1979), 'A political economy of the family in capitalism: women, reproduction and wage labour', Mimeo, Department of Sociology, Bristol University, and published in T. Nichols (ed.) (1980), *Capital and Labour: Essays in the Capitalist Labour Process*, London, Fontana.

Westergaard, J.H. (1970), 'The rediscovery of the cash nexus', in R. Miliband and J. Saville (eds), *The Socialist Register 1970*, London, Merlin, pp. 111–38.

Westergaard, J.H. (1975), 'Radical class-consciousness: a comment', in M. Bulmer (ed.), *Working-Class Images of Society*, London, Routledge & Kegan Paul, pp. 251–6.

Westergaard, J., and Resler, H. (1976), *Class in a Capitalist Society*, Harmondsworth, Penguin.

Wilson, E. (1977), *Women and the Welfare State*, London, Tavistock.

Working Party of Housing Directors (1976), *Housing in Multi-Racial Areas*, London, Community Relations Commission.

Worsley, P. (1976), 'Proletarians, sub-proletarians, lumpen proletarians, marginalidados, migrants, urban peasants and urban poor', *Sociology*, 10, pp. 133–42.

Wright, E.O. (1976), 'Class boundaries in advanced capitalist societies', *New Left Review*, no. 98, pp. 3–41.

Wright, P.L. (1968), *The Coloured Worker in British Industry*, London, Oxford University Press.

Yannopoulos, G.N. (1975), 'Migrant labour and economic growth: the post-war experience of the EEC countries', *Proceedings of International Conference on Migrant Workers*, International Institute for Comparative Social Studies of the Science Centre, Berlin.

INDEX